Conjuring is a demanding art ruled by a Muse of bizarre whimsy,
one given to great generosity with some of her disciples
and yet capable of cruel indifference with others.
We who serve her accept her rules and recognize that she,
of all those we aspire to please,
sees instantly through our every artifice and ruse.

We would have no other mistress and we serve her willingly.
In so doing, we trust that we also serve you, our patrons.
We hope to deserve the support and acclaim
which we are awarded when we properly delight you.
If you will, look upon us with understanding,
forgive our occasional errors
and grant us your tolerance.

And while I have your attention,
may I ask you, please,
to choose a card?
Any card...

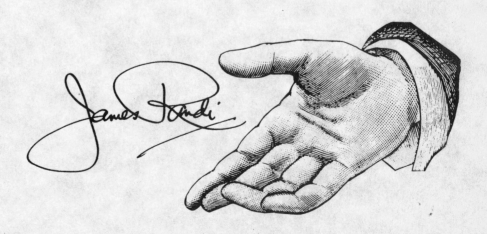

CONJURING

CONJURING

BEING A DEFINITIVE ACCOUNT OF THE

VENERABLE ARTS

OF

SORCERY, PRESTIDIGITATION, WIZARDRY, DECEPTION, & CHICANERY

AND OF THE

MOUNTEBANKS & SCOUNDRELS

WHO HAVE

PERPETRATED THESE SUBTERFUGES

ON A

BEWILDERED PUBLIC

BY

JAMES RANDI, ESQ.,

A CONTRITE RASCAL

ONCE DEDICATED

TO THESE WICKED PRACTICES

BUT NOW

ALMOST TOTALLY REFORMED

ST. MARTIN'S PRESS   NEW YORK

Library of Congress Cataloging-in-Publication Data
Randi, James.
    Conjuring / James Randi.
        p.   cm.
    "Being a definitive history of the venerable arts of sorcery, prestidigitation, wizardry, deception, and chicanery and of the mountebanks and scoundrels who have perpetuated these subterfuges on a bewildered public, in short, magic!"
        ISBN 0-312-08634-2
        1. Conjuring—History.—I. Title
GV1543.R36 / 1992
793.8—dc20   92-21042
                                                              CIP

Design by Janet Tingey

FIRST EDITION: DECEMBER 1992

10 9 8 7 6 5 4 3 2 1

DEDICATION

A number of folks influenced my life in Magic and guided me through professional and personal crises. In the 1940s Harry and Sophie Smith ran the Arcade Magic and Novelty Store in Toronto, Canada, where I spent so many long Saturday afternoons puzzling over obscure directions for some miracle or other. Those were golden hours presided over by the irascible Harry, who squinted at my bumbling efforts and sighed mightily as he once more showed me my errors. Dai Vernon—a minor god—would sometimes drop by to offer a suggestion, and Sid Lorraine, ever ready with a gag, might be there to propose a bon mot or two that could add some entertainment value to what I was doing. In the T. Eaton Company store a few blocks away, the diminutive Johnny Giordemaine held court from behind a counter in the toy department, freely offering his wisdom and criticism to the neophytes. Sometimes we listened.

Then there were the giants who gave of their time and consideration so that I might not be a total embarrassment to the profession. Robert (The Great) Morton took me on the road with him as an opening act, and sweated through a couple of jailbreaks with me, never faltering as he assured the assembled reporters that he knew I could do it. I'm proud to say that I never let him down. That magnificent rascal Joe Dunninger tolerated my chatter through many long evenings at his home, no doubt wishing that I had enough ESP to sense his surfeit.

And then there was Harry Blackstone. I admired the others; I worshipped Harry. His eyes still twinkle at me over the years since he's been gone, and I still hear his voice in moments of reverie. I miss him very, very much.

All those folks, with the exception of Dai Vernon, are gone now, though their shadows fall over the scene occasionally. I have thought of them frequently as I prepared this book, and I humbly dedicate this effort to their memories. With all their faults and glories, they were my gods, and I think I could not have chosen better. I only hope that they acted wisely when they encouraged me to embrace my strange and fickle Muse.

Only recently, a young man named Sándor Horváth, who as "Alex" works his magic in the streets of Budapest, restored my faith in the integrity of basic simple traditional magic by proving that it still works to attract, amuse, and captivate new audiences of all cultures, all ages, and all political opinions. Alex is the shaman, the mountebank, the warlock, and the enchanter of the world's storybooks. He is Magic.

James Randi
Plantation, Florida
January 1992

CONTENTS

Contents

AN APOLOGY

Choosing what artists would appear in this book was a very difficult task. The number of persons who might have been included is very large indeed, and many suggestions have been offered by those of my colleagues who knew that I was preparing the volume. Of course I could not include all who might have been selected because of their performing record or their other contributions to the art of magic, but those major figures who I felt best represented various aspects of the trade have been incorporated. If some favorite artist, writer, or inventor in the field has been omitted, please forgive me.

If you are in the profession and find that you are not in these pages, it's not because I ignored you; I may have been unaware of your value to magic, or may have been forced to omit you for other reasons. Some of my personal friends will not appear here, for any of many reasons, mostly because of limited space; I have tried to create a history of the subject rather than a catalog of performers. I know that I will go to print having offended some of you, and for that, I am sorry. However, in spite of any disappointments, I hope that you will enjoy this effort to bring to the public some of the excitement and joy that we share in this remarkable profession.

To at least show my good intentions, I have produced a list of conjurors, along with their real names (where they have adopted stage names) and their dates of birth and death. Some of those names may have been included in the text when submitted to the publisher, but have been chopped out by a cruel editor to make room.

It has been a rather tiresome custom, in other histories of this subject, for the author to reveal some of the major secrets of the conjuring profession in order to make the book more attractive to the buyer. I have chosen to break this tradition, believing that the personalities, the events, and the growth of this art should provide entertainment enough to the reader. My publishers, too, have agreed to discard the formula, under threat of being vanished into that place to which magicians' assistants go and from which they never return . . .

The old Empire Theatre in Montreal was converted to a supper club, the Folies Royales. I had the pleasure of reopening the place in 1965, well assisted by these attractive helpers. Happy days!

INTRODUCTION

Conjuring is said to be the second-oldest profession, and may well be the oldest of the theatrical arts. Once the carefully guarded weapon of the priesthood, by which it was used to establish a belief in supernatural powers among an uninformed public, it progressed uneasily through the Middle Ages from a largely scorned though tolerated street-corner diversion, to become a popular and generally respected branch of modern theater.

The word "magic" is derived from the word "magi," referring to the priest-scholars of ancient Chaldea and Media. The word is largely misused, especially in America. In one dictionary it is defined as "an attempt to control nature by means of spells and incantations." That same dictionary tells us that a "conjuror" is "one who [summons] spirits and pretends to perform miracles by their aid." This definition almost accepts that spirits can be invoked, but denies that the performer really makes use of their supernatural assistance. Another source defines conjuring as the art of "producing the appearance of genuine magic by means of trickery and deception." The line between natural and supernatural is often poorly drawn, but those who appear in this book are more correctly referred to as conjurors, rather than as magicians.

In the United Kingdom, the term "conjuror" is widely understood and used. In the United States and Canada, conjurors are referred to as magicians and their art is "magic." I will use the terminology interchangeably so as not to show bias, though I admit I prefer the purer usage. The conjuror is, simply put, an actor who plays the part of a wizard.

A recent journal from China defined the art rather well, though clinically. It said:

> Magic is a comprehensive, scientific performance. Magicians use their knowledge of science, specialized equipment and considerable skill in order to "openly deceive" their audiences.
>
> A magic performance is actually a competition of wits between the audience and the magician. The audience is trying to solve the tricks, but that is difficult for them to do. The magician is an expert at observing and shrewdly evaluating the audience's thoughts.
>
> One valuable quality of the magician is being creative. . . .

This present book is not concerned with witchcraft, "occult sciences," fortune-telling (such as astrology and biorhythm), or the many and various religious figures who claim divine contact that empowers them to heal the sick, cure poverty, or confer immortality of diverse sorts. There are cases where persons believed to be genuinely supernatural have used common conjuring modalities to establish that belief, and some of them will be included here as conjurors. It is correct that they be encompassed here, though my honest fellow conjurors may resent such neighbors.

There was a time—not quite passed, I regret to say—when folks did not trouble to differentiate between "real" magic and the trickery sort. Of course, an obvious difference was that the latter usually worked, while the former never did manage to live up to its promises. Certainly, the distinction between the two sorts of magic is not always clear. Modern performers, with few exceptions, do not insult their audiences by claiming supernatural powers, though one well-known artist is known to have said, following a series of clever tricks that strongly suggested he might have used genuine occult powers, "If I wanted to, I could perform *all* of these things by trickery!" You are allowed to make your own assessment of his meaning.

Conjuring is, along with mime, acrobatics, juggling, and dance, international in its appeal and understood by all. Fortunately, the effect of much of the magician's performance is due to the sense of sight. Problems arise when the effect relies on language, though world-class conjurors have often mastered a number of languages or have memorized their patter well enough to get their ideas across. On one occasion, with the aid of a taped translation, I myself had to laboriously commit to memory a three-minute speech in Danish, a language with which I am still totally unacquainted, and with much trepidation I delivered my piece on my opening night in Copenhagen with Circus Moreno. To my great relief, the audience reaction to my rendition seemed excellent, and the director assured me that I had "a great American accent." The following night, confident that I had mastered the language, I delivered the speech in *exactly* the way that I'd heard it on the recording I'd learned it from. The director was near apoplexy as I left the stage. "You've lost your accent!" he exclaimed, "Go back to doing it the way it was! Otherwise, they'll think you're Danish!" You just can't please some people.

This book deals with tricksters and their trickery. It is a grand, noble sort of trickery, a skilled imposture that fascinates, puzzles, and entertains by confounding the sensory system in a delicious and titillating fashion. Conjuring is specialized acting, a performing art, an entertainment. It is inherently honest, though it deceives. That statement requires clarification, which may be achieved by discussing a parallel.

Most of us are familiar with the actor Hal Holbrook, and many of us have had the privilege of seeing his one-man presentation of *An Evening with*

Mark Twain. It is, in my memory, one of the more captivating and entertaining evenings that the theater can offer, a veritable tour de force. During the presentation, the actor looks, talks, dresses, walks, and gestures like Mark Twain. He uses the words of Twain—and much of the success of the performance, I'm sure he will admit, is due to that fact. But consider this: If Mr. Holbrook tried to tell us that he actually *is* Mark Twain, we would be insulted. We know better, I hope, and we must credit our temporary suspension of disbelief to the superlative skill of the actor. We willingly agree, for an hour or so, to be taken into the presence of a famous personality recreated for us on a stage.

Similarly, the honest conjuror is an actor, employing his or her deftness of characterization, consummate dexterity, and general charm, often but not always assisted by certain concealed technologies, to win the attention and the appreciation of an audience. The conjuror is a character actor, a juggler of the senses and a master of psychology, and makes no attempt to *be* a guru, saint, clairvoyant, or messiah. Entertainment is the goal.

It is not difficult to imagine that a group of early Egyptian scholars had discovered, through patient observation and record-keeping, that the Nile would rise and inundate the land at certain dates, calculable by a system known only to them. Assuming—quite safely, I believe—that these clever men were driven by the same thirst for wealth and power that their descendants worldwide experience today, a further extrapolation of their probable actions might suggest that they then announced the alarming probability that the Nile's failure to rise and nourish the next season's crops was imminent, unless the proper ceremonies were performed by them in the temples. What threat would more effectively elicit generous donations from the farming community, if not from the very rulers of Egypt? In this or in some similar manner was born the first priesthood.

We know from history that early temples of worship were ruled by priests of both genders. The Oracle at Delphi was run by women, as were various sects of Roman times. In Egypt, several women attained positions of high temporal and religious power, though they had to adopt the trappings of male costume to occupy such stations. However, the conjuring trade is essentially represented by the male gender, in past times and today. Some notable exceptions will be noted in this history. I have always felt that women have been poorly represented in magic, I believe because they have not been able to command the respect for authority to which males have had access. Part of the reason for the failure of women to gain entry to the trade in greater proportion may be found in the most fundamental rule for success in conjuring: The magician is, first and always, in charge of the performance. Without appearing to do so, he disallows questioning of his actions

Above left: Cleopatra was the wife of a Greek magician, Anastasius Kasfikis. He was killed when a crated illusion fell on him, and Valeria—Cleopatra—immediately took over the show. She performed internationally for many decades. Above right: Dell O'Dell was a nightclub performer who ran a large and very successful fan club. She was very knowledgeable about the conjuring art, and a proficient performer.

or claims, he overrides all interference, and he plows through delays and distractions to accomplish his ends. He runs the show. A failure to be in charge can be disastrous.

There have been prominent women in the trade featured as stars: Adelaide Herrmann; Cleopatra (Valeria Kasfikis or Cherni), as The Goddess of the Nile; Okita (Julia Ferret or De Vere); Lady Frances (Frances E. Hess); Ionia (Elsie Williams); Mercedes Talma; Diana Zimmerman, as Diana the Enchantress; Dell O'Dell (Dell Newton); Tina Lenert; Paula Paul; and Celeste Evans are only a few. But generally speaking, women have mainly served as the foils for male prestidigitators, being torn to shreds, severed in two or more pieces, cremated or otherwise brutalized to entertain the masses. That uncomfortable situation may well be nearing its end, even as I write. Recently, Margaret Daily was elected president of the Society of American Magicians. Several Las Vegas showplaces have signed up women like the beautiful and talented Melinda as featured magical performers, not just as box-jumpers. Magic clubs are going out to enlist women as members. Even the prestigious Magic Circle of England has finally not only accepted a female member, but actually appointed Charlotte Pendragon directly to the distinguished highest position in that organization, Member of the Inner Magic Circle (MIMC). This positive step must be credited to the Circle president, Mr. David Berglas.

As we will see, a few conjurors have attained positions of great influence in society, often by using the simplest trickery. I came upon evidence of just such a situation when Dr. Morton Smith, a renowned scholar of religion and languages at Columbia University in New York, presented me with a translation of a very old Greek document that appeared to make little sense but clearly dealt with a method of producing the "human volcano" phenomenon. Unclear references to a "nutshell" and various fuzzy procedures had Dr. Smith understandably puzzled.

Armed as I was with rather specialized expertise, I was able to provide Dr. Smith with enough information about the modus of accomplishing the trick, and he soon had, to his great delight, an adequate interpretation. He then revealed to me that the scamp who had employed this trick in 135 B.C. in Sicily, a Syrian slave named Eunus, attained enough occult reputation with it to lead a major revolt. Eunus became a king for a while, but after a short reign, perished miserably. It is said that in 132 A.D., Bar Kokhba, leader of a Jewish revolt against Rome, attained a similarly powerful reputation with exactly the same simple trick.

Many tens of thousands of conjurors have appeared on the world scene. There may be some mentioned here who are not easily recognized by the lay reader, but whose names are revered by those in the trade. These are the "magicians' magicians," who have set standards, perfected sleights, invented

Above left: Tina Lenert with her mop-headed character in the "Maid in Heaven" number. Magic and mime are cleverly woven into this internationally acclaimed presentation. Above right: Celeste Evans conquered the image of women as the assistants to magicians by becoming a magic star in her own right. Her costume made certain standard procedures unavailable to her, so she successfully created new methods.

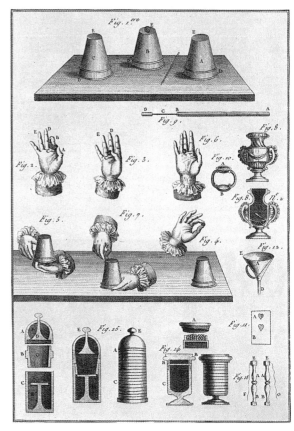

Above left: A woodcut from the 1470 book, Wirkungen der Planeten *("Effects of the Planets") showing that the moon rules such trades as fishing, milling, and conjuring. Above right: The moves for executing the Cups & Balls trick are described and illustrated in many old books.*

principles, designed illusions, or theorized on our art.

I will draw upon information obtained from other histories, friends, specialized libraries, personal interviews, published biographies, historical documents, letters, posters, playbills, and certain secret sources, in order to present to my reader a history of conjuring that reflects the changing tastes of the public as well as the adaptations made by the artists themselves as new technology has become available to be applied to the art. In some ways, what would have seemed wonderful to audiences only a decade ago has been superseded by technological miracles of a greater magnitude, yet a wizard who snatches a rabbit from an empty hat need hardly improve upon that trick to satisfy his customers.

In a very interesting but somewhat naïve book, *The Lives of the Conjurors,* author Thomas Frost declares that

> performing singly, . . . [the conjurors] have few opportunities of association, and those peculiarities which are the product of gregariousness are, in consequence, not developed.

Today, nothing could be further from the truth, and though Mr. Frost was writing in 1876, the situation was very much the same then as now. For the very reason that we are few in number, we seek one another out with great

diligence. Except for those very, very few among us who choose to adopt the appearance of divine or otherwise supernatural affiliations, we are convivial to excess. I cannot imagine a colleague of mine refusing to assist me in any way possible with technical advice, the loan of equipment or tools, or sources of information. Nor could I ever fail to reciprocate.

We magicians constitute an admittedly strange sector of humanity. I have found, generally, that each of us marches to one of those different drummers postulated by Thoreau, and we all, perhaps, are seeking some sort of control over a slightly foreign world. We are, in some cases, misfits from a parallel universe. What strange mistuning of character could inspire an otherwise ordinary person to step out before a critical audience and claim to demonstrate godlike powers? The answer to that profound question has always eluded me.

To enter this profession, one needs to be a little mad. After years of being flooded out, burned out, chased out, and tired out, working with carnivals and ten-in-one sideshows, laboring long hours in very minor, smoky nightclubs in which the bimbos were of much more interest to the patrons than anything I could offer them, I could have easily turned to any of a score of other professions. When unscrupulous agents and managers swindled me and club owners short-paid me, I stayed with it. When unpleasant substances and objects were thrown my way as very obvious expressions of dissatisfaction, I adjusted to the problem. Following reviews in which questions were raised about the wisdom of my remaining in the business, I bravely managed to ignore the obvious message. I persisted, in spite of very good reasons to abandon my Muse.

Robbed of money and wardrobe in Ottawa, Canada, as a teenager many years ago, unable to pay the hotel, I abandoned my props and slipped away late at night out of a back window to return to my parents in Toronto. This process is referred to in show business as "doing a raincoat and whiskers."

Above left: A 1493 German version of Circe turning the crew of Odysseus into swine also shows divination (scrying) taking place along with the Cups and Balls. The lady was, apparently, the complete sorceress. Above right: James Randi, at age seventeen, seems to imagine that he has something captured. A ghost, perhaps . . . ?

Oleg and Kate Medvedev are young Russian artists who combine traditional and very modern magic with song and dance.

Only a week later I was in Buffalo, New York, wearing a cheap new suit and breaking in an equally new deck of playing cards, not at all aware that I was about to be asked to appear on a major U.S. television show and to learn that I apparently had something to offer the public after all. I had been "discovered," and I haven't looked back since. It doesn't always happen that way. I know a number of young folks who have become quite proficient in the art of conjuring, but have never attained success as performers. Those are the breaks.

A certain number of artists in magic are strict amateurs, exceedingly skilled but not professional. From this segment of the conjuring population have come a number of very valuable artistic contributions, without which certain aspects of the art might not yet have developed. By definition, an amateur is "one who loves," and some amateur conjurors are known to specialize in a limited number of carefully selected tricks that are the admiration of all who see them. Happily, they choose to remain attached to conjuring as amateurs, contributing to the history, techniques, and innovations of magic. They are valued for their contributions, which need not be made from behind the footlights.

Conjuring is, to most of those we will read of here, a business. There are matters of advertising, pricing, hiring and firing, design, transportation, and management to consider in order that the conjuror may successfully compete against other attractions that seek to part the spectator from his money. Jealousy, detraction, and plagiarism are not unheard-of in the trade, and in sorting out the truth about any performer one often has to bypass a great number of canards created by contemporary competitors.

As in any art, there are dilettantes and outright bunglers who certainly should have been included on the "little list" of the Mikado's Lord High Executioner. Now here is a controversial and daring statement of opinion

Armando Vera is from Mexico. He specializes in close-up and card magic, and is much in demand at magicians' conventions around the world.

for me to make: Most of these monsters are safely cocooned away in magic clubs that keep them insulated, never to become butterflies. Please understand; I do not in any way disparage the numerous magic clubs that are found around the world. On the contrary, I visit them regularly and make many new and valued friends from their ranks. Most of their members are skilled performers. They are dedicated to the art of conjuring, and frequently contribute to it. These clubs serve as a valuable means of introducing young people—neophytes—to the art, and help to train them. But the clubs often perform another valued, though unintended, service. They satisfy the fumblers who will not or cannot see that they are inept as performers and would do better as collectors or historians of conjuring, rather than dismaying and embarrassing audiences with their floundering attempts. They are thus effectively quarantined, and conjuring is better off for that fact.

As in any profession, the old must make way for the young. In the past twenty years, many bright young stars of magic have come into prominence. I have often admitted my relief that these ambitious beginners were not around when I myself first broke into the field, or my progress might have been much slower. We have been blessed—particularly by the Orient—with

Above left: The Playboy Clubs gave Harry Maurer his start in magic, and now he is a Vegas and Atlantic City regular with his fast-paced comedy-and-magic act. Above right: One of my favorite photographs of a magician at work. Here is shown the ecstatic reaction of a young spectator when he finds that conjuror Tony Albano, himself not yet out of his teens in this photo, can make the trick work right up close. This is what our art is all about, what it attempts to achieve and why we do it.

new ideas, exciting innovations, and a spectrum of new talents that have given our art renewed strength and inspiration. A revolution is taking place today in magic, and it is headed by the young.

The pursuit of conjuring as a profession requires long practice sessions, some suffering, and a lot of self-criticism. The Muse of Magic is particularly severe and quite intolerant of incompetents, who are weeded out early in the game. Those who survive are usually unselfish, caring folks, patient with newcomers and willing to help. I'm very proud to be part of the community of conjurors, and I hope in this book to parade before the reader some of the glory, the heartache, the wonder, and the pure fun in which we specialize.

I am happy in my profession, and delighted that I was foolish enough to embrace this particular Muse. She has venomous snakes for hair, sharp claws, cloven feet, a barbed tail . . . Aha! for a moment there, you accepted the illusion. My Muse is in actuality a delight, a beauty in many ways, a demanding but often generous mistress, an enigma in herself.

The poet Goethe said, "The highest problem of any art is to cause, by appearance, the illusion of a higher reality." If that is true, then conjuring takes on this task more directly, and with generally greater success, than any other art. The practitioners— curious, peculiar, whimsical, some somewhat eccentric, many of them misfits, but artists all—are the subjects of this book.

This is the world of magic and of magicians. It is my world, for better or for worse. Welcome to my world!

CONJURING

The author, James Randi.

CHAPTER 1

IN THE BEGINNING...

Egypt and India are perhaps the countries most often connected in the public mind with wizardry. The Arabian Nights' tales, gypsy legends, Ali Baba, and biblical stories all take us to the Far and Middle East for magical adventures.

In the last century, magician Robert Heller claimed that he had discovered evidence concerning the biblical account of Aaron's battle with two sorcerers of Egypt, who are identified in the Arabian version of this encounter as Jambres and Jannes. In this story it was said that each of the magi cast down rods that became snakes. Heller said he had seen drugged or hypnotized snakes that first looked like sticks, and then became mobile again when stroked by the conjurors. Since this trick seems to be lost to modern Egyptian artists, I seriously doubt magus Heller's story. Such secrets are seldom lost to performers. Furthermore, it seems likely that biologists would have discovered such remarkable behavior by now.

However, there exists an Egyptian document, some twenty-five centuries older, that would seem to be much more believable, since it describes a trick still known and used by some modern street performers. This manuscript is known as the Westcar Papyrus, after its 1823 discoverer, Henry Westcar, who sold it to Egyptologist Richard Lepsius. It is currently in the Berlin State Museum. It was written thirty-eight hundred to four thousand years ago, but relates events that are said to have occurred five hundred years earlier, in the reign of the pharaoh Khufu, more popularly known as Cheops. He was probably the builder of the Great Pyramid at Gizeh, near Cairo.

The Westcar Papyrus relates a series of tales told at the court of Cheops to the pharaoh by his sons. Since the beginning of the document is missing, we have only a tantalizing end to the first account of an unknown marvel said to have taken place in the reign of Pharaoh Djoser.

Following that is a miracle of Pharaoh Nebka's time, described by Cheops' son Khafre (Cephren), who was to attain immortality through his construction of the second-largest pyramid at Gizeh. This story tells of one Webaoner, a court magician-scholar faced with the problem of an adulterous wife who was sending expensive gifts to a townsman who had attracted her. This Lothario, who was holding trysts with the errant wife in an enclosed garden area, was known to bathe in the lake at a certain time, so Webaoner cunningly sculpted a wax crocodile "seven fingers long," which he cast into the water at the proper moment. It immediately became seven cubits (twelve feet) long, and dutifully swallowed the hapless bather.

Pharaoh Nebka, a witness to this wonder, was fearful of the beast, but when Webaoner reached down to pick it up, it was once again a harmless wax model. I regret to report that the faithless wife was taken, on the command of the pharaoh, and burned.

Next on the Westcar Papyrus we have a story told to Cheops by his second son about the reign of Cheops' father, Snefru. This bored pharaoh, on the suggestion of his magician-scholar Djadjaemonkh, had arranged to view a bevy of twenty naked ladies rowing three of his boats, a sight which Djadjaemonkh had assured him would "gladden his heart." It did indeed, but Snefru became concerned when one of the ladies ceased rowing, and he inquired about the reason for this failing. The maiden sobbed that she had dropped a "fish-shaped charm of new turquoise" overboard into the lake. The ruler offered to replace the bauble, but she was distraught, wanting the original back. Pharaoh's magician was commanded by his ruler to recover the amulet.

Ever ingenious and willing to please, Djadjaemonkh simply folded the lake! He "placed one side of the water of the lake upon the other, and lying upon a potsherd he found the fish-shaped charm."

Personally, I find both the crocodile and the lake-folding tricks rather hard to accept. Mind you, I wasn't there, but I reserve the right to make informed judgments.

The papyrus reveals that Cheops' third son, Hardedef, was the wisest son by far. Pointing out to his father that the former tales involved only the past and the dead, he told Cheops that there was a magician known as Dedi, from the town of Ded-Snefru,* who was very much alive and available to perform for Pharaoh. One of Dedi's specialties, said Hardedef, consisted of wringing the head off a goose, then restoring it again. This description so fascinated Cheops that the ruler immediately dispatched his son to fetch the wizard, and Hardedef took several boats up the Nile to Ded-Snefru. Dedi

---

* Believed to be a site now known as Medūm, forty miles south of Cairo, known for its collapsed pyramid constructed by Snefru.

was duly boarded, along with several of his helpers and many books, and arrived at the royal court.

In the pillared hall of the palace, Cheops met the wizard, and the following exchange occurred:

PHARAOH: How is it, Dedi, that I have not seen you before?

DEDI: It is only the one who is summoned who comes, Pharaoh. I have been summoned, and see, I have come.

PHARAOH: Is it true, the saying that you know how to reattach the head that has been cut off?

DEDI: Yes, I do know how, Pharaoh.

PHARAOH: Let there be brought to me the prisoner who is in confinement, that his punishment may be inflicted.

DEDI: But not indeed to a man, Pharaoh, for the doing of the like is not done even to the august cattle.

Cheops thought about this for a while. They apparently compromised, and a goose was brought and decapitated. The papyrus continues:

The goose was placed on the western side of the pillared court, and its head on the eastern side. Dedi said his magic words. The goose arose and waddled and so did its head. The one reached the other and the goose stood up and cackled. Next he caused a waterfowl to be brought, and the like was done with it. Then His Majesty caused that there be brought to him an ox, and its head was felled to the ground. Dedi said his magic words, and the ox stood up behind him with its tether fallen to the ground.

Dedi then followed his conjuring demonstration by making some potent prophecies for Cheops, which need not concern us here. The lake-folding and wax-crocodile stories are certainly not accounts of conjuring but tales of sorcery, and do not belong in our discussion. However, the bird's-head-off-and-back-on trick and the method for doing it are well known to conjurors, though not currently popular in most drawing rooms, and not done *quite* as described here. Where the papyrus relates that the same feat was performed with an ox, it may be simply a bit of hyperbole—not entirely unheard-of in descriptions of conjuring—and likely to creep into the story. Bear in mind that this document was written by a scribe from secondhand reports nearly five hundred years after the event.

In the Westcar Papyrus we find the additional claim that Dedi was a bit of a lion tamer as well, being able to make wild animals follow him about quite docilely. We are not told whether he entertained Pharaoh with this performance.

Also, the scribe recorded that this same Dedi was 110 years old and that he consumed every day five hundred loaves of bread, a side of beef, and a hundred jugs of beer. I find that claim hard to swallow. The time required to eat all that bread and chug down all that beer would leave little time or coordination for any other activity, especially at that advanced age.

Note that Dedi was not willing to perform with a human being as the victim, perhaps because one of the necessary props would be rather difficult to obtain, especially on short notice. And, more importantly, he appears to have been manipulating Pharaoh into doing things *his* way, as would be expected of any competent conjuror.

We have no record in the Westcar Papyrus of what reward Dedi received for his show. That portion of the document is also missing. We are only told that Cheops kept Dedi on hand, and his retainer was a thousand loaves of bread plus other necessities. According to the consumption ascribed to Dedi, that would have fed him for only two days. Perhaps Pharaoh was not that impressed with the performance after all.

In reconstructing this account, author Henry Ridgely Evans, apparently relying on an early translation of the Westcar Papyrus, has misnamed Dedi and ascribed his control of animals to "hypnosis." Not very likely. Evans also naïvely assumed that later sixteenth-century conjurors (he mentions Nostradamus) used huge concave mirrors to produce illusionary effects that were far beyond their means.

(I am appalled by this strange preoccupation with curved mirrors as a means by which the ancients created certain claimed illusionary effects, when we have no adequate evidence to establish that the described events ever took place at all—no more than we know that the Red Sea parted as described in religious writings. This dependence on huge curved reflectors was very thoroughly perpetuated by Sir David Brewster (1781–1868) in his book *Letters on Natural Magic*, and many writers on magic have repeated his declarations uncritically. His opinions in this respect show that he was not at all well informed about the subject, though he professed far-reaching expertise. He certainly had adequate knowledge of the optical properties of various devices, but did not recognize that the technical problems of constructing the large, properly curved reflectors needed were insoluble in early times. Such a mirror could not have been made, any more than Da Vinci could have constructed the helicopter he designed—brilliantly—on paper. It is such poorly derived opinions as Brewster's that detract from proper treatment of these subjects.)

The bird trick was an advertised specialty of a British performer named Moon, who was active around 1800. His card read:

> MR. MOON, the celebrated conjuror, whose dexterity in command of the cards is unanimously acknowledged, will undertake to convey the contents of any gentleman's purse into his (Mr. Moon's) pockets with surprising facility. He will also cut a cock's head off without injuring that noble bird.

Moon, billing himself as "Ingleby, Emperor of all Conjurors," appeared in London in 1807. He advertised "the amazing trick of cutting a fowl's head off, and restoring it to life and animation, for no man knows the real way but himself."

Soon afterward, he found it necessary to declare that

there are numbers of wandering people performing at Bartholemew fair, and some in the Metropolis, and other parts of England, saying they will expose the method of cutting the fowl's head off; yes, for a very good reason, because they cannot do it without exposing it; but if they come to the Minor Theatre, they shall see the Emperor execute it without exposition, in the first style of superlative excellence.

By 1830, the trick was so well known that Thomas Frost, in his 1876 book, *The Lives of the Conjurors*, says that it was "in the repertoire of every conjuror who exhibited at a country fair."

Howard Thurston in the 1920s featured in his stage show a trick very similar to Dedi's. He seemed to remove the heads of a duck and chicken, then switched them. Fu Manchu in Mexico used the trick in 1935, using a black and a white duck. Modern conjuror David Copperfield has taken the cue and also uses the same trick today in his full stage show. So the oldest trick in recorded history is still with us, and appears to have never left!

In 1584, English writer Reginald Scot's *The Discouerie of Witchcraft* published details of a decapitation trick using a human being. Poorly diagrammed, it would have been a difficult trick to get away with, in my estimation. As we will see in Chapter 29, Chinese conjurors were familiar with this illusion as well.

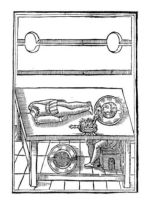

The "Beheading of John the Baptist" trick as revealed in Scot's Discouerie of Witchcraft.

This drawing on an Egyptian tomb wall does not, *despite several assertions by writers on the subject, depict an early performance of the Cups & Balls trick. It illustrates a popular game of the day.*

The Cups & Balls routine, in which small stones or balls made of wood, cork, or fabric are caused to congregate in or travel through, under, and out of three metal or wooden cups that are slid about mouth-down on a table, is one of the most popular and artful tricks in the conjurors' repertoire. It has been claimed that this most venerable trick was represented in a Middle Kingdom tomb wall painting at Beni-Hasan, on the river Nile, in an area now flooded by the Aswan Dam project. This drawing, however, is merely an illustration of a game known as Up from Under, which was played at that time, four thousand years ago. It is not proof that ancient Egyptians were conjuring, though they doubtless were.

Certainly, the Cups & Balls was performed by conjurors in imperial Rome, and there was a word, *acetabularii,* to describe the many masters of the trick who performed in the streets. Later Italians used the term *giuoco di bussolotti* ("game of measures") referring to the measuring cups often used. The Greeks called a manipulator of these materials a *psephopaikteo,* the French said he was an *escamoteur* or *joueur de goubelets,* and the ever-direct

Above left: Johannes Brigg, though born without legs and one hand, played several musical instruments and performed difficult sleights such as the Cups & Balls. Above right: The remarkable Matthias Buchinger, "The Little Man From Nuremberg," was married four times and had eleven children, but still found time to earn a great reputation as an engraver, artist, and accomplished conjuror. He was substantially handicapped but overcame his disabilities in a dramatic fashion.

Germans derived their word, *Taschenspieler* ("pocket-player"), from the frequent trips to the pocket made by the performer's unnoticed hand. In days before clothing had regular pockets, the hand visited the conjuror's apron for the same secret purposes.

The great Latin philosopher and writer Seneca (4 B.C.?–A.D. 65) commented on the methods of semantic trickery used by orators of his day and provided proof that the Cups & Balls was familiar to people of his time:

Such [semantic tricks] are as harmlessly misleading as the juggler's cups and pebbles, in which it is the trickery itself which pleases me. But, show how the trickery is done, and I have lost my interest in it.

Seneca is voicing an interesting observation here. He recognizes that the revelation of the modus operandi behind a conjuring trick brings no delight, but results instead in a certain dissatisfaction for the observer.

The Greek observer Alciphron (second or third century A.D.) left us quite an excellent account of a performance of this classic trick.

One thing that I saw made me almost speechless and caused me to gape in surprise. A man approached and set on a tripod table three small dishes, beneath which he then concealed some small round white pebbles. He placed them one by one under the dishes, then—I do not know how—he made them come all together under one! At other

The conjuror Bussolti entertains a street crowd with the classic Cups & Balls trick.

times he made them disappear from beneath the dishes and then showed them in his mouth. Next, after he swallowed them, he brought those persons who stood nearest him into the middle area, and pulled one stone from the nose, another from the ear and another from out of the head of the man standing near him. Finally he caused the stones to vanish from the sight of all.

Alciphron was quite astonished at the dexterity of the conjuror, but was easily able to ascribe his performance to sleight-of-hand and did not need to invoke diabolic forces as an explanation of what he had seen.

When the Cups & Balls routine was performed in China, after the balls or pebbles had gone through their acrobatics, live baby mice often appeared beneath the cups, and even today the Egyptian performers prefer to materialize baby chicks this way. At the beginning of this century a father-and-son succession of magicians named Gali-Gali toured the world doing this specialty. Other performers will conjure up a lump of coal, metal balls,* oranges or tennis balls as a climax to the routine.

Still widely performed today, and regarded as the test of a conjuror's basic skill, a version of this venerable trick is actually used by U.K. magician Paul

* American sleight-of-hand artist Paul Gertner uses huge steel ball bearings in his superlative performance of Cups & Balls.

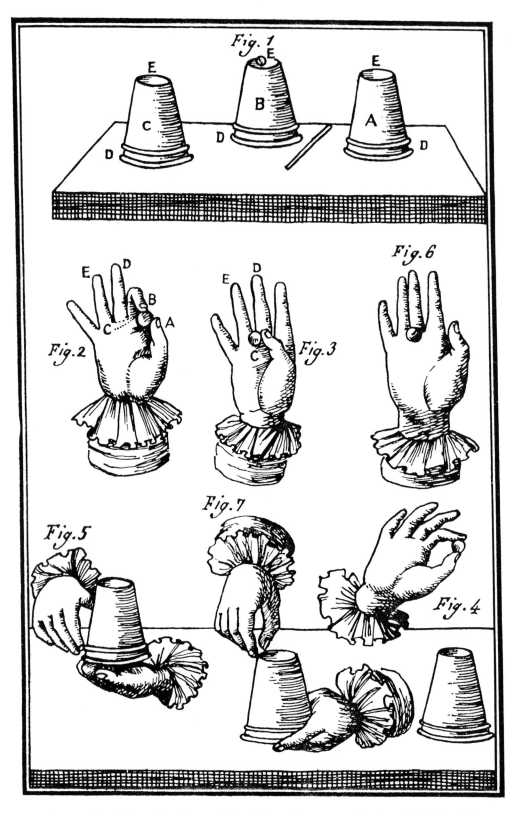

A copperplate illustration, from 1786, of the performance of the Cups & Balls trick.

Daniels to *open* his full stage show, where other performers might have chosen a flashy Pomp-and-Circumstance opening. I think Mr. Daniels has chosen well. When HRH Prince Charles was inducted into the prestigious Magic Circle of London, he was required to perform a trick to demonstrate his skill. He chose the Cups & Balls.

Not a small part of the reason for the persistent popularity of the Cups & Balls lies in a basic fact of the theater, and particularly in conjuring: illusions created with familiar, simple, everyday objects will invariably be more appealing and effective than those that require strange, red-boxes-with-gold-dragons-painted-on-them types of props. Since a spectator knows what a small cloth or cork ball will do when brought into play with wooden or metal measuring cups, any unusual behavior can be a miracle rather than just a puzzle. The public, accustomed to wondrous effects brought about by technology beyond its understanding, will relate more effectively to a performance using ordinary objects. The Cups & Balls trick satisfies this "simplicity" criterion perfectly.

The Greek philosopher Hero described a number of devices driven by hydraulic and thermal power which he said were used in various temples to open doors, sound trumpets, and turn statues, in response to offerings made by worshippers. Later historians devised working diagrams for these machines, only briefly sketched by Hero, and thus freely ascribed to Greek technology the ability to actually build them. Had they ever worked, they would have been cumbersome, undependable contraptions in need of constant attention and repair. A better modus operandi would have been to simply have a concealed person to operate the mechanisms.

I must admit that we conjurors, accustomed to inventing stories to fit our presentations, have applied that skill to create a certain mythology about our own profession and its history. Writers in the trade have freely accepted unlikely tales told by and about their colleagues when those tales have fitted well. I don't know that our account has needed such fluffing, being, as it is, a fascinating enough history. No, the Cups & Balls trick was not described on the walls at Beni-Hasan, Albertus Magnus had no conjuror's cup, and Houdini was not trapped beneath the ice of the Detroit River.

The real people, and the real lives they led, are far more interesting than that.

CHAPTER 2

A RABBIT FROM A HAT & THE FABULOUS INDIAN ROPE TRICK

The magician, at least in the Western world, is irrevocably connected with the famous Rabbit-from-the-Hat trick. I recall the wonderment I experienced as a child, seeing little Johnny Giordemaine on the stage of the Eaton Auditorium in Toronto, Canada. He removed his hat from his head, looked inside with astonishment, and began removing a great number of silk handkerchiefs from the previously empty topper. Then, to my openmouthed delight, he reached inside and pulled a live, squirming bunny from that hat! You can keep your bending spoons and disappearing playing cards; getting a live rabbit from Nowhere is *real* magic!

The origin of this classic is obscure. We know that Professor Anderson, the Great Wizard of the North, was advertising the trick in the 1840s. Whether he originated it is not certain. There is a notion that it might have first been performed by some enterprising English conjuror following a cause célèbre in Godalming, Surrey, in 1726. A housewife named Mary Tofts claimed that she had been attacked and raped in the woods by a giant white rabbit, and though her neighbors—and husband, no doubt—doubted the tale, they all had second thoughts when she began to deliver many small rabbits some weeks later. Ever her doctor, responding to inquiries launched by a very curious King George I, certified that the deliveries were genuine. When Mary later announced a second pregnancy, she was isolated for careful observation and alas! she was found to be perpetrating a fraud. Really? Yep.

In any case, the Rabbit-from-the-Hat trick is very difficult to perform,

demanding great skill and timing. Most magicians I know have never done it, preferring docile doves to kicking coneys. But, to this day, I have never been able to consume any dish prepared with the unwilling cooperation and participation of a rabbit. One must show respect for one's colleagues.

The much-discussed Indian Rope trick is a rather ubiquitous staple of early conjuring history. The famous Indian magician Protul Chandra Sorcar, in his book, *Indian Magic*, devoted thirty-eight pages to establishing that the trick actually was performed by the street "Jadu-wallahs" (itinerant conjurors) long ago, though most of those others who examine the evidence find that it is essentially anecdotal. Interestingly enough, Sorcar never attempted to perform the trick.

A century ago hardly a traveler returned from the East who did not claim to have seen this wonder, in one form or another. Under close questioning, those who told the tale often admitted that they didn't actually *see* the trick, but were told about it by a person they trusted.

More than one thousand years ago, both Pantajali and Sankarācārya, early religious writers of India, referred to the trick wherein "the juggler . . . climbs up the rope and disappears." It is also described in Sutra 17 of the

The East Indian Rope trick wasn't quite what it promised in this poster, but Thurston pleased his audiences with it.

Vedanta, and the Indian poet Kālidāsa recounted how an early king named Vikramaditya was fooled by it, so it is certainly established in history that *something* was being done from time to time that has come down to us in a probably vastly hyperbolized account.

Many variations of the story exist. In one basic version, the wizard is said to throw a rope into the air, where it remains rigid. A small boy then climbs up the rope, balances on the end, then vanishes at the command of the conjuror. The boy then reappears in the crowd gathered to witness the feat. In another more involved scenario, after the boy climbs the rope, he is enveloped in a cloud and refuses to descend at the conjuror's order, whereupon he is pursued up the rope by his angry master. He is heard to cry out in terror, after which pieces of him—arms, legs and other parts—rain down from the cloud. The conjuror descends to the ground, gathers together the pieces and places them in a large basket, from which the intact boy then emerges to take up a collection from the gratified spectators.

It appears that the frequent visits of Chinese Buddhist pilgrims to India during the T'ang dynasty (A.D. 618-906) brought the story of the Rope Trick to China very early. The T'ang was one of the most culturally adventurous periods of that vast country, during which was recorded the first known printing, and travel and exchange of foreign ideas at that time was much encouraged. One account tells us that in a magic contest in Jiaxin city, a prisoner at the local jail was allowed to compete. He threw one end of a long coil of rope up into the air and it stood erect. The rope continued up until it was extended to a length of twenty *zhang*s (about 110 feet) and the prisoner climbed up the rope and thereupon disappeared. And you thought magic was impractical!

The basic tale of the Indian Rope trick was told much later, about 1700, by Chinese author P'u (Sung) Chu-Ling, in his story "The Theft of the Peach," though in this case the scenario was that the magician sent his son up the rope to steal a peach from heaven. The boy was caught and dismembered by heavenly guards who threw him down from the sky in pieces. He was similarly happily restored, but this time in a bamboo box. Unlike his Indian counterpart he was not privileged at this point to collect the offering; his prudent father had already done so in advance. The author of that version credited the trick to a sect known as the White Lily, which was active in China about A.D. 1350. At about the same time, in his *Volume of Travels*,

Sheik Abu Abdullah Mohammad of Tangiers wrote about being in Hang-chow (Hangzhou), China, and witnessing the same miracle.

This "Peach Boy" theme is found repeated in Japanese fairy tales, as well.

P. C. Sorcar, in his long recitation of accounts of the Rope trick, failed to note a few important aspects about the data he'd recorded. They indicate that the witnesses were either seeing very different performances or that they were not capable of recounting what they actually saw. It is vital to point out that observers of conjuring tricks *very often* misreport what occurred, not necessarily because they are witless or are lying, but more often simply because they have been misdirected so effectively that they do not have an accurate memory of the event, and unconsciously fill in details that were not there. It is a common failing.

First, in Sorcar's many stories told by "reputable" witnesses, the trick is said to be done, in most cases, with a *thread* rather than a rope, and in some reports it is only the standing of the thread that is described. A red rope, a string, a golden rope, a "thicksome" rope, and a "thin" rope are all reported as having been used. In some other cases, it is not a boy, but a monkey, a horse, a hare or "a winsome young woman, at all points adorned," who is said to have ascended the rope or thread. (In the case of the horse, it is claimed that the magician, "himself taking hold of the horse's tail, would follow him [up the rope]." That I have to see.) The Rope trick is sometimes done outdoors, often indoors. The boy either is dismembered and/or re-assembled and/or he vanishes, or any two or all three.

The Indian emperor Jāhangir related to Sir Thomas Roe, an official of the East India Company in 1615, several highly unbelievable feats that he said he'd seen performed by conjurors of Bengal. His description of another classic, the Mango Tree trick, would be almost correct if the singing birds in the branches had been left out. This trick consists of causing a tree to grow in stages beginning with a seed, each new growth being covered with a cloth before the next is revealed. Finally, fruit can be picked by spectators.

In recounting his witnessing of the Rope trick, His Imperial Highness reported that the conjurors he saw brought out

> a chain fifty cubits in length, and in my presence threw one end of it towards the sky, where it remained as if fastened to something in the air. A dog was then brought forward, and, being placed at the lower end of the chain, immediately ran up, and, reaching the other end, dis-appeared in the air. In the same manner a hog, a panther, a lion, and a tiger were successively sent up the chain, and all disappeared at the other end. At last they took down the chain, and put it into a bag, no one ever discerning in what way the animals were made to vanish into the air in the mysterious manner described.

No one in 1615 chose to doubt the emperor's tale, but now that he is very deceased, I think I may safely state that in my opinion he was talking through his turban.

And so it goes. There seems to be a great latitude in what constitutes the Indian Rope/Thread/String trick.

An amazing offer was made in 1934 by Dr. Alexander Cannon, K.C.A., M.D., Ph.D., M.A., of the London County Council Mental Hospital Service. He said that he had seen a version of this trick done "in Indo-China." It is not quite clear, especially after we read his report, whether Cannon was a physician serving the hospital or a patient in that facility. He outlined his offer in detail at a meeting of the British College of Psychic Science in London. His description of the trick has the boy climbing a red rope, which goes so high that the lower end is actually off the ground as well. The performer follows the lad up the rope and hacks him to bits, all of which drop to the ground, still individually "quivering." The magician reassembles the boy by setting the bits together on the ground and stomping on them, then sends the ever-tolerant lad back up the rope, whereupon he vanishes. Cannon offered to perform the trick under certain incredible conditions:

> I can produce the Rope Trick in the Albert Hall, London. . . . Providing you are willing to lay down enough money to bring over a shipload of special sand, to heat up the Albert Hall to tropical temperature, and to provide my own tropical lighting—and also to place with a bank £50,000 to be handed over to me as soon as I have produced the phenomenon, I will do it.

It was Cannon's naïve idea that hypnosis was responsible for the stories of the Indian Rope trick. He opined that "in hot climates the cortex of the brain is much more passive and the unconscious mind easier to deal with."

I have serious doubts that Dr. Cannon, even with his K.C.A., M.D., Ph.D., and M.A. degrees, could have done anything useful with all his sand and lighting other than possibly opening a branch of Club Med within the Albert Hall. Nor, I think, did he seriously intend to actually do so.

Even two prominent and accomplished English conjurors, Jasper Maskelyne and Will Goldston, offered the explanation that spectators of the Indian Rope trick were deceived by having a hot tropical sun shining in their eyes! But American John Mulholland, a careful and intelligent researcher into such matters, summed it up with his findings:

> After forty years of trailing the Indian Rope Trick, I have finally found what I was looking for: the reasons why the legend refuses to die. One answer is that after people have been fooled, they are incapable of giving an accurate description of what actually happened during the

magician's performance. Given time, their descriptions often become fantastic. They confuse two or more tricks, and even describe something the magician hasn't done—and couldn't do. . . . Take the enchantment lent by distance, add the embroidery of secondhand hearsay, hemstitch with the 'mystery' of the East—and you come up with a fabric as far from truth as the Magic Carpet. The Indian Rope trick is pure fiction. But Mankind has always had an instinctive urge to manufacture the myth that it exists. The idea of a stairway to heaven is a universal dream.

Years ago, when I had a radio show on station WOR in New York City, the subject of the Indian Rope trick came up for discussion. There followed a letter from a listener who was amazed at my naïveté in not having an explanation for the trick. Claiming all sorts of scientific credentials, he then described how it was done:

> The [Indian Rope] trick is always performed in a valley between mountains. Some time before, the magician's assistants stretch a fine steel wire between the two mountain peaks. Late at night, a huge fire is made which causes a lot of smoke to fill the valley, and the magician throws up a rope with a small steel hook on the end which catches the overhead wire. The boy climbs up into the smoke, slides along the wire behind the crowd, and drops to the ground, unseen. . . .

This remarkable description goes on, getting sillier and sillier. The author, in common with so many who have come up with impossible solutions for the secrets of the conjurors, failed to consider even so simple a problem as the "fine steel wire" he postulated. That wire would have to be a monstrous, thick, braided cable weighing many tons, and anchoring it to each mountain would be a major engineering feat in itself. Even if such a plan with a steel wire were attempted between two buildings rather than mountains, the physical requirements would be beyond any ordinarily available technology, even today.

Regrettably, I must report that P. C. Sorcar himself believed that early Indian street Jadu-wallahs had performed this famous illusion by means of braided human hairs. This is simply not possible, especially when he states that the magician climbed a rope hooked to such a horizontal human-hair cable and then descended with the boy assistant concealed within his robes!

This Indian Rope trick tale seems to be one that has become an enduring bit of folklore, and there is no good evidence that the illusion was ever actually performed, in the generally accepted version. And—who knows—it is perhaps the source of the popular Western children's tale "Jack and the Beanstalk."

Even today, when it might be expected that modern India, with its great contributions to science and mathematics, would be free of belief in medieval notions, there is a ubiquitous belief in astrology and other forms of magic in general. (It embarrasses me to confess that a modern U.S. president also employed an astrologer quite recently!) There actually exists a large international religious cult built up around a "baba" in India who performs—as a miracle—the Holy Ash trick, which has always been a part of the repertoire of the street performers there. He also "materializes" wristwatches for especially important or generous spectators, and films made of this wonder easily reveal the standard methods at work. His "miracles" are accepted by persons of widely differing educational backgrounds and he is treated as an important political power by the government of that country.

Professional conjurors, aware of the attraction of the Indian Rope trick legend, have advertised it in their programes, though there has often been disappointment from the audience that the performance did not meet expectations. Carl Hertz, Horace Goldin, Thurston, Kalanag, and Harry Blackstone, Sr., used it as a publicity draw. Fu Manchu reported that Le Roy, De Biere, Chang, and others had also used it, and that, in his opinion, "[the versions] were all lousy."

As a myth, the Indian Rope trick is a charmer. It should stay in the storybooks where it belongs.

CHAPTER 3

CONJURING IN EARLY EUROPE

Acceptance of tricksters as important personages by ruling powers is not unheard of in history. In England, conjurors gained the attention of Elizabeth I. One of them, Girolamo (Hieronymus) Scotto, entertained the queen regularly and was rewarded handsomely for his talents, even being entrusted as a special secret agent of the Crown to obtain and deliver information as he traveled about the Continent. He attained a considerable reputation through this royal endorsement, and was a celebrated figure of his day. Though Elizabeth seems to have accepted Scotto's talents, another unnamed juggler of her time was condemned as a wizard and escaped the pillory only as a result of pleadings to the queen by the Earl of Leicester, according to writer Reginald Scot.

Dr. John Dee (1527–1608), was more a "real" magician, who practiced astrology and searched for the legendary Philosopher's Stone, a substance that could heal all ills and transmute base metals into gold. The Earl of Leicester was even sent to him by the queen-to-be Elizabeth to ask him to determine—by astrology—a propitious date for her coronation. He became a very trusted servant to Elizabeth, and indeed served her well as a cartographer, navigator, and general advisor, aside from any conjuring or occult shenanigans he might have been asked to perform in her service.

Most early conjurors amplified their programs with such skills as ventriloquism, juggling, sword-swallowing, fire-eating, and tumbling.*

---

*To Oriental performers, conjuring was for a time only a variety of juggling, and an astonishing demonstration was given by some who turned a full somersault and came to an upright position holding a bowl of water that had not been there at the beginning of the acrobatic. This stunt, also done by Ching Ling Foo and Chung Ling Soo, became a specialty of Long Tack Sam, a Chinese variety artist of the 1920s. Early conjurors sold various medications and aphrodisiacs as part of their "pitch," a tradition carried into the twentieth century by mountebanks/quacks (often referred to as "snake-oil salesmen") of the American West.

Above left: Girolamo Scotto, the chosen conjuror of Elizabeth I of England, attained great fame in his day and was a court favorite. Above right: The Satsuma troupe was a typical Oriental act, with jugglers, magicians, and acrobats. Usually, these were family groups working under an American manager.

In about A.D. 1240 the Franciscan monk Roger Bacon (nicknamed Dr. Mirabilis) briefly described the tricks of the conjurors and declared them to be harmless amusements. Bacon was noted as a medieval advocate of experimentation and observation as a means to learning, an advanced idea for his time. His learned opinion on magic tricks was largely ignored, and conjurors continued to be sporadically persecuted by secular and ecclesiastic authorities as minions of Satan.

In English writer Reginald Scot's *The Discouerie of Witchcraft* (1584), we find an in-depth, serious attempt to refute the superstitious belief in witchcraft, demons, and devils. The book, written in the vernacular, consists of sixteen divisions, with the last four devoted to charms and the tricks of jugglers and conjurors; in the sixteenth century, even street performers were suspected of demonic powers, and Scot wished to show that what they did was merely clever trickery. Conjurors will smile to recognize many familiar and still-popular tricks among those Scot mentioned: swallowing a knife, burning a playing card and re-producing it from the spectator's pocket, transferring a coin from one pocket to another, converting coins into tokens and back again into money, making a coin appear in a spectator's hand, passing a coin through a tabletop, making a coin vanish when wrapped into a handkerchief, tying a knot in a handkerchief and making it untie itself, removing beads threaded onto a cord while both ends of the cord are held, transferring rice from one container to another, turning wheat into flour, burning a thread and restoring it, pulling yards of ribbon from the mouth, sticking a knife into the arm, passing a ring through the cheek, and decapitating a person and restoring him.

In Basel, Switzerland, twenty years earlier, Johann Wier's *De praestigiis*

THE
Diſcovery of Witchcraft:

PROVING,

That the Compacts and Contracts of WITCHES
with *Devils* and all *Infernal Spirits* or *Familiars*, are but
Erroneous Novelties and Imaginary Conceptions.

Also diſcovering, How far their Power extendeth in Killing, Tormenting,
Conſuming, or Curing the bodies of Men, Women, Children, or Animals,
by Charms, Philtres, Periapts, Pentacles, Curſes, and Conjurations.

WHEREIN, LIKEWISE

The Unchriſtian Practices and Inhumane Dealings of
Searchers and *Witch-tryers* upon *Aged, Melancholly,* and *Superſtitious*
people, in extorting Confeſſions by Terrors and Tortures,
and in deviſing falſe Marks and Symptoms, are notably Detected.

And the Knavery of *Juglers,* *Conjurers,* *Charmers,* *Soothſayers,* *Figure-Caſters,*
Dreamers, *Alchymiſts* and *Philterers*; with many other things
that have long lain hidden, fully Opened and Deciphered.

ALL WHICH

Are very neceſſary to be known for the undeceiving of *Judges, Juſtices,*
and *Jurors,* before they paſs Sentence upon Poor, Miſerable and Ignorant People;
who are frequently Arraigned, Condemned, and Executed for *Witches* and *Wizzards.*

IN SIXTEEN BOOKS.

By REGINALD SCOT *Eſquire.*

Whereunto is added
An excellent Diſcourſe of the *Nature* and *Subſtance*
OF

DEVILS and SPIRITS,

IN TWO BOOKS:

The *Firſt* by the aforeſaid *Author:* The *Second* now
added in this *Third Edition,* as Succedaneous to the *former,*
and conducing to the compleating of the *Whole Work:*
With *Nine Chapters* at the beginning of the *Fifteenth Book*
of the *DISCOVERY.*

LONDON:

Printed for *Andrew Clark,* and are to be ſold at Mris. *Cotes's* near
the *Golden-Ball* in *Alderſgateſtreet,* 1 6 6 5.

The second edition title page of Reginald Scot's Discouerie of Witchcraft, *in which
he attacked belief in supernatural powers ascribed to old women, and their
subsequent punishment. The book also tried to take suspicion away from conjurors,
who were thought to possess occult powers.*

daemonum had tried to perform the same educational service, but it did not deal with the art of the conjurors. In any case, both books were essentially ignored.

The Scot book is very rare in its first edition, because when James I of England succeeded Elizabeth I to the throne in 1603, he ordered all copies burned. James was most zealous to hang anyone suspected of witchcraft, and since Scot claimed that belief in witches was silly and illogical, his book might have interfered with His Majesty's religious work of torturing and murdering old ladies and misfits—and conjurors as well, we suspect. It was sixty-seven years later, in 1651, that the Scot book again appeared in print, well after the death of King James.

In 1612, *The Art of Juggling* was published, amplifying and improving on Scot's rather poor description of standard tricks of the day but with no philosophical message. It was followed in 1614 by *The Art of Juggling, or Legerdemaine* [*sic*], probably written by one Samuel Rid. Up to this point, books on the subject consisted mostly of exposures of methods, usually very poorly described. Then in 1634, under the nom de plume Hocus Pocus, Jr. (the first time the expression, "hocus-pocus" is known to have been used), the book *The Anatomy of Legerdemain: The Art of Jugling* [*sic*] appeared. Printed in London, it was the first really complete how-to-do-it book on the subject, rather than being just an exposure of tricks. Rules for the successful conjuror were given. In the following extract, "conveyance" refers to the sleight-of-hand action:

> First, he must be one of an impudent and audacious spirit, so that he may set a good face upon the matter.
> Secondly, he must have a nimble and cleanly conveyance.
> Thirdly, he must have strange terms, and emphatical words, to grace and adorn his actions, and the more, to astonish the beholders.
> Fourthly and lastly, such gestures of body as may lead away the spectators' eyes from a strict and diligent beholding of his manner of conveyance.

That set of rules can hardly be improved upon today.

In 1716, an author named Richard Neve published the same set of rules as if he had originated them, adding one more:

> He must have none of his trinkets wanting when he is to use them, lest he be put to a *non-plus*.

Sounds sensible to me.

It is recorded that in 1640 an amateur conjuror named Lamb so worried his neighbors that they began blaming every misfortune of nature on him,

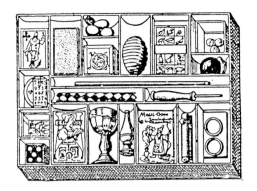

and finally rose as a mob and murdered him. The tricks, too, might have been pretty bad. We will never know.

The next known mention of the words, "hocus pocus" appears in a 1641 pamphlet describing the sights that were seen at Bartholemew Fair that year. The words were apparently the name by which a local conjuror was known. This may be the same man referred to in *A Candle in the Dark*, a 1656 book written by a man named Ady, where we find a still-popular trick in which the conjuror or a spectator drinks some liquid like wine or milk, then recovers that liquid from the forehead or elbow by means of a funnel. Ady tells us:

> I will speak of one man more excelling in that craft than others, that went about in King James's time, and long since, who called himself the King's Majesty's most excellent Hocus Pocus; and so was he called because at playing every trick he used to say, *Hocus pocus tontus talontus, vade celerite jubeo*, a dark composition of words, to blind the eyes of the beholders, to make his trick pass the more currently without discovery, because when the eye and ear of the beholder are both earnestly busied, the trick is not so easily discovered, nor the imposture discerned.

Most magic in early times was performed in the street. Either taking up positions on busy corners, or working at small booths or enclosures or from the backs of well-equipped wagons, the conjurors were mobile and efficient as they took their wares to fairs and marketplaces. Most wore what appeared to be only a convenient apronlike affair around their waists. This was called a *gibecière* (the word for "game-bag") or *servante* ("serving-board"). In actuality, more than serving only as a convenient pocket in which to store small pieces of apparatus, it was made use of as an active prop.

That prop is most prominent in the well-known (circa 1490) painting by

Above left: The title page of this 1745 German book on magic promises "natural" magic and new revelations. Above right: This was a common layout in 1920 for a child's box of tricks. Tried and true items (Cups & Balls, Ball and Vase, etc.) were always part of such sets.

Hieronymus Bosch in St. Germain-en-Laye, which depicts the *Taschen-spieler* amazing his audience while a distracted spectator is having a free purse-lift performed. A book published in Madrid in 1733—*Engaños a Ojos Vistas*, by Pablo Minguet e Yrol—gave detailed instructions on the use of the apron.

One of these conjurors, who actually had an enclosed area to which he charged admission, was Britain's Isaac Fawkes, active in the early 1700s. At first performing mostly at fairs, he eventually rented a room in James Street near the Haymarket, and worked before packed houses. His repertoire included a masterful handling of the Egg Bag trick, in which a number of gold coins, then many eggs, were taken from a small cloth bag that had previously been conclusively shown to be empty; then, a live chicken was produced. Another feature was the old Indian Mango Tree trick, along with several mechanical wonders. Some of those devices were originated by Fawkes' partner Mr. Pinchbeck, who was also very clever at sleight-of-hand.

Fawkes died in 1732 an exceedingly wealthy man, with an estate of more than £10,000, in a day when a pound sterling was much more than a week's income. His son, in partnership with Pinchbeck, carried on the act beginning in 1730 and continuing through the 1740s. An advertisement for the Southwark Fair in 1733 told potential clients that they might see

> the diverting and incomparable dexterity of hand, performed by Mr. Pinchbeck, who causes a tree to grow out of a flower-pot, on the table, which blossoms and bears ripe fruit in a minute; also a man in a maze, or a perpetual motion, where he makes a little ball to run continually which would last was it for seven years together only by the word of command. He has several tricks entirely new, which were never done by any other person than himself.

The versatile Mr. Pinchbeck had also invested in a shop in Fleet Street where he sold various mechanical curiosities, and he and Fawkes Junior sponsored shows using marionettes and a waxworks. Though Pinchbeck broke off his partnership with Fawkes by 1746, Fawkes continued on with other colleagues.

The next important conjuror on the scene was Comus, a French artist who stayed three months in Panton Street in 1765. He returned in 1766 and again in 1770, exhibiting automata.* A second Comus made his appearance in London in 1793, also featuring automata and performing the Bullet Catch along with various mental tricks. A master of word coinage, Comus II advertised that he would feature his Thaumaturgic Horologium, a "self-acting machine"—the "only one existent"—which, he said,

* Robotlike performing machines. See Chapter 4.

Isaac Fawkes was a popular performer at English fairs and in his own indoor theater about 1700, with his magic bag that produced quantities of balls as well as eggs, birds, and gold and silver coins.

by the means of an Alhadida moving on a Cathetus, discovers to the company the exact time of day or night by any proposed watch, though the watch may be in any gentleman's pocket, or five miles distant, if required; it also points out the colour of any lady or gentleman's clothes, by the wearer only touching it with a finger, and is further possessed of such occult qualities as to discover the thoughts of one person to another, even at an unlimited distance.

This marvelous device was accompanied in performance by the Pyxidees Literarum, the Stenanographical Operation, and the one-and-only Teretopæst Figure. Such descriptions make one want to rush out and buy the latest model of the Thaumaturgic Horologium, don't they?

There were two conjurors named Jonas, a Breslaw, a Boaz and a Ray active in London at this same time, all quite successful, and one named Cosmopolita, who most decidedly was not a success. Breslaw was a superior performer, who worked from 1764 to 1784 and upon his retirement published his *Last Legacy* explaining his tricks and the working of his equipment. His announced purpose was to end the notion that the public still harbored, that conjurors were diabolically assisted and driven. He hoped that the knowledge which the book conveys will wipe away many ill-grounded notions which ignorant people have imbibed. Some imagine that many deceptions cannot be performed without the assistance of the gentleman of the cloven foot, long since distinguished by the appellation of Old Nick, from whence the original of this amusing science gained the name of the Black Art. Indeed, some ages back, when learning was confined to a few, self-interested and designing persons pretended to enchantment and to hold intelligence with supernatural beings, and, by their skill in chemistry and mathematics, so worked upon the senses that many were brought to believe in conjuration.

It can be seen from Breslaw's statement of intention, as well as from a newspaper item of the day, that the influence of Wier, Scot, and Ady had not yet been felt as those authors might have hoped; people still sought conjurors out for supernatural assistance. The newspaper reported that "a man in the shameful disguise of a conjuror, with a large wig, a hat of extraordinary size, and an old night-gown on," had been locked up in prison for his efforts to deceive His Majesty's subjects. It added that

the mischiefs which these impostors cause to the public are as shocking as they are inconceivable, and persons, foolishly desirous to be familiar with future events relative to themselves, establish a credulity in their own minds, to which nothing appears improbable that these conjurors relate.

Gustavus Katterfelto, born about 1765, claimed to be the son of a Prussian colonel of hussars. He made his debut in London in the spring of 1781, and captured an audience who appreciated his rather new approach to conjuring. He presented an hour of "philosophical" lecture followed by two hours of entertainment, into which he wove pretentious assertions of scientific principles. He seems to have had a wide though not deep knowledge of various sciences, so he may have educated his audiences somewhat. He declared that he was intent upon protecting his clients and to that end would "discover and lay open those various impositions, for the benefit and satisfaction of the public." He directed these comments at the "many ladies and gentlemen [who] lose their fortunes by cards and dice." He was very popular.

Katterfelto made great use of the fact that he had a beautiful black cat with him at all times, and he obviously did not mind if some persons whispered that the beast was his "familiar," an animal companion to witches and warlocks. He usually prefixed his name with the title "Dr." or "Col.," and his fame was so great that he was eventually brought to the attention of George III of England, who asked to see this wonder-worker at a command performance.

PHANTASMAGORIA
THIS and every EVENING,
AT THE
LYCEUM, STRAND.

Conjuror Philipstal used this flyer to draw crowds to his highly successful optical show in 1803. The actor is seen on the stage within the traditional protective "magic circle" interacting with a transparent "ghost" figure that appears and vanishes.

When it came to most optical effects, the completely enclosed theater was a necessary environment. The simple slide projector, often doubling as an "opaque" projector as well, was then known as the magic lantern. This device was first described in detail by the Dutch scientist Christian Huygens in 1659, but existed before that time, since it was mentioned by the Jesuit Athanasius Kircher in the 1646 edition of his book, *Ars Magna Lucis et Umbrae* ("The Great Art of Light and Shadow"). It evolved over the next century, and in 1784, Belgian showman Étienne-Gaspard Robertson, an adventurous performer, was very successful with his innovative presentation of this novelty, using it to great advantage by projecting wondrous images on smoke and on undulating fabric screens.

As early as 1796, a variety of optical tricks were being shown by major performers. Robert, a French conjuror, Philipstal in Edinburgh, a German named Moritz, and the Italian performer named Bologna all showed illusions generally known as Phantasmagoria.

As novel and exciting as the magic lantern was, it shortly afterward gave way to other forms of fashionable diversion, though in 1847 conjuror Henri Robin briefly restored the apparitions to popularity under the name Living Phantasmagoria.

The innovator named Philipstal and his successor, Cross, combined more than one projector to provide the "dissolving views" effect, which went through many changes until it became a distinct art form. In 1833, the presentation by a French artist, De Berar, of his "Optikali Illusio" was the big attraction at Bartholemew Fair. In this same year a book was published in New York exposing many choice secrets of the magical art such as the projector innovation. It was titled

THE WHOLE ART OF LEGERDEMAIN

OR HOCUS POCUS

LAID OPEN AND EXPLAINED

BY THOSE RENOWNED [*sic*] MASTERS

SENA SAMA, HAMED BEN-ALLA

For a few years, regular conjuring shows were almost eclipsed by projector novelties. Then in 1862 the magic lantern was put on the shelf permanently when the public was astonished by "Pepper's Ghost," based on an idea first developed by a Liverpool civil engineer named Henry Dircks, though in his version it would have been difficult for a large audience to view it. John Henry Pepper was a professor of chemistry at London Polytechnic Institute who developed several improvements on the Dircks design. That design itself might have been inspired by a bad description of a similar illusion that had been published in 1588 by author Giambattista della Porta in his book *Magia naturalis*.

Pepper's Ghost was a stunning optical effect in which living actors could be seen to interact with semitransparent ghostly figures who appeared to stand with them on the stage, faded in and out of sight, and behaved very much as real phantoms are expected to do. This theatrical presentation was featured not only at the Polytechnic Institute but also at London's Egyptian Hall and the Musée Grévin in Paris, as well as in stage productions of *Hamlet* (for the ghost of Hamlet's father) and *Macbeth* (for Banquo's ghost). A stage version of Charles Dickens' story "A Christmas Carol" made good use of the Pepper's Ghost effect.

The *Times* (London) of August 6, 1863, ran these two advertisements, one after the other:

> POLYTECHNIC.—Notice.—The fashionable SATURDAY MORNING ENTERTAINMENTS. Admission 2s. 6d. Commencing at 1 o'clock, and terminating at 5 o'clock—In consequence of the very great and distinguished patronage which these entertainments have received, there will be a few more given, when every effort will be made to increase the amusement and comfort of the visitors. JOHN HENRY PEPPER, Hon. Director.

> POLYTECHNIC.—All the Lectures and Entertainments as delivered before their Royal Highnesses the Prince and Princess of Wales, the Prince and Princess of Hesse. Professor Pepper's adaptation of Mr. Dirck's [*sic*] Ghost Illusion, Saturday, at 1 and 8, and every other day at half past 1 and 8. Von Weber's Grand Opera of "Der Freischutz." Engagement of Herr Susman for his remarkable Imitations of Birds

and Animals. Entirely New Series of Dissolving Views of Poland and the Poles, with lecture by J. Millard, Esq., describing the Rights and Wrongs of that Country. Pneumatic Wonders, by J. L. King, Esq.

We may note in passing that in the same newspaper column a conjuror named Kinsbergen-Maju was teamed at the Coliseum Theatre with "Master Arlidge the juvenile Flautist," along with "Cycloramas of Lisbon," "London by Day and Paris by Night," "Neopolitan [*sic*] Minstrels," "Stalactite Caverns," "Swiss Scenery," and "Mountain Torrents." And all that was to be seen for a mere one shilling!

The original inventor, Henry Dircks, was not happy at the success attained by Pepper's improvement of his illusion effect. Immediately following the running of the advertisements quoted above, he published a lament titled

THE GHOST!

AS PRODUCED IN THE

SPECTRE DRAMA,

POPULARLY ILLUSTRATING THE

MARVELOUS OPTICAL ILLUSIONS

OBTAINED BY THE APPARATUS CALLED

THE DIRKSIAN PHANTASMAGORIA:

BEING A FULL ACCOUNT OF ITS

HISTORY, CONSTRUCTION, AND VARIOUS ADAPTATIONS.

A version of the Ghost illusion is used today to fill a ballroom with semi-transparent dancers at Disney World in Florida. This production, however, is much closer to the original Dircks design.

Dircks was not the only one to claim the invention of this illusion, though he certainly made the biggest fuss about it. The team of Poole & Young, a Mr. Gompertz, and a magician named Silvester all came up with fanciful names for their versions of ghosts produced by similar optical illusions.

One wonders what these gentlemen would have thought of the motion picture as it was to develop eventually. But even when the huge advances in technology—sound, color film, then Cinerama, stereo, and wide-screen—became available to motion picture producers in this century, it was still evident that it was the actors themselves, the stars, who attracted the audiences and brought them back again. And so it was, and is, with conjuring. Though all the newest technical and artistic developments were snapped up by ambitious conjurors and incorporated into their shows, no amount of fancy equipment, no matter how novel and marvelous, ever made anyone into a magician.

CHAPTER 4

THE AMERICAN PHILADELPHIA, PROFESSOR PINETTI, & L'ESCAMOTEUR PHILIPPE

PHILADELPHIA

The first American-born (1735) magician to attain any fame was probably Jacob Meyer, who took his new name Philadelphia from the city in which he was born when his family converted from Judaism to Christianity. He chose not to perform in America, instead exporting his talent to Europe, where he toured the British Isles, Germany, Portugal, and Spain. In Russia, he was invited to perform before Empress Catherine, and in Turkey for Sultan Mustafa III.

In common with several other shows of the day, Philadelphia's production featured new scientific novelties along with the conjuring tricks. These were often referred to as "Philosophical Experiments," though neither philosophy nor experimentation was involved. Displays via magic lantern (opaque or transparency projector), mirror effects, and various magnetic and electrical (usually high-voltage) demonstrations were, to the observers, essentially of the same nature as the tricks achieved by sleight-of-hand or specialized conjuring apparatus.

Philadelphia earned a rather questionable degree in what can only be described as occult medicine. From then on, he adopted all sorts of titles and his conjuring performances were never admitted to be such, though he quite obviously used sleight-of-hand and common tricks of the day, specializing in the oldest trick of all, the ever popular one with the birds' heads. He dressed up his illusions as if they were demonstrations of obscure mathematical, physical, and natural laws, and even notified his audiences at one German town that he was not to be placed in the class of charlatans and imitators, or to be compared with them as he dares, without boasting, to say that his skill has been applauded by the Royal Imperial as well as by the Prussian and Swedish Courts with gracious acceptance. He therefore flatters himself that he will be appreciated and applauded here at Luneberg.

Perhaps he did well at that town, but when this pretentious braggart appeared at Göttingen in 1777, he came up against a scientist named Lichtenberg, who issued a printed satire on Philadelphia that listed his seven best tricks, among which was one in which he said the conjuror

takes all the watches, rings and other ornaments of the company, and even money if they wish, and gives every one a receipt for his property. He then puts them in a trunk, and brings them off to Cassel.* In a week after, each person tears his receipt, and that moment finds whatever he gave in his hands again. He has made a great deal of money on this trick.

Philadelphia's pretensions were almost unlimited. In 1783 he tried to interest Frederick the Great in a grandiose business proposition to which his occult powers could be usefully applied. The monarch declined to take up this generous offer to get rich.

After many attempts at various bombastic business ventures, Philadelphia retired to his home in Köthen, Germany, and died at the turn of the century.

PINETTI

One late-eighteenth-century Italian magician brought a new elegance to his art by sporting a wide variety of colorful and elegant costumes. His name was Giuseppe Pinetti.

Though he was a contemporary of Cagliostro, the all-time champion of humbugs, Pinetti refused the role of charlatan. He was academically proficient, having been a professor of physics and mathematics and a member of the Royal Academy of Sciences at Bordeaux, who as an instructor had devised entertaining ways of illustrating principles of these sciences to his students in Italy and France. He left the pedagogical profession for conjuring, and fifteen years later he had the distinction of having become a famous and popular conjuror who roamed Europe, even making command appearances before Louis XVI of France and the royal family; George III of England; and the barons of Germany.

Along the way, he gave himself a few fake titles ("Chevalier M. Josêph

* Modern Kassel, north of Frankfurt-am-Main.

Des génies placent le buste de M. le Professeur PINETTI dans le temple des Arts, au milieu des instruments de Phisique et de Mathematique.

Professeur et Démonstrateur de Physique amusante, qui après avoir réduit en cendres une Carte choisie au hazard, jette le Jeu en l'air pour la faire reparaître en la clouant au mur d'un coup de Pistolet.

Above left: The title page of Pinetti's 1784 book left no doubt about his divine connection. Later editions added a third cherub crowning him with laurel. Perhaps this version is all you can stand. Above right: This illustration in the 1784 Decremps "exposé" of Pinetti describes one of his most famous tricks: "Professor and demonstrator of entertaining physics, who, after having reduced to ashes a playing card chosen at random, throws the pack in the air to restore [the card] by pinning it to the wall with a pistol shot."

Pinetti Willedale de Merci, Knight of the German Order of Merit of Saint Philip, Professor of Mathematics and Natural Philosophy, Pensioned by the Court of Prussia, Patronized by All the Royal Family of France, Aggregate of the Royal Academy of Sciences and Belles Lettres of Bordeaux," etc. etc.) but it was all for theatrical purposes and was so taken by his clients.

In 1783 he opened a huge, colorful show in Paris. The public was dazzled by props made of silver and gold, rather than of brass and tin. His costumes were straight out of mythology and fantasy: tall conical hats topped with stars; embroidered and jeweled robes and flowing capes.

He featured a version of the Thumb-Tie trick,* which was very well received by his clients. But perhaps the strongest items on his show were the

*The performers thumbs were tied together, yet he was able to catch hoops over his arms.

automata, among which were the "Grand Sultan" and a marvelous mechanical bird, both of which were the talk of Paris. The show was sold out weeks in advance, and Pinetti stayed at that theater for more than a year.

Signor Pinetti arrived in London in 1784, bringing with him one of his most famous automata creations, "The Wise Little Turk," a figure about two feet high which answered questions concerning articles offered to him by the audience. The advertisement for his show at the Haymarket theater has particular interest. Among promises that he would "exhibit most wonderful, stupendous, and absolutely inimitable, mechanical, physical, and philosophical pieces," there is an interesting item about his wife's participation in the show:

> Signora Pinetti will have the special honor and satisfaction of exhibiting various experiments of new discovery, no less curious than seemingly incredible, particularly that of her being seated in one of the front boxes, with a handkerchief over her eyes, and guessing at everything imagined and proposed to her by any person in the company.

This was more than sixty years before Robert-Houdin, who is usually credited with the creation of the Second Sight trick, ever performed it!

Returning to Paris again after publishing in both English and French a booklet explaining thirty-three of his tricks, Pinetti ran into a problem in the form of one Henri Decremps, who for some reason felt that the Italian wizard should not be allowed to continue entertaining the public of France. Decremps claimed to be able to expose Pinetti's tricks, and published a book, *La Magie blanche dévoilée* (published in English as *The Conjuror Unmasked*), which purported to do just that.

Decremps was himself a conjuror of ability. The feud was senseless, but Pinetti moved off to the Continent to reopen his show without the nagging of M. Decremps, who seems to have had no good reason to have denounced him. The conjuror was not claiming any divine or supernatural powers, after all.

Pinetti performed in other parts of France and in Italy, where he stayed for several years. He wisely avoided Rome, knowing that zealous Vatican officials might provide him with a prison stay if he could not satisfy the Inquisition concerning his conjuring abilities. He next went through Austria and Poland, then, in 1796, to Russia. It was there that he contracted some sort of fever and died.

L'ESCAMOTEUR PHILIPPE

After seeing a troupe of Chinese conjurors, a French confectioner in Aberdeen named Jacques André Noé Talon decided that he would abandon his profession for the stage. He became the conjuror Philippe, and made his debut in Glasgow in 1840. From there he toured the north of England, then made two lengthy stays in Paris and in Vienna. In 1845 he appeared in London to great acclaim.

He performed in what he said was Chinese costume, though it was only what he had dreamed up himself. However, the inaccuracy was overlooked by his audiences, and his dress was certainly effective. A very tall, conical peaked hat that Philippe wore may have been the basis for the legend that witches and other magical personages wear such hats.

The costumes—especially the hats—worn by the various professions in early times were carefully designated by tradition. Starting in the fifteenth century, physicians were permitted to wear a low, four-cornered hat that was specific to the healing arts. Michel de Nostredame, who became the famous Nostradamus, was a physician by profession, so was always seen in this headgear. The conjurors, aside from those such as the street workers wearing the specialized apron that served as a catchall and a source of supply for various props, wore a great variety of costumes, partly dictated by their individual requirements. Philippe took full advantage of this freedom of attire.

Quickly attaining success in France and the British Isles, he featured in his show the production of large numbers of animals—chickens, ducks, pigeons, geese, and goldfish (in bowls)—as well as a trick that was destined to become one of the most famous and enduring of all manipulatory numbers, the Linking Rings. This trick was already very, very old when Philippe brought it to the stages of Europe, and it is still seen frequently today.

Philippe also showed various "automata" to his audieces. These were human-shaped constructions, often miniature, that performed such simple tasks as trapeze acrobatics or selecting a playing card. In more complicated modes, a figure wrote a name or even played whist or chess. Now, the fabrication of "intelligent" machines was well beyond the abilities of even such clever technicians as Robert-Houdin and J. N. Maskelyne, who were both originally trained as watchmakers. While a figure could be made that did relatively simple tasks, chess- and card-playing were, at this point in time, quite impossible, and we might even suspect that any automata that were presented as such, were possibly powered and directed by unseen human agencies. Alas, all too possibly!

After a very long and successful career, the pastry chef–turned–wizard died in 1878.

THE FABULOUS AUTOMATA

It would be well to insert here a history of the automaton, one of the staples of the early conjurors which Philippe, Robert-Houdin, Maskelyne, and many others used to such advantage.

There are, technically speaking, two major types of automata and one

Philippe, in his striking costume as the "Physicien Chinois." His pièce de résistance was the production of a bowl full of water and goldfish from a thin silk foulard, the trick shown in this illustration.

Pseudo-Automaton. An Automaton of the First Kind, if I may invent these terms, is a truly automatic device that acts in accordance to preset instructions and signals, or that goes through a programmed sequence. A striking clock would be a very simple example of this, while a toy automobile that reacts to obstacles would be a better example. An Automaton of the Second Kind appears to the observer to be one of the First Kind, but is actually operated by another agency, usually an offstage human being. A remotely controlled toy automobile would serve as an example of this class.

The Pseudo-Automaton, however, is actually just a person concealed within a figure who carries out the tasks as if the machine were performing them. A man in a robot suit—Robbie the Robot of *Forbidden Planet* fame comes to mind—could represent this kind.

Robert-Houdin featured a number of Automata of the First Kind. This sort was very popular with conjurors of that time; the difference between technology and artistry was blurred. A very famous Pseudo-Automaton, the Kempelen Chess Player, had been first publicly demonstrated in 1770. It was named after a Hungarian noble, Baron Wolfgang Von Kempelen, who had constructed it to satisfy a promise he'd made to Empress Maria Theresa. Only six months after he began construction, the baron astonished the empress by having it successfully play chess against members of her court.

It was a dangerous move by Von Kempelen. Had the empress discovered that the figure was a fake, she might have shown her displeasure in a dramatic fashion. It appears that the baron was aware of that fact, for he promptly partially disassembled the apparatus, refusing to further demonstrate it, especially since he was being besieged by visitors to his home who wanted to see the device. Only upon the personal request of Maria Theresa and Emperor Joseph II did he put it back together to demonstrate the wonder to their friends Grand Duke Paul of Russia and his consort. Perhaps encouraged by the further success of his device, and the failure of his clients to detect the imposture, Von Kempelen then put the chess player on public exhibition.

In operation, the apparatus was quite impressive. It consisted of a figure resembling a Turk, seated behind a square cabinet thirty inches high, forty-two inches long, and twenty-four inches deep. It slid about on casters to eliminate any suspicion that it might be connected to any source of intelligence through the floor. On top of the table was a chessboard, and the eyes of the Turk were directed there. The right arm was held above the board, the fingers extended.

Two doors in the front of the cabinet, two in the back, two small doors in the figure itself, and a drawer in the bottom, were all opened in turn to reveal the strange machinery and the chess pieces. A cushion supported the figure's arm.

The apparatus was wound up by the operator, using a key similar to that employed to wind a clock. In play, the Turk always got the first (white) move, the fingers opening and the arm descending to the board to pick up and move the piece. The opponent was then allowed to make his move. If the Turk checked the black king, it made an appropriate move of its head. If the opponent made an illegal move, the Turk tapped repeatedly on the board, and replaced the black piece. The Turk almost always won the game.

Following the game, the Pseudo-Automaton performed the Knight's Tour, a complicated maneuver in which a knight is moved—in the proper manner—about the chess board, not missing any of the sixty-four squares and not landing on any square twice.

In 1778 the Kempelen chess player was in England, and Paris saw it in 1783 when Benjamin Franklin, then ambassador to France, saw and played

Kempelen's Automaton Chess Player, as seen in The Illustrated London News *on December 20, 1815.*

the device. He lost. It was back in London in 1785. All this time, there was much suspicion that the automaton was a fake, and that opinion was often expressed. Blanche Dévoilée, who had written the book *La Magie blanche dévoilée*, attempted to explain it and was almost right, and a chap named Thicknesse was also almost right. But, no cigar. In 1789, Freiherr von Racknitz, who had seen the device six years earlier, made a similar Pseudo-Automaton, but it was not much publicized.

Von Kempelen himself died in 1804, and his son sold the chess player to a man named Maelzel, who put it back on tour. In 1809 the figure played Napoleon I, who tried illegal moves and was corrected. It was purchased by a wealthy nobleman in 1812, but as soon as he knew its secret, he lost interest in it. In 1817, Maelzel bought it back and visited London with it again in 1819, then the United States in 1826, where it held forth twice a day at the National Hotel at 112 Broadway in New York City. Boston and Baltimore followed, and several times the Turk was beaten at the game. And, to Maelzel's dismay, spies detected the secret and it was published. The public, as usual, preferred not to know about that and largely ignored the exposures.

Maelzel died in 1838, aboard a steamer leaving Havana, after his machine had failed to attract customers in Cuba. Robert-Houdin saw the device in 1844; it was eventually sold at auction to a Dr. J. K. Mitchell, and finally given to the Chinese Museum in Philadelphia. It was destroyed in 1854 in a fire.

A close imitation of the Kempelen figure was exhibited in London at the Crystal Palace in 1870, but its fate is unknown.

A Hungarian postage stamp issued in 1974 depicts a chess automaton, though it is not clear whether it is supposed to be a genuine calculating machine.

We will come upon other interesting automata in Chapters 10 and 17.

At this period of history, there was strong public fascination with the possibility of cyborgs (Mary Shelley's monster, as assembled by her fictional Dr. Frankenstein, is a good example) and with what we know today as the concept of Artificial Intelligence. Charles Babbage, in England, was busily designing his "analytic engine," the mechanical forerunner of the modern calculator. But it was beyond any genius of the day to construct a chess-player, mainly because of the enormous amount of data that would have had to be stored and accessed. The true chess robot has only now become available to us and is still being improved upon so that it may someday regularly defeat—in chess, at least—the so far superior computer that nature has evolved inside the human skull.

CHAPTER 5

ANDERSON, WONDERFUL WIZARD OF THE NORTH

John Henry Anderson, a Scotsman from Aberdeen, called himself The Great Wizard of the North, a title he said was given him by Sir Walter Scott. The son of a mason, he was orphaned at the age of ten and to stay alive he took a job at a theater as a call-boy, the lowest rung of the hierarchy in such an institution. His responsibilities included polishing shoes, running errands, notifying actors of their cues, and generally being useful. He kept his eyes open and learned from the experience, eventually taking up acting himself and playing small parts with the company. He soon turned to the study of conjuring and at seventeen began performing. His efforts met with immediate success.

A fortunate appearance before Lord Panmure at Brechin Castle in 1837, when Anderson was twenty-three years old, brought him an invitation to dinner there, at which time he made a great impression and was rewarded with the magnificent sum of ten pounds, more money than he'd ever had at one time. Lord Panmure also provided him with a glowing testimonial:

Sir, Our party here last night witnessed your performance with the greatest satisfaction; and I have no hesitation in saying that you far excel any other necromancer that I ever saw, either at home or abroad.

Armed with this endorsement, Anderson used his savings to put a larger show together and began a three-year tour that took him all through Scotland and Ireland and finally to London where he opened to great acclaim at the New Strand Theatre in January 1840.

It was Anderson who really brought magic off the streets and into the

The Great Wizard of the North performed many times before royalty, and made full use of such honors in his advertising, this illustration appearing in 1851.

theater. He was one of the first great advocates of advertising promotion, holding parades and plastering very wordy posters everywhere that there was an open space. His stage, which he dubbed the Cabalistic Laboratory, was a splendid array of equipment, velvet-draped tables, and glittering crystal vases. He made it known that he used very costly apparatus, much of it, he claimed, of solid gold and silver. In this, he was following Pinetti's lead. He also referred to himself as "Professor" and adopted other colorful titles. He was bombastic in word and deed, but he had the show to back up his advertising.

Anderson recognized the publicity value of such daring stunts as The Bullet Catch (he called it the Gun trick) and indeed it was so effective that the London *Courier*'s reviewer rhapsodized that

> we have never been so completely spellbound as on Monday evening, while subjected to the magic influence of Mr. J. H. Anderson, that unrivalled master in what is commonly termed the "black art." . . . his Gun Trick is alone sufficient to warrant our recommending Mr. Anderson to the patronage of our townsmen.

The Gun trick (which he falsely claimed to have invented), was used successfully by Anderson all his professional life without a mishap. This was not always the case with others who performed it, as we will see up ahead in Chapter 11.

Anderson thoroughly comprehended the basic rule of the successful performer of his art. "It is the duty of all magicians to give entertainment," he declared, and he was not at all interested in merely demonstrating that he could perform tricks that the spectator could not explain. If the entertainment value was not there, the trick was discarded.

Flushed with success, the Wizard turned his thoughts to marriage, and in 1842 he walked the aisle with Hannah Longhurst, a lady friend from Aberdeen who was working with his show. They produced a son, John Henry, Jr., the next year. Two years later a clandestine romance with a Miss Prentice resulted in another son, though the mother died in childbirth. Anderson supported the child faithfully, and Philip Prentice Anderson eventually graduated from the University of Aberdeen as a doctor.

By 1844, Anderson was very famous and very rich. He decided to invest his money and time in the erection of a theater in Glasgow, which was completed in 1845 as the City Theatre. It held five thousand persons and was the largest theater in Scotland. It opened on July 12, with Anderson, of course, as the star attraction.

Phineas T. Barnum, the famous American showman, told an amusing story about his friend Anderson in connection with this show. Barnum was visiting him and Anderson decided to play a little joke on the local inhabitants at the hotel where the two were staying. In the smoking room, Anderson introduced Barnum to the assemblage as The Great Wizard of the North. Barnum went along with it, and was besieged with questions by all present, while Anderson sat aside and enjoyed the joke. Then Barnum turned the tables. He told his admirers that he wished to give them all free passes to the show, and had made out some thirty slips before an alarmed Anderson stepped in, admitted his imposture, and agreed to honor those passes, but no more.

As misfortune would have it, disaster struck after only four months of operation at the City Theatre. In November the building burned down in an early morning fire of suspicious origin. Anderson had not operated there long enough to recoup his investment; he was only partly insured; and his loss was considerable.

His friends in show business sprang to his assistance and held a benefit for him. Soon back in business, he leased the Covent Garden Theatre in London and by next April he opened a gala show there. Rapidly recovering from his setback, he next toured Europe in 1846, taking off for Hamburg, Copenhagen, and Stockholm and finally arriving in St. Petersburg. He had a very successful season there, and an event at the Russian court had a lasting effect on his career. He accidentally bumped a uniformed general at the Bolshoi Theater, and profusely apologized, only to find that the officer was Czar Nicholas, and that it was not proper protocol to ever directly address any comment to His Imperial Highness. Apprehensive about what might occur as a result of his gaffe, Anderson was pleasantly surprised the next day when he was informed that the czar, rather than requiring the Wizard to do some prolonged mining in Siberia, had graciously arranged a command performance for him at the Winter Palace. This, of course, brought great honor and distinction to the Wizard, and he immediately found himself in great demand at every important soirée.

In 1849, back in London, he performed for Queen Victoria, Prince Albert, and the Prince of Wales at Balmoral Castle. Visiting America next, he was a great success in New York, then toured Australia, Canada, Hawaii, San Francisco, and, again, Russia.

A review of his London show in 1851 said:

> we are bound to entertain the conviction, that if Professor Anderson had deliberately set himself to prove that white was black . . . he would have succeeded in doing it. To say that handkerchiefs were torn to ribands, put in water, and hey presto! produced from some totally unexpected quarter, washed, folded, ironed and perfumed . . . that geese, children, bird-cages, and we know not what, were produced from between the covers of a "scrapbook," three inches thick; that watches appeared to be suddenly endowed with sentience and vitality, and to obey the mandate of this arch-conjuror and that a bottle was full or empty, and full again, nay, gave out an unbroken stream of two different colored liquids at the same time . . . would be to convey but a vague notion of the perplexing operations of this disciple of the black art.

Anderson's travels eventually took him back to England, where he found he had a great rival in Robert-Houdin, just then the toast of the kingdom. Wisely avoiding that competition, he sailed for America. By 1853, at the early age of thirty-nine, he was thinking seriously of retirement.

His run at the Melodeon Theatre in Boston was marked by a hilarious encounter with civic bureaucracy. It was the result of a conflict between one of Anderson's feature tricks and the local blue laws. The "Inexhaustible Bottle" was rather a required item on the program of any major conjuror of the day. Pinetti, Robert-Houdin, Philippe, and others made much of the trick, which consisted of producing a seemingly endless variety and quantity of potable liquids from a single bottle. Members of the audience would call out their choices, and the conjuror would oblige by pouring out glasses of the required beverages, which would then be distributed to the thirsty clients for their validation and approval. Sometimes the trick was done with a kettle rather than a bottle.

Anderson's presentation of this trick was amusing and amazing. Of course, there was always some wag present who would demand a glass of milk in an effort to confound the performer, and if one did not voluntarily make that request, Anderson supplied an assistant who would oblige by

Professor Anderson, the Great Wizard of the North, and his son, preparing to serve drinks from the Inexhaustible Bottle, a required item in the repertoire of the day's conjurors. It also got the professor into a bit of trouble.

doing so. Naturally, he was ready with the required substance. In his Boston show, the Wizard chose to have nine-year-old John Henry Junior, in Highland Scottish dress, serve up the drinks. No sooner had the lad given out the first glass of wine than a bevy of policemen charged down the aisle and onto the stage, armed with a warrant for the immediate seizure of the Wizard himself and his wonderful Inexhaustible Bottle. It seemed that both John Henrys had violated the Massachusetts liquor laws and had offended the Temperance Association by this flagrant action.

The audience, mostly persons from the Scottish community in Boston, were incensed. They shouted their support of the Wizard, and a riot was imminent. Cool as ever, Anderson took control and addressed his audience. He assured them that he intended to conform with the law, and asked if the officer in charge had to take the bottle as well as his person to the police station. The officer insisted that the bottle had to go, too. The *London Journal* described what ensued:

> The Professor handed him the "bottle" and no sooner was it in his hands, than the "bottle" commenced to emit streams of liquid fire. As soon as he dropped it, the fire became extinguished. Another officer lifted it up, when the fire again made its appearance; of course, he was also glad to drop it. The audience screamed, roared and never was such a scene witnessed. At last the Professor lifted up the "bottle," and giv-

ing the audience thanks, and bidding them good night, he walked off with his "bottle" to the police office, followed by two or three thousand persons, whose shouts, going to Washington Street, soon augmented the crowd to many thousands, all calling out "Shame on the liquor law."

I note that no mention was made of the other criminal in this case, John Henry Junior, who was probably left standing in the center of the stage with an empty tray. I'd have clapped that malefactor into irons, dragged him from the theater and tossed him into a dungeon to await the thumbscrews in the morning. A bad one, that!

To return to the *London Journal* account:

> In the morning, every available inch of the police court was crowded long before the usual hour of opening. . . . A long indictment was read, setting forth that Professor Anderson, better known as the "wizard of the North," had been in the habit of nightly supplying the citizens of Boston during the last five weeks, with all kinds of spirituous liquor without a license, and against the laws of the Commonwealth of Massachusetts, and was therefore liable for the first offence: to the penalty of ten dollars fine, and securities for one thousand dollars; the second offence double the fine and forfeiture of bonds; the third offence, imprisonment in the penitentiary.

Being somewhat familiar with the English press, and assuming that their present penchant for hyperbole is a constant and has been our burden to bear back to the day when this account was written, I must regard the entire tale with a certain detachment. The reader will perhaps better understand my caution when reading the conclusion of the *London Journal* version of this event.

Anderson won the day, the magistrate deciding that his license to perform covered the production of the liquor, which was an established part of the regular show. He granted Anderson permission to continue to dispense his magical beverages from the stage, and offered to return his bottle to him.

> No sooner did the magistrate touch the "bottle" than he dropped it again, stating it was red hot . . . and told the Professor that he did not care how soon he left the court. The Wizard asked the magistrate to hand him the "bottle." The magistrate, taking his handkerchief from his pocket, for the purpose of taking the bottle by the neck, was about to lift it, when, lo, it vanished! to the utter astonishment of his honour and all present.

Sure.

Anderson's Boston appearance was the last he intended to make in America. Returning to Aberdeen, he was confronted by his wife, Hannah, who stated that she was no longer able to look after the children and also travel with the show. John Henry held his "Farewell to Magic" show in Aberdeen in February of 1854, but the response was so enthusiastic that he altered his plan. Changing the nature of his show to feature an exposé of spiritualism and to place less emphasis upon the conjuring, he continued to perform.

Having come upon the very active spiritualist movement in the United States, Anderson was appalled at the number of people taken in by the imposture, which he referred to as "a delusion so absurd, yet so fraught with danger." In his shows, he relied heavily upon his spiritualist exposures, using his daughters to duplicate the tricks. He was one of the magicians of his day who replicated the claimed mediumistic demonstrations of the infamous Davenport Brothers, who we will meet in Chapter 7, and even wrote a book, *The Magic of Spirit Rapping, Table Turning, Etc. Etc.*, in which he called all psychic fakers "the most unprincipled of all jugglers." His daughter Louise did an early two-person mental act with Anderson, billed as the "Second-Sighted Sybil and Retro-Reminiscent Mnemosyne." Try saying that!

Anderson's combination magic-and-spirit show was a huge success, and his advertising was never more flamboyant and overdone. A poster stated that he had surpassed

> Hermes the Wizard of Greece
> Zoroaster the Wizard of Persia
> Dr. Faustus the Wizard of Germany
> Michael Scott the Wizard of Scotland
> Mephistopheles the Wizard of Heligland
> Dr. Donne the Wizard of England
> Count Cagliostro the Wizard of France
> Obi the Wizard of Van Demon Land.

With this show, he played 214 successive nights before capacity audiences at the London Lyceum, then found that the Covent Garden Theatre was available, not having had a paying tenant in some time. He moved the show there at Christmas of 1855.

It was announced that the Anderson show at Covent Garden was intended as his *very* final performance. It was extended sixty days. On the morning of March 5, at 5 A.M., as a special gala show was closing, fire broke out and the theater was entirely consumed in flames, though no lives were lost. Anderson's props were a total loss, and the second fire in his professional life again forced him into bankruptcy. The newspapers gave very strong hints that Anderson was suspected of having caused the fire, but his response was appropriately logical, arguing that in no way could he have benefited from

Professor Anderson and his daughter Louise in "The World of Magic and Second Sight" in 1867. This was a typical two-person mentalism act.

the disaster. He was, in fact, a heavy loser, not having learned from his former experience and being once again underinsured.

His announced retirement was postponed, and yet again he was forced back onto the boards, reopening in London's East End to enthusiastic crowds. Misfortune followed him there, for just as he was recouping his losses, the bank in which he had deposited his money failed. He was ruined again, with less than £200 to his name.

Changing his tactics, the Wizard turned temporarily to acting. One of his favorite pastimes had been playing the part of Rob Roy in an operatic play about the Scottish folk hero, and for a while he played that part with some success. Then, in 1858, he returned to the role of Wizard and did an extensive tour of Australia, going on to Hawaii, San Francisco, Boston, and New York, where he was just in time to witness the beginning of the American Civil War. He originated a satire of Shakespeare's *Tempest,* which failed mightily in New York. A young lady named Antonia who had become part of the troupe for the Australian tour, had borne another Anderson and was a further drain on the means and time of the Wizard. As if those burdens were not enough, young John Henry, now eighteen and a capable performer, left the show and struck out on his own, forming his own company.

The defection of young Anderson was a great blow to the Wizard. In 1862, he desperately planned a tour of Canada to keep afloat financially, only to find that his son, using the title "Great Wizard of the North," was intending to visit the same area. John Henry Senior posted a notice warning the public to "not confound him with any who have usurped the same title, nor with any who plagiarize his bills and announcements." From that moment on, the two, father and son, never met again.

Anderson's fortunes were at a very low point. He owed much money in America, and returned to England in 1864 after promising to pay his creditors as soon as he could.

Always a frequent and bountiful donor to charities, he went bankrupt again in 1866. He seemed to have little skill at managing his money. One more tour followed, this time of India and Australia.

The Great Wizard of the North finally laid down his wand for the last time in 1874. He was buried beside his mother, in St. Nicholas Churchyard near Aberdeen. In 1909 the site was visited by Harry Houdini, who was then at the height of his success. Houdini had been born just thirty days after Anderson's death. The grave was in a deplorable state, and Houdini arranged for it to be restored. It is still maintained today by the city of Aberdeen.

Anderson's legitimate son, John Henry Anderson, Jr., stayed in the United States and was a popular and successful magic star there for several years, using his father's titles. Suffering from a marked mental problem, he was often severely depressed; he died at the early age of thirty-six. One daughter of Anderson Senior, Alice Hannah Anderson, is believed to have worked as a magician. However, "Jennie the Magicienne," who met her death by accidental drowning in 1875 in New Zealand, though she used the name Anderson and is sometimes said to have been Alice, was actually Jennie Whiteside, who also used various other names professionally (Blanche Fane, Blanche Anderson) as a magician and trapeze performer. This has been well established by James V. Reilly of New Zealand, who has chronicled magic in that country. A second daughter, Mary Antoinette Anderson, became the most famous American Shakespearean actress of the nineteenth century, being particularly admired by George Bernard Shaw. The second son, Philip Prentice Anderson, borne by Senior's companion Miss Prentice, gave up his plans to be a doctor and performed, not only as "Rubini" but also as the Great Wizard of the North. This Anderson Junior died in 1920.

CHAPTER 6

ROBERT-HOUDIN, THE INNOVATOR

Jean Eugène Robert (pronounced "ro-bayr") was born in 1805, and was early inclined to be a watchmaker, his father's profession. That had not been his parents' intention, since they provided him with an excellent classical education at the University of Orléans. The young man was for a short time a practicing watchmaker, but seeing the performance of an itinerant conjuror named Carlosbach and coming upon a book on conjuring, he became much interested in the art, which at that period frequently made use of clever mechanical props. Because of his training and natural aptitude, he was quite capable of constructing such devices.

He took sleight-of-hand lessons from a local amateur who was also a chiropodist, and when he felt himself sufficiently independent he moved to Tours and set up in the watchmaking business, doing conjuring on the side.

An accident in which he came under the care of a traveling magician named De Grisi, also known as Torrini, sealed his future. Young Robert was known to suffer from hallucinations. On this occasion he'd imagined that he was being poisoned, and for some reason he set out to travel by foot to the town of Blois. Along the way he collapsed, and when he regained his senses found himself with De Grisi. He was invited to travel with the show, and did so for many months, learning much about the business. However, De Grisi's tour (as Torrini) was rather unsuccessful, and Robert soon left. De Grisi continued on for a short while and died soon afterward at Lyons, France.

De Grisi had an interesting background. He was the son of a French count, and he first studied medicine when his family fortune was lost in the French Revolution. Then, in Naples, he met the Italian conjuror Pinetti, with whom he became associated. He was soon quite proficient as a performer, and began working on his own. De Grisi believed that Pinetti later betrayed him, fearful that he might now have a rival. The feud between the two continued for years, and De Grisi suffered greatly from the run-in with Pinetti.

De Grisi was one of those who performed the dangerous Bullet Catch trick; he had a version in which he acted a William Tell part, firing at his son. The boy was shot dead in error, and De Grisi stood trial. He was sentenced to six months in prison, during which time his wife died. Freed, he adopted his wife's maiden name, Torrini, and at that point he met Robert. De Grisi-Torrini had employed the young watchmaker to repair one of his automata, a featured part of his act.

(It should be mentioned here that some authorities believe De Grisi-Torrini to have been a character totally invented by Robert-Houdin to fluff up his biography. I doubt this claim.)

Jean Eugène told the story that after leaving De Grisi's service, he was at the Fair of Angers when he saw a magician named Castelli, from Normandy. This mountebank had advertised that he would eat a man alive in view of all the spectators who would attend his show. Naturally, the place was packed and young Robert *had* to attend such a remarkable exhibition. When Castelli asked for a volunteer, two men mounted the stage. One was rejected as being too fat, but the other seemed quite suitable for the performance. The Norman smacked his lips, sprinkled the seated man with pepper and vinegar, turned down the victim's collar, and bit him in the back of the neck. The volunteer howled, leaped up and left the stage nursing his nape. Castelli, with a great show of annoyance, impatiently called for another volunteer, but failed to obtain one. The spectators, Robert reported, were understandably disappointed.

Robert met and married the daughter of a well-known Parisian watchmaker named Houdin. He changed his last name to mark this event, and was thereafter known as Jean Eugène Robert-Houdin.*

Our hero spent several years manufacturing mechanical toys, intricate clocks, and various automata. It was a thriving business, and he took time out to occasionally give magic shows. Then in 1845 he gave the first of his "Soirées Fantastiques" in Paris, receiving rave reviews. He was launched on his conjuring career. In 1848 he stormed London to great acclaim, and was seen by fifteen-year-old William Palmer, who was to be so inspired that he became the conjuror Heller as a result.

His mechanical skills enabled him to produce wonderful magical effects such as the Orange Tree, probably inspired by the Indian Mango Tree trick,

Robert-Houdin, the famous and respected master of magic, in his prime.

* Pronounced "ro-bayr-oo-dan."

**ROBERT-HOUDIN,
ST. JAMES'S THEATRE.**

MONS.ᴿ

ROBERT-HOUDIN,

THE CELEBRATED

PRESTIDIGITATEUR

AND

FRENCH CONJURER,

WILL CONTINUE HIS ORIGINAL

EXPERIMENTS

AND WONDERS OF

NATURAL MAGIC,

As Invented by him, and Performed for Ten Consecutive Seasons at his Théâtre
Palais Royal, Paris, under the title of

" SÉANCES FANTASTIQUES,"

THESE EXTRAORDINARY REPRESENTATIONS WILL BE CONTINUED

AT THE ABOVE THEATRE,

FOR A LIMITED NUMBER OF REPRESENTATIONS,

EVERY

TUESDAY AND THURSDAY EVENING,

At Half-past Eight o'Clock,

AND A

DAY PERFORMANCE

ON

WEDNESDAY & SATURDAY MORNINGS

Commencing at Half-past Two o'Clock.

Above left: London was host to Robert-Houdin's very successful English visit. He changed his show frequently to attract new patrons. Above right: Robert-Houdin's Orange Tree illusion was based upon the story of the Indian Mango Tree trick. His version was a mechanical wonder which he built himself.

in which the street performers would grow a tree by stages right before their audiences, covering a seed, then a sprout, and then various stages of a small mango tree, complete with fruit. Philippe featured such a trick, too. Robert-Houdin's device consisted of a box in which a small tree was planted. He would borrow a handkerchief from a lady spectator, cause it to vanish, then call attention to the tree. Slowly, blossoms would emerge, then fall to the floor one by one. This miracle was followed by the appearance of fully ripe oranges, one of which opened of its own accord to reveal a handkerchief within. Two mechanical butterflies took the lady's handkerchief into the air and it was returned to its owner.

Another of the great illusions introduced to Western magic by Robert-Houdin was his Aerial Suspension. The use of ether as an anaesthetic agent had just been discovered (in 1842). The magician spilled this liquid freely about the stage, and it put his suspension effect into the Big Illusion class. A reviewer of his show in London described it thus:

> [Robert-Houdin's] most impressive illusion was the "Escamotage de Robert-Houdin, fils," with his son suspended in equilibrium by atmospheric air, through the action of concentrated Ether, which concluded by showing the boy horizontal in the air and apparently supported by nothing except his elbow on the top of a walking stick.

The implication was that the ether had made the boy (Émile) light, and a rather flimsy "scientific" premise was thus established.

The innovative Suspension Éthéréene devised by Robert-Houdin, with his young son Émile as the subject of this "experiment in natural physics."

This illusion was first shown by Robert-Houdin in 1848, but the idea was not original to him. In 1836 Ling Lau Lauro, a pseudo-Oriental, had been the first to introduce it in the Occident. A few years earlier than that, in the city of Madras, India, an old Brahmin conjuror was reported to have done a suspension effect, but in his version he sat in the air cross-legged. The report had him using

no better apparatus than a piece of plank, which, with four legs, he formed into an oblong stool; and upon which, in a little brass socket, he placed, in a perpendicular position, a hollow bamboo, from which projected a kind of crutch, covered with a piece of common hide. These properties he carried with him in a little bag, which was shown to those who went to see him exhibit. The servants of the house held a blanket before him, and when it was withdrawn he was discovered poised in the air, about four feet from the ground, in a sitting attitude, the outer edge of one hand merely touching the crutch, with the fingers deliberately counting beads, and the other hand and arm held up in an erect posture. The blanket was then held up before him, and the spectators heard a gurgling noise, like that occasioned by wind escaping from a bladder or tube, and when the screen was withdrawn he was again standing on the floor or ground.

The effect can be seen from the accompanying illustration. The report went on to say that

Above left: The Brahmin conjuror's Levitation appeared like this to observers in the 1820s. Above right: This photo of the classic suspension trick appeared in The London Illustrated News *in June of 1936. The editor was convinced that this demonstrated genuine Indian magic, but it was just the old Brahmin conjuring trick.*

this performer died at Madras in 1830, without imparting to any one the secret of the trick, which was said, however, by a knowing native, to be effected by holding the breath, clearing the tubular organs, and a peculiar mode of respiration.

Even Thomas Frost, the gentleman making this report, found this difficult to accept. Frost said the explanation was "too vague to be satisfactory." I agree.

In passing, I must report that in 1931, *Time* magazine ran a series of photos of exactly this trick being done in India, and quite seriously reported that no scientific explanation was available for it. This shows what can happen when there is no "knowing native" available.

At that time in history, France occupied Algeria, to the considerable profit of the occupiers. Unrest was constantly being stirred up by the Marabout priests, who performed various magical feats to keep alive the idea that they had divine connections. The French government called upon their most famous conjuror to pit his skills against that of the Marabout performers, and though the account as given in Robert-Houdin's *Mémoires* may be somewhat hyperbolized in favor of the conjuror, it is a historical fact that he

Above left: The Second Sight act as performed by Robert-Houdin and his son, Émile. Above right: Robert-Houdin, the great innovator in magic, late in life.

did visit Algeria and bested the competition with his Light and Heavy Chest trick. This consisted of a small wooden box with a metal handle on the top. Robert-Houdin asked a Marabout to lift it, saying that it could only be lifted if he, the great wizard, willed it so. The Marabout easily lifted it with one hand, then set it down again. Now, announced the Frenchman, he willed that the Marabout had not even the strength of a woman, and was unable to lift the box. Try as he might, straining with both hands, the fakir found that the box would not budge until Robert-Houdin bent down to lift it with one hand. It is reported that this demonstration did much to consolidate the reputation of the French in that part of the world. *Hélas!* That is past history, and the Algerians have discovered that they can do without the French, though they still enjoy a good conjuring show.

For this, and for various inventions connected with timekeeping, Robert-Houdin received numerous medals and commendations from his government. He retired, disappointed that only one of his sons chose to take up conjuring, and that with little enthusiasm; one joined the army, another became a watchmaker.

The master magician died at his home in Blois, France, in 1871. The high esteem of the French nation for their conjuring son was shown in 1971, when a postage stamp was issued there honoring the hundredth anniversary of his death.

From descriptions of his act, we know that Robert-Houdin was not dependent only upon the ingenious mechanical marvels he was able to create. Without his shomanship, humor, and artistic handling, the "Soirées" would have been merely exhibitions of interesting machinery. Modern conjurors, often far too preoccupied with owning the latest hardware of their art, would do well to note this fact.

CHAPTER 7

CONJURING IN THE NEW WORLD: THE BROTHERS DAVENPORT & THEIR SPIRIT CABINET

The first recorded advertisement for a magic show in America was in 1734. The *Weekly Journal* of New York announced that a German conjuror named Joseph Broome could be seen there. It read:

> This is to give notice to all Gentlemen Ladies and others, that on Monday the 18 of March at the House of Charles Sleigh, in Duke-Street is to be seen the famous German Artist, who is to perform the Wonders of the World by Dexterity of Hand: The Things he performs are too many to be enumerated here. He here with invites all to be Spectators of his Ingenuity, 1 s. 9 d. & 6 d. is the Price for Admitance [*sic*]. He begins at 7 o' Clock in the Evening. To be continued every Night in the Week. Saturday Nights excepted. to be performed by. Joseph Broome.

(I suspect that there were three prices of "Admitance," rather than only two. The typesetter probably meant (a) one shilling; (b) ninepence; (c) sixpence, rather than what appears to be (a) one shilling, ninepence, (b) sixpence, as prices.)

Many more followed Herr Broome, and the trade, for better or worse, became established in the New World.

Fantastic and highly embellished claims were made by early performers. Audiences often did not see what they were promised, and it was doubtless a major occupation of the conjuror to charm customers into accepting what he showed them as being close enough to the advertised wonders, and a wonder in itself that he was not lynched there and then. The language was overblown and rather ludicrous, as witness this 1836 declaration by the same Ingleby Moon whom we previously met in England doing the head-off-the-bird trick:

> Mr. I. Lunar, has in modern times acquired more celebrity than any of the ancient Magicians, and rendered himself in those places through which he passed, more famous than Memus-Cyrus, mighty son, or the witch of Endor did in the habitation of old. . . . The mother of wonder, the nurse that gives suck to the saplings of Genius was pleased to complete by her approbation that fame he is so anxious to immortalize.

Advanced dental caries may result from reading such blather.

In the late 1800s the American Davenport Brothers, Ira Erastus and William Henry, caused a major sensation, first in the United States and then around the world, with a spectacular and puzzling vaudeville stage act. Tied hand and foot, and facing one another from each end of a long wooden bench, they were then locked into a large cabinet with an assortment of props, after which bells would sound, musical instruments would be played, hands would appear through openings in the cabinet, and a bewildered person taken from the audience would have his clothes turned inside-out and suffer various other indignities. The cabinet was often opened quickly—by one of the brothers' assistants—in the midst of these events, and the two Davenports were always found to be still securely bound.

Many who saw this act attributed the effects to spirit forces; to them, it seemed impossible for the Davenports—and others who imitated their act—to have done the tricks by other than supernatural means. But we must remember that magicians today regularly perform equally confounding feats, and we do not ascribe to *them* any diabolical powers or collusion.

The Davenport phenomena had all started just six years after spirits were said to have appeared for the famous Fox sisters, Margaret and Catherine, in Hydesville, New York. These were the two who launched the whole "spiritualism" craze, from which we are not yet recovered. The Davenports, sons of a Buffalo, New York, policeman, began reporting very similar miracles happening to them, and as with the Fox children, everyone believed what they wanted to hear.

Before long the father of the two "mediums" resigned from the police force and took over managing what quickly got to be a very profitable operation. They were joined by William Fay, another Buffalo resident who became an important agent of their miracles. They developed their tied-in-

Above left: The famous Davenport Brothers traveled the world demonstrating their wonderful Spirit Cabinet to record audiences. Above right: This unreal representation shows what the Davenports would have their audiences believe happened within the closed cabinet.

a-box routine and for the next ten years toured the United States with it. Then they arrived in England, a country that had accepted spiritualism enthusiastically even after its popularity had begun to wane in the country where it was born. England was fully primed for belief in the Davenports.

An important part of the Davenport act was their spokesman, Dr. J. B. Ferguson, a Presbyterian minister with a wonderfully sepulchral voice. He assured the audience that the Davenports were given divine powers and worked by spirit power alone, not by "the wit-craft of the commercial." Ferguson said that the bell-ringing and other phenomena happened independently of the brothers, and that they occurred "for the glory of God and the greater enlightenment of weak humanity."

In 1868, a young magician named Harry Keller (later Kellar) joined the show and toured with the Davenports. He was to go on to great fame after leaving the brothers, for a while even doing his own version of their spirit-cabinet act with William Fay, who would similarly defect.

The Davenports were hugely successful in spite of many exposés offered by such prominent conjurors as J. N. Maskelyne, who got his own start in the conjuring profession by debunking the brothers. Many other magicians, such as John Henry Anderson, Redmond, and Tolmaque, also featured Davenport exposures as part of their programs.

The Davenport Brothers' career was anything but unchallenged. In Liverpool, two amateur magicians came up with a "special knot" that defeated the brothers. The expected phenomena did not occur, and the Davenports had to be cut loose. On that occasion, a riot ensued, in which the cabinet was destroyed by the audience, the police arrived, and the price of admission was refunded. The two mischief-makers followed the Davenports to Huddersfield and Leeds, performing the same service for them in both those cities; wisely, the brothers opted to begin a tour of the Continent, far from these rascals.

There they ran into Robert-Houdin, the leading French conjuror, though he was by then retired. He wrote *Magie et physique amusante*, a complete, detailed exposé of their act, which was published posthumously. Back in England, the Maskelyne & Cooke team continually burlesqued the Davenports so effectively that the spiritualists in that country were forced to claim that Maskelyne & Cooke were actually "very powerful mediums" since they could not solve their tricks, and if they—the spiritualists—*had* solved and revealed the tricks, they'd have been cutting their own throats! In 1902, the pioneer filmmaker, Georges Méliès, even produced a short feature titled, *The Cabinet Trick of the Davenport Brothers*, which left no doubt about the nature of their performance. Méliès himself was a very accomplished conjuror, and many of his films show his expertise.

It might be thought that the reputation and drawing power of the Davenports' act would diminish quite dramatically following such exposures and continued ridicule. However, the public tendency has always been to persist in belief despite such efforts. The Davenports, appearing as they did in variety theaters, should not have ever been taken seriously. The high jinks that occurred in the cabinet on stage should have indicated to any sensible person that not divine forces but vaudeville was behind the wonders.

Back in America for a final tour, the Davenports were rejoined by William Fay, who had by then left his partnership with Harry Kellar. The trio took off for Australia, where the younger of the two brothers, William Henry, died in 1877. Fay settled down in Australia as a wealthy man and Ira Erastus returned to America and dropped out of sight for the next eighteen years.

Then, for some strange reason, Ira and Mr. Fay decided to revive the whole act again in 1895, but apparently the public had had enough of their particular brand of humbug and the tour was given up after they failed to attract sufficient audiences. Fay returned to Australia and Ira Erastus died in New York in 1911.

Ira Erastus was interviewed by the famous American magician and escape artist Harry Houdini in 1909 and offered his explanation of the Davenport philosophy. Since it was Reverend Ferguson, and not the brothers themselves, who made the statements at the beginning of their stage act, we can perhaps be charitable enough to accept what the remaining Davenport, in 1909, told Houdini:

Georges Méliès issued this poster to advertise his magic shows held at the Robert-Houdin theater before he became totally involved in making films, many of them based on magical illusions.

Okita,* among others—who both used their own routines and acted in Méliès' filmed reconstructions of some of J. N. Maskelyne's illusions.

Abandoning his own direct performance of live magic and the employment of visiting conjurors, Méliès switched his attention to the production of motion pictures, and it is for his work in this field that he is best known. In all, he produced some five hundred films in the period from 1896 to

* A female magician of some skill.

1912. He painted the remarkably three-dimensional-seeming sets himself, in a day when cinema lenses would not permit very much depth of field and everything that was to be in focus had to be about the same distance from the camera. Many of his scenes appear to go off into the distance, but were actually quite flat, a tribute to his artistic skill.

This man was one of highly varied talents, whose works are still available to be seen and wondered at. A fantasist at heart, he took conjuring and put it onto moving film, providing us with valuable documentation of the art that is still entertaining to see. He was an accomplished conjuror, a graphic artist, and a mechanic whose career overlapped the Golden Age of Magic and the advent of motion pictures. He took advantage of the new medium that was soon to replace vaudeville, beginning in 1929, as the primary entertainment resource of the public. He had, and used, the best of both worlds.

In 1971, the French government commemorated the centenary of his birth with a postage stamp.

CHAPTER 9

THE MASKELYNE DYNASTY

It appears that a scientific or technical background played an important part in the genius of some nineteenth-century conjurors. Robert-Houdin, the French magician who so strongly influenced the trade—largely by his mechanical approach—was an experienced watchmaker when he decided to step behind the footlights as a wizard. Twenty-five years later, an English boy, John Nevil Maskelyne, was apprenticed to a watchmaker at the age of thirteen, and spent the next three years learning that trade. He later applied his considerable talents, including those of the watchmaker-mechanic, to magic and also began a family tradition that eventually involved his four sons and a grandson, Jasper. The Maskelyne family was already of some note, including in its history an astronomer royal to King George III.

John Nevil was an amateur conjuror well known in his hometown of Cheltenham, England, when an encounter with the Davenport Brothers became his first serious foray into magic. It was 1855, and interest in spiritualism was at its height. The Davenports had just had a successful season in London at the Hanover Square rooms, and were passing through Cheltenham. John Nevil and George Cooke, an older colleague from the local magic club, didn't believe for a moment that the Davenports were using spirit powers when they caused objects to fly about after being tied up and locked away by the audience. The two amateurs set out to establish the fraudulent nature of the performance.

They were close observers at a performance by the Davenport Brothers at the Cheltenham Town Hall, and they made careful notes. Two months later, the team of Maskelyne & Cooke was born when the two appeared at Jessop's Aviary Gardens with some success, duplicating the entire Daven-

The Maskelyne & Cooke magic show created a new and lasting awareness of the art in Britain that persists to this day.

port act from beginning to end and throwing in a few innovations of their own. Then, under the management of a perceptive gentleman named William Morton, the team began playing small halls all over England, calling their show an "entertainment of pure trickery." They operated under often harrowing conditions and in a state of perpetual near bankruptcy, and barely held on for two years.

Just when it seemed they would have to fold the show, they were summoned to perform at London's Crystal Palace. The Palace was famous for what we would call "freak" shows, then labeled "scientific curiosities." Most of what was exhibited was of a caliber acceptable today to the *National Enquirer*, but even then not quite believable. Maskelyne & Cooke were to change all that by introducing superb entertainment. They took their first-night audience by storm and established a new standard for conjuring performances. They had arrived, in grand style.

Manager William Morton was ecstatic. Out-of-town theater owners who had thrown him out for suggesting that his clients appear on their stages were now begging for a one- or two-week booking following the fabulous London opening. But Morton had not forgotten their insults and abuse. He had the distinct pleasure of responding to one fellow who had been particularly offensive to him by writing:

My dear Sir:
> We have received your offer to engage Messrs. Maskelyne & Cooke's company for two weeks. Oh, my dear Sir!
>> Yours incredulously . . .

And Morton immediately, with great glee, proceeded to book the team into that very town—but at a rival theater.

After touring the provinces for six years to polish up their skills, Maskelyne & Cooke returned to the Crystal Palace in London in 1873. They graduated almost immediately to the St. James's Great Hall in Piccadilly, where they packed in thousands, and finally moved to what was to become more or less their permanent home. They signed a long lease with the Egyptian Hall, at 171 Piccadilly, where they were to reign as monarchs of magic for an incredible twenty-nine years.

London's Egyptian Hall, a sort of museum with lecture halls and theaters on several floors, was host to many, many magicians over the years. The Egyptian Hall had first featured a full-evening show of magic back in 1861, with a Dutch conjuror known as Robin (Henri Joseph Donckèle) who wanted to be thought of as French. He specialized in "Living Phantasmagoria" produced with the aid of projectors and mirrors. The first purely conjuring show at the hall appears to have been that of Charles Bertram (born 1853), who was known as "The King's Conjuror" owing to the fact that he

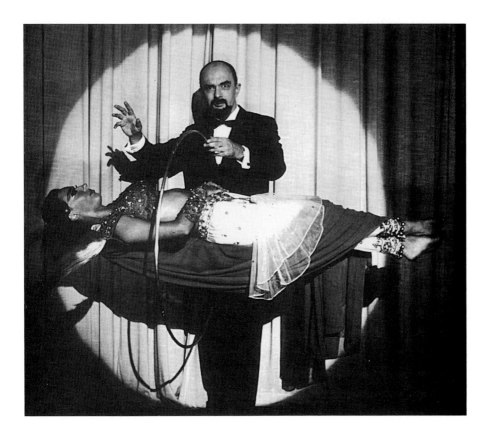

*The Amazing Randi,
many years back,
performing the classic
Levitation illusion.
The hoop is seamless,
made from steel.*

had appeared before King Edward VII twenty-two times. He was followed soon after by Bautier De Kolta and then by a never-ending stream of conjurors, minor and major. Londoners always associated the Egyptian Hall with conjuring attractions, especially after Maskelyne moved in.

John Nevil Maskelyne is credited with having invented a major illusion, the Levitation. This differed from the previous "suspensions" in that the subject actually moved up into and then through the air, rather than being positioned there manually and staying in place. At the first presentation in 1867, Maskelyne's wife was made to float into the air in a standing position; then she was returned safely to the stage. In a later version, the lady rose from a prone position, and still later, in 1898, a great improvement was made by J.N.'s son Nevil, who introduced the use of a large metal hoop that was passed over the floating person to quiet suspicions of supports.

(That illusion, in common with other successful routines that have been created from time to time by various magicians, was soon copied by competitors. The American magician, Harry Kellar, called his version Princess Karnac, and it passed from his hands to those of Howard Thurston, his successor. The Blackstones made of it an even greater miracle, and a score of major magicians today have improved upon the effect in many ways. In Russia, Rafael has a levitation in which his assistant, Elena, floats in the original upright position. The most recent developments are by André Kole, who floats himself through a huge arch while seated in the lotus position,

Above left: The Microphone Suspension is an adaptation of the Robert-Houdin Aerial Suspension. All suspension tricks differ from Levitations in that the subject is placed in position, rather than rising independently. Here, the author suspends assistant Pua aboard the French liner Liberté *crossing the Atlantic. Above right: The automaton Psycho was an important feature of the Maskelyne & Cooke show, as was their antispiritualist campaign, which exposed the flummery behind the popular séances of that day.*

Lance Burton, with an X-rated version in his spectacular Las Vegas show, and David Copperfield's free-flying production.)

The orchestra that played the sepulchral music during the Maskelyne & Cooke show was invisible to the audience. Musical instruments were suspended at the ceiling as if they were the source, and in a day when recorded music was unheard-of, the mystery of the Egyptian Hall was much enhanced by this clever innovation.

Another very successful invention by Maskelyne, introduced in 1875 during a command performance for the Prince of Wales, was Psycho, a twenty-two-inch-high automaton resembling a Hindu boy, which sat on a cushion atop a wide clear-glass cylinder in the center of the stage. The cylinder served to isolate the figure from the floor, and thus from any wires or strings that might be thought to activate his wonderful abilities, which included smoking a cigarette, adding and subtracting numbers, spelling words, and actually playing a game of whist! One conjuror who felt he had solved the mystery of Psycho's operation appeared onstage during the show and probed the area with a sensitive compass, suspecting that a powerful magnet was somehow involved. He was quite wrong.

The basic idea for Psycho had originated with John Algernon Clarke, an ingenious Lincolnshire farmer who had constructed a prototype in his spare time. He offered the idea to Maskelyne, who improved vastly on the original; Psycho became a great hit in the show, making some four thousand appearances before being retired in favor of other automata that Maskelyne

CHUNG LING SOO

THE WORLD'S GREATEST CONJURER

The cauldron of Chung Ling Soo produced endless quantities of flags, silk foulards, animals, and finally a human being.

devised. Today, it is in the London Museum in the Barbican, not on permanent display but available to scholars for reference. The operating principle is exceedingly clever, and has kept more than one magician guessing.

Besides inventing stage props, J.N. obtained patents for other devices. He designed a cash register and several other machines for keeping track of money and records. Until the 1950s penny-operated toilet locks that bore his name as inventor were in use in London, giving rise to the English euphemism, "to spend a penny." A model of his 1889 typewriter, the first to produce proportional spacing, is now in the London Science Museum. In all, J.N. held forty patents on various machines and ideas that came from his fertile mind.

Above left: Maskelyne's automata were varied. Psycho, his most famous, was the seated Hindu figure. Others played musical instruments. The figure in the center is Maskelyne himself, and the others are Psycho, Fanfare, Labial, and Zoe.

Above right: Spiritualist faker Henry Slade lost a case brought against him in a London court when magician Maskelyne showed how his tricks were done.

In 1876, Maskelyne was a prominent witness against Henry Slade, a faker who pretended to produce spirit messages on sealed school slates. The British court case caused great excitement, and Slade was convicted. Sentenced to three months at hard labor, he managed to get out of England and avoid the penalty. Washington Irving Bishop, an American mentalist who was famous for his "blindfold drive" and other astounding feats, was also challenged by Maskelyne. This provoked libelous remarks from the American, and J.N. promptly sued him, winning the case and driving Bishop from England to escape paying the £10,000 penalty.

J.N. was a litigious sort, seeming to enjoy the notoriety lawsuits brought. When he was sued in 1898 by two men who tried to collect his £500 reward for duplication of his box trick, the jury had a difficult time but decided, after two trials, that the duplication had indeed been achieved. Maskelyne appealed the decision, but finally had to pay the plaintiffs. He was in his element when a subsequent case enabled him to demonstrate in court that he could duplicate an involved scenario described by a clergyman named Colley as having been performed for him by a spiritualist. Maskelyne had unwisely responded to this challenge, accepting the story told by Colley of an event that he said had occurred twenty-nine years earlier. Though his replication of this probably hyperbolized anecdote was effective, and he was awarded the £1,000 that Colley had offered him if he could meet the challenge, there was a technical difference that the court decided disallowed the award, and Maskelyne ended up paying the clergyman £75 in damages for libel. It was an excellent investment for the conjuror, as the Egyptian Hall was jammed for months afterward.

Maskelyne promoted the careers of many deserving young magicians, hiring them to appear in his Egyptian Hall shows and encouraging them to create their own associations in order to establish a secret fraternity that could nurture the art of magic. He was very successful in this offstage activity, to which he devoted much time and effort. At this time, he formed the Magic Circle of London, a most prestigious organization of conjurors which is still flourishing, at present under the leadership of mentalist David Berglas.

Though the real star of the Maskelyne & Cooke act was always J.N. himself, he never forgot that it was his early partnership with George Cooke that had gotten the whole organization started. Cooke, fourteen years older than Maskelyne, always played a relatively minor part onstage, but was a full partner. He was often the subject of the famous Levitation trick, a position not without some very real risk. When Cooke retired in 1904 and the Egyptian Hall was torn down, another conjuror named David Devant, a former student of Maskelyne, joined him at St. George's Hall, which had to be almost rebuilt by the new occupants before it could be used. Devant was much more of an active participant and performer.

A spectacular new show featured J.N.'s son Nevil. It opened at St. George's while an additional Maskelyne & Devant unit was playing in Paris, too.

The partnership of Maskelyne & Devant lasted for nine years, until Devant, suffering from a "nervous ailment," was forced to retire. J.N., well on in years, continued with his son Nevil as a partner. In 1917, still active at the age of eighty-eight, he died, after making an agreement—not the only one to be designed by a magician—with Nevil that he would try to communicate with him from beyond the grave. The attempt was not successful.

The show, now known as *Maskelyne's Mysteries*, was still wildly popular with London audiences, and continued for years at St. George's (which was blitzed in World War II) by Nevil Maskelyne, along with Clive, Jasper, and Noel, all Maskelynes. Jasper Maskelyne, the third generation of the family, carried it on at the Westminster Theatre for several years before he moved his family to Kenya. The show finally closed down in 1933, and seventy-eight years of wizardry by the Maskelyne dynasty was at an end.

An interesting book titled *White Magic* was written by Jasper Maskelyne, who proved himself somewhat naïve on some matters. He ran on about all sorts of black magic and Satanic wonders, even accepting that poltergeist powers were genuine. Describing a fire-eating act (he called it "fire-swallowing"), he declared that in order to do it "the tongue is coated with powdered sugar and soap before the performance, when it becomes perfectly insensible to heat."

Don't try it. It's not only very, very nasty tasting, but it doesn't work. And don't use the formula that Jasper gave for climbing up a ladder of sharp swords:

> The secret is really very simple. The performer first bathes his feet in a very strong alum solution, to which zinc sulphate is added. The feet are gently dabbed dry, and then plunged into ice-cold water, and dabbed dry once more. They will then resist almost any cutting edge.

The mind boggles at such naïveté, especially from someone who should have known better. Much better.

CHAPTER 10

THE UBIQUITOUS HERRMANNS

Samuel Herrmann, an industrious physician of Hanover, Germany, at the turn of the century, had a second, clandestine life that was a matter of some concern to his patients. Closing up his practice every now and then, he would make off for distant parts of Europe, taking on a new and colorful avocation as a conjuror. It is said that his skill was great enough to attract the attention of the sultan of Turkey, who would periodically summon him to entertain specially favored guests at his palace.

When Compars (known as Carl), the eldest of Samuel's eight sons, began to show an interest in his father's secret vice, that young man was quickly packed off to the University of Paris to study cadavers and pills, rather than the trapdoors and card-sleights in which he found much more fascination. Resolutely, Carl abandoned his study of medicine in 1838, when he was twenty-two, and fell in with a troupe of actors.

His father was distraught. Hoping that his other children (there were sixteen in all!) would show more respect for his wishes, and determined to bring the real world to Carl's attention, he cut off all financial support and waited for his son's return to sanity. It never came. Within a decade, as a result of Carl Hermann's diligent application to the study of the art he had chosen, his name was known to society all over Europe, and French aristocrats were vying for his presence at their soirées and garden parties. Borrowing freely from Robert-Houdin's repertoire, Carl built up a great full stage show, with huge, colorful props and an effective supporting cast. The financial rewards, too, were great. Royalty showered him with gifts and money, and he was hosted at the finest mansions of the Continent.

Adelaide Herrmann in one of her spectacular costumes. She took over her famous husband's show after his death, and toured with it for many years very successfully.

He was famous, wealthy, and content, the more so when his skills were suddenly in demand in South America and, eventually, in the United States. There, too, he was a smashing success, traveling from Cuba to New Orleans in 1861, and thence to New York, then as now the mecca of successful artists. During his American tour, he entertained President Abraham Lincoln at the White House and then, two years later, sailed for England once more. He had made a strong impression in America, but his fame was greatest in Europe; America was to become the grazing ground of yet another Herrmann.

Herrmann *père* could hardly have known what he was starting by indulging his amateur theatrical distractions before his children. Carl, hav-

Herrmann the Great as he appeared at the height of his career. His distinctive appearance earned him recognition everywhere he went.

ing so shocked his father at the very beginning of his adult life, served as a model for Alexander, the eighth of the Herrmann sons, born twenty-seven years after Carl. Young Alex brought Samuel close to apoplexy when he announced at age ten that he, too, would "tread the boards" as a professional prestidigitator; he promptly ran off and joined his brother's show. His major function in that production, besides working backstage, was to serve as the "levitated" subject in Carl's presentation of the popular Aerial Suspension number originated by Robert-Houdin. Young Alex had been thus used in his brother's act as early as age eight; at the age of sixteen, he made his debut as a full-fledged professional before the approving eyes of Queen Isabella II of Spain.

For a few years, it was the Brothers Herrmann who toured the world with great success; then they went their separate ways, Carl to Europe, leaving the Western Hemisphere to his younger brother.

Alexander became an American citizen and was known as Herrmann the Great. Shortly after this, in 1876, his full stage show was seen by a seminary student named Howard Thurston, and the performance had such a powerful effect on that young man that he decided to take up the profession himself, which he did with eventual resounding success.

Leon Herrmann and his aunt Adelaide, as seen in the center of one of their lavish stage productions of an Oriental flavor, A Night in Japan.

Both Herrmanns were tall, thin, and handsome with Mephistophelian beards, and they didn't mind invoking the delicious suspicion that they just might be connected with dark powers. Carl eventually retired to Austria, where he died in 1887, but the Herrmann legend continued with Alexander, who not only equaled his older brother's success, but set new records for the name. With a great flair for publicity methods, Alexander would show up in towns where he played, driving a magnificent carriage and team of horses, stopping to pluck gold coins from the ears of passersby and to slice open fruit in the markets, thus revealing more coins within. He occupied a huge

Grand Opera House.

HARRY L. HAMLIN, Manager.

Announcement Extraordinary !

SUNDAY, SEPT. 5.   BY SPECIAL REQUEST.

ADELAIDE HERRMANN

Will on this night only perform her late husband's

ORIGINAL AND SENSATIONAL BULLET CATCHING ACT.

She stands as a target and catches the bullets fired point blank at her by six local Militia-men under the command of a Sergeant. The regular military rifles and the regular United States Government ammunition will be used in this test. Adelaide Herrmann will not handle or even touch the ammunition, which goes directly from the hands of the parties from the audience, who will mark the bullets, to the soldiers composing the firing party. The rifles will be then loaded by the soldiers, who, at the word of command, will face Adelaide Herrmann and fire at her point blank. Adelaide Herrman will catch the previously marked bullets in her hand and return them to those who marked them, still warm from the barrels of the rifles.

Even Adelaide Herrmann used the Bullet Catch to attract new audiences. She never had an accident, unlike many others who tried the routine.

some cases it has been caught between the teeth, or so the artists would have you believe. Many artists have featured it. Even female performers such as Adelaide Herrmann performed the stunt, as did one Annie Vernone, who in 1857 was advertised at the Theatre Royal in Hull.

In recent years Mr. Paul Daniels, the prominent British conjuror, has given a reenactment of the Chung Ling Soo routine on his popular television series in the U.K., even locating Jack Grossman, one of the two original riflemen who had fired at Soo on a fatal night in 1918, to re-create his part in the scene. One can only wonder what went through Mr. Grossman's mind when he fired at Daniels, though he was not the one who had held the faulty firearm that killed Soo. I'm glad to report that Paul Daniels survived his excellent presentation quite nicely.

Maurice Fogel was a powerful and effective U.K. performer who specialized in mentalism. He had started his career as assistant to a magician called Rameses. Maurice had a wonderful routine, which he performed between 1941 and 1960, in which he offered a spectator the choice between firing a rifle at a suspended china plate or at the conjuror's heart. If the plate was the chosen target, it shattered. If not, Fogel caught the bullet on a plate held in his hands. On one occasion, Fogel was hit in the forehead by stray wadding from the gun, and a portion of his skull was subsequently removed in surgery. The accident very nearly killed him, and left him scarred and somewhat incapacitated though still performing in top form, and certainly a lot wiser.

For some time during World War II, Britisher Peter Warlock performed the trick in the army, but wisely gave it up and is happily still with us.

Harry Kellar, in a fatherly attempt at advising escape artist Harry Houdini on the matter, wrote to him:

> Now, my dear boy, this is advice from the heart. DON'T TRY THE BULLET-CATCHING TRICK. There is always the biggest kind of risk that some dog will "job" you. And we can't afford to lose Houdini. Harry, listen to your friend Kellar, who loves you as his own son, and DON'T DO IT!

"Some dog" referred to any unknown enemy or smart aleck who might wish to do mischief to the performer; to "job" means to sabotage. Houdini, who'd had experience with such situations, apparently listened to Kellar, and neither artist ever did the Bullet Catch.

The trick, as might be expected, has had a deadly history. Examining what magic historian Will Dexter calls "the black record of the ill-starred gun trick," we find that Coullew of Lorraine was, in 1613, encouraging people to fire pistols at him. He appeared to catch the bullets in his hand. Though he survived many performances of the trick, this worthy was killed by an angry servant who clubbed him with the other end of the pistol. Ironic, isn't it?

Though Reverend Beard explained the secret of the trick in his 1631 book, it continued to be performed.

An unnamed troupe of Indian jugglers in 1814 performed at a room in Pall Mall, London, going on from there to continued success around the British Isles for the next three years. They were in Dublin when one of them was instantly shot dead while doing the gun trick, pretending to catch the bullet between his teeth. Kia Khan Kruse, a performer in Dublin in 1818, handed his loaded pistol to a spectator, took up his position onstage, and

CHAPTER 12

CHUNG LING SOO, THE MARVELOUS CHINESE CONJUROR

It is the evening of Saturday, March 23, 1918. The scene is the Wood Green Empire, a fine theater in London, and the remarkable Chinese magician Chung Ling Soo stands at the right side of the stage with a willow-pattern china plate in his hands. Opposite him across the stage are two Chinese warriors costumed in brass and leather armor, each with an old-fashioned muzzle-loading rifle aimed at the silken-robed magician.

The hushed crowd is about to witness a trick that has been a standard part of Soo's act for most of the eighteen years he has been a magical headliner. It is called Defying the Bullets. Two lead bullets, carefully marked by audience members for later identification, have been loaded into the rifles now pointed at the magician, who holds the china plate out at arm's length toward the riflemen, in line with the rifles and his heart. In a moment, he intends to exhibit those two bullets, caught on the plate, and it will be just one more triumph of the conjuring art.

But not this time. His luck has run out. For, as the two shots echo in the theater, Chung Ling Soo pauses a second as if in surprise. He spins forward and falls in a pile of confused silken splendor on the stage. Across his chest and at his back, a crimson stain begins to spread. The curtain drops rapidly across the unexpected scene, and the audience sits stunned. The projection screen quickly drops into place, and in seconds the scheduled motion picture is on the screen.

Backstage, beyond the gaze of the audience and behind the huge red front

curtain, a little lady named Suee Seen, Soo's* wife, kneels at his side. He whispers to her in agony, and he is tenderly wrapped in a portion of border curtain hastily ripped down by a stagehand. Moments later, the doctors arrive and the "Marvelous Chinese Conjuror," as the marquee outside describes him, is rushed off to the Wood Green Cottage Hospital nearby.

His wife sits with him all through the night, while he weakens. As dawn arrives, Chung Ling Soo gives a mighty sigh and is dead.

And the mystery begins.

Above left: Formal, signed portrait of William E. Robinson as Chung Ling Soo. Above right: The same man when he was known as Robinson, the "Man of Mystery."

The Sunday newspapers reveal the greatest secret guarded by Chung Ling Soo: He was not Chinese. He was an American named William Ellsworth Robinson, a master of makeup and magic. For nearly two decades he masqueraded as an Oriental wizard, never speaking in public, but having a genuine Chinese "interpreter" delivering all of his words to the audience. His wife, Suee Seen, was actually the Caucasian Olive "Dot" Path. The stage decor was magnificent in its Eastern extravagance, the beautiful costumes were delights, and the finely crafted apparatus transported his audiences into the world of Aladdin, where they saw miracles such as the production

*I am quoting accounts of the day, which err in using the third part of the name as the family name. My Oriental friends will know that I am aware of the correct usage. The family name, in this case, would be "Chung," and the performer would be correctly called "Mr. Chung."

The Defying the Bullets trick that eventually took Chung Ling Soo's life used the familiar and popular willow pattern of china plate. Cardboard replicas of such plates were used by Soo as advertising giveaways and also in his poster designs.

of a huge bowl of water in the center of the bare stage. "Chung Ling Soo" toured the world with the show, always returning to England, where he lived in a sumptuous estate done up in Chinese magnificence.

His famous trick with the rifles failed him due to a mechanical defect, and he was shot—with one bullet—through the lung. The projectile passed completely through his body.

But immediately, as might be expected, stories began to circulate about strange tong revenge motives, secret societies, and even rival magicians who had arranged to have Chung murdered. There were even hints of suicide and thwarted love, promoted by someone who had known Robinson and should have known better. So many versions of this man's life have been produced that he could be a dozen different persons. American author Fulton Oursler, in an unforgivable burst of hyperbole, wrote a 1947 account that summed up all the nonsense about Chung and presented it as fact.

In *The Riddle of Chung Ling Soo*, surely the definitive account of the matter, author Will Dexter went into the mystery in great detail. Like so many great mysteries, this one was actually a simple, direct event. It was tragic but hardly as involved and devious as so many would have it.

Billy Robinson was born in 1861, and as a youth was apprenticed to a mechanic and metalworker. He learned the trade, one which helped him greatly when he later entered the magic business. At age nineteen he began his magic career as "Robinson, the Man of Mystery." No Oriental trappings here, just an American conjuror breaking into the business, working variety theaters. He was described in one newspaper review as, "a good allround performer," doing "magic, spiritualism, mind reading, etc." There were no superlatives for him—not yet.

At age twenty-six, Robinson met a tiny lady named Olive "Dot" Path, and they began doing a "Black Art" act, one in which the artists work against a dead black background in very light-colored costumes. This act, which opened at the Keith's Gaiety Theater in Providence, Rhode Island, with Robinson using the stage name of Achmed Ben Ali, elicited praise from a local critic. It was, he said, "the most profound sensation of any performance placed before the public." That accolade brought Robinson to the attention of magician Harry Kellar, who was always looking for fresh talent to travel with his lavish productions, and Kellar vied with Alexander Herrmann for Robinson's services. Kellar won the competition, and used Robinson and some of his original inventions such as the Cocoon and Astarte, both spectacular effects, in his full stage show.

When he actually got an opportunity to perform onstage in the Kellar show, Robinson changed into yet another Easterner, Nana Sahib. At one point, he left the active stage work entirely and worked as Kellar's manager and mechanic for a while.

Inescapably, Chung Ling Soo had to feature the Chinese Linking Rings as part of his repertoire. In this, as in all aspects of Oriental conjuring, he was a master.

The bowl was marked "Lot 58." If it had not been for that bowl, many things might never have happened, for it was the original Water Bowl with which Soo first won fame as a Chinese magician. It was bracketted with a tray, pail and three glue pots. This "lot" should have been the star item; conjurors should have fought for its possession; instead, it was passed by like the breathing of the common wind.

The cauldron of Chung Ling Soo produced endless quantities of flags, silk foulards, animals, and finally a human being.

Lot 58 fetched fourteen shillings—a dollar or so. The bowl was not seen again.

The death of Chung Ling Soo, a tragedy that occurred because of a mechanical failure, has been thoroughly and correctly solved and explained. There was never any great mystery about it. But it involved a fascinating, enigmatic character. In much the way that the death of John F. Kennedy gave rise to all manner of insane theories, Robinson's demise begged to attract the lunatic fringe of the profession. Writers have sought conspiracy, suicide, murder, romantic frustration, and international intrigue in Robinson's accidental death, ignoring the simple facts that have been established. His wonderful illusions were enough mystery for us to remember the man by; let us not sully his memory with fanciful conjectures.

CHAPTER 13

LAFAYETTE, THE QUICK-CHANGE ARTIST, & THE BOSCOS

LAFAYETTE

Sigmund Neuberger was born in 1872, in Munich, Germany. He emigrated to the United States in 1884 and at the age of nineteen was performing in vaudeville as an archery marksman. Then he came upon the skill that was to make his future in show business: As The Great Lafayette, he became known as a quick-change artist. His entrance to the conjuring world was as an impersonator of the famous Chinese magician Ching Ling Foo. In 1900 he took that act to the London Hippodrome.

Lafayette was the highest-paid conjuror of his time, employing forty-five people in his extravagant stage show. The passion of his life was a dog named Beauty, which had been given to him by Harry Houdini in 1899. He was a martinet to his staff, a teetotaler, a stern master in all ways.

His show featured a particularly spectacular number titled "Dr. Kremser—Vivisectionist." It was a macabre little playlet in which Lafayette, as Dr. Kremser, came close to experimenting on his dog in order to save his daughter's life. Then, as now, the English were fervent antivivisectionists, and this dramatic number was very popular.

But the single strongest illusion he produced was known as "The Lion's Bride." It was a pantomime in which a lovely Christian princess was ship-wrecked and captured by an evil pasha. Her choice was to become his bride or to be thrown to the sacred royal lion. The appropriate decision was obvi-ous to Edwardian audiences; the lion would soon be dining. The hero, played by Lafayette, entered on a charging horse and bravely did in a huge Nubian guard, then disguised himself as the beleaguered princess. He was thrown into the lion's cage by a fresh set of guards, and when the lion charged out of the cage to terrify everyone, its head fell off to reveal Lafayette himself.

On May 1, 1911, at the Empire Palace Theatre in Edinburgh, Lafayette began his Scottish tour. Three days later, the dog Beauty suddenly died (at age twelve), and the conjuror was inconsolable. He barely made it through his shows. Funeral arrangements for Beauty were made, with the embalmed body in a metal-lined oak casket with silk trim and a glass lid. Lafayette purchased a cemetery plot in which he himself was to be placed beside his beloved dog when his time came. The canine funeral was set for May 10.

But on May 9, at the conclusion of "The Lion's Bride" illusion, fire broke out onstage from a short-circuited electric cable. A partially blocked fire curtain was lowered, and the audience of three thousand escaped safely to the street. Nine people backstage were killed, including The Great Lafayette, along with a midget named Alice Dakle and her understudy, Joseph Coats. The real horse and lion used in the illusion also died. Lafayette's body was taken to Glasgow for cremation.

Then the real mystery unfolded. A second body was discovered later in the evening, beneath the stage. This was unquestionably the actual body of Lafayette. During the performance of "The Lion's Bride," a double had been introduced at one point so that the audience would believe that their hero was onstage. Actually, he was below the stage, preparing to make his appearance costumed as the lion. The first body discovered and identified as Lafayette was that of a man named Richards, employed in the show because of his close physical resemblance to Lafayette.

It was a tragedy that need not have happened. In contravention of the fire laws, Lafayette had ordered that three of the five fire exits backstage be locked to ensure security for his secrets; a fourth exit was blocked by scenery. The artists were effectively trapped, though some forced open one locked door to escape. It is believed that Lafayette himself turned back to save the horse, but was overcome by smoke and fumes.

That Saturday, sixty coaches in a three-mile cortège traveled to the cemetery past a crowd of thousands of mourners in the grandest funeral ever seen in Glasgow. Four coaches were required to carry the wreaths alone. The urn containing the ashes of the conjuror was placed between the paws of Beauty, and two stones, still to be seen today at Piershill Cemetery, were raised in memory.

BARTOLOMEO & THE OTHER BOSCOS

There have been quite a number of conjurors in the business using the name "Bosco." The first of the prominent ones, Bartolomeo Bosco (1793–1863) had an early career as a soldier under Napoleon Bonaparte, was wounded in

The Great Lafayette's feature playlet was an antivivisectionist number that featured the fearsome Dr. Kremser, a villain if ever there was one.

Here the three of this famous troupe are shown in their respective specialties. They issued a great number of such posters to advertise their long and successful association.

The Queen of Coins, Mercedes Talma, of the team Le Roy, Talma & Bosco, as she appeared doing her remarkable coin manipulations. This was a departure for female performers, who were usually mere dressing to a magic act.

audience of magicians. It was a fiasco, since Le Roy had lost his coordination and he fumbled through it miserably. Following that performance, he destroyed all of his equipment and notes. He faded away and died in poverty in 1953.

CHAPTER 16

KELLAR, THE MAN WHO SPOKE WITH DEVILS, & THURSTON, KING OF CARDS

HARRY KELLAR

The first major American-born stage illusionist of truly international fame was an adventuresome chap named Harry Kellar. The product of an unhappy home, he ran away at a very early age. He was taken in by a minister, who attempted to prepare him for a life in the church; but, like Howard Thurston, Kellar was not at all ready for such a life, and at age twelve he accepted a job as an assistant to a well-known magician, I. H. Hughes, an Englishman known as "The Fakir of Ava." Six years later, he struck out to become "The World's Best Magician," as he billed himself. Clumsy, thick of speech—with a slight impediment—and quite uneducated, he did not cut the figure that his audiences expected. They were accustomed to the fine manners and speech of the Herrmanns, and rejected young Kellar.

Then in 1868, as fortune would have it, he became the agent for the Davenport Brothers, with their traveling "spirit" show, in which he also worked a spot. The act traveled widely, covering the United States and Canada, as well as Europe. Harry learned what it was to tour with a highly organized and successful show, and he also discovered a lot about putting before the audience a carefully rehearsed pattern of speech and dress.

Having learned from these highly skilled people, but not getting along well with the cantankerous Davenports, he was soon on his own, doing a Davenport-style act himself, accompanied by one William Fay, another disenchanted colleague of the Davenports. (As has been mentioned, his name was originally Keller, but to avoid the possibility of being confused with the magician Heller, who was then enjoying great acclaim, he'd changed the spelling.)

*Only one word explains this powerful poster. It was all that was needed. Here, Harry Kellar
again made use of the in-league-with-Satan implication that so titillated his audiences.*

The famous Karnac Levitation as shown in this beautiful Kellar poster from 1904. The illusion underwent many improvements in the hands of Kellar.

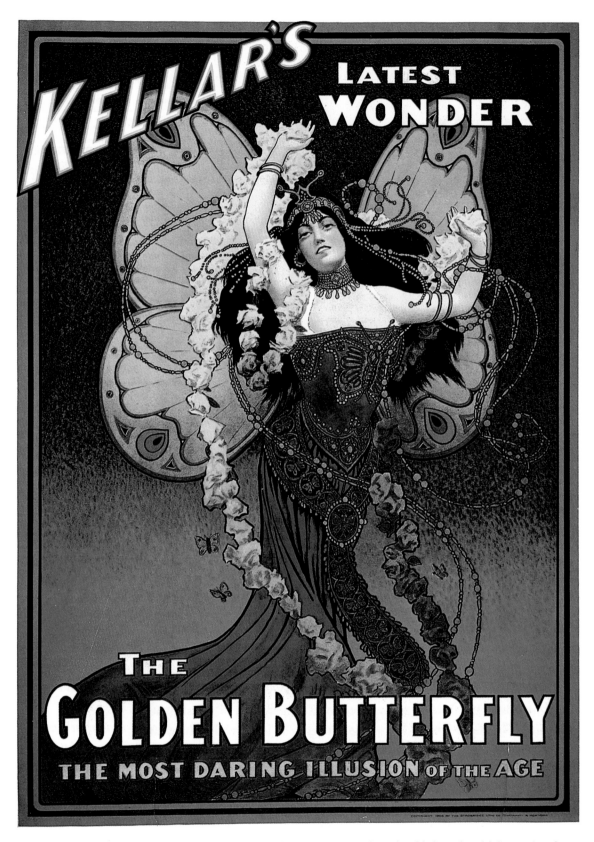

One of the most effective and attractive posters of the golden age of magic, this item is widely sought after
by collectors. Kellar was famous enough that he did not need to be portrayed by the artist.

America only fueled his audiences' need to see with what wonders he would attempt to outdo his rival. This competition led to bitter actions such as overpasting each other's posters and delivering insulting remarks to the press. Eventually the two were reconciled, and upon Herrmann's death Kellar was genuinely sympathetic to his widow, Adelaide.

In 1908, approaching sixty years of age, Harry Kellar formally transferred the huge show to Howard Thurston, twenty years his junior, who was embraced by the public with just as much enthusiasm as had been shown his mentor. Harry Kellar died, in retirement and full of honors, in 1922.

The books of "Professor Hoffman" are still on sale through magic dealers. Here is an advertisement from a 1912 catalog.

HOWARD THURSTON

Varied early careers as a race tout, a newspaper boy, and a medical missionary would hardly seem suitable preparation for a professional magician, but that's how the great Howard Thurston got his start. As a child, he'd witnessed a performance by Herrmann the Great in Columbus, Ohio, and he soon took to practicing sleight of hand as described in Professor Louis Hoffmann's* *Modern Magic.* His mother, a religious woman, saw the devil's work in such studies, and when young Howard happened to come under the influence of one Dwight Moody, a fiery Bible-thumping evangelist of the day, it seemed that the life of a conjuror was not to be his.

Howard was shipped off by his mother to attend Mount Hermon School in Massachusetts, where he began his Bible studies. Leaving that school to enroll in advanced studies at the University of Pennsylvania, he was suddenly switched off track by an impetuous decision to wait in Albany, New York, between trains. He'd seen by posters that Herrmann the Great was then showing in Albany, and what he intended to be a mere stopover to see the show just once more, led to permanent abandonment of a life in religion and the beginning of a brilliant career as the foremost magician of his day.

During the very hard years that followed, Thurston perfected the trick that was to be his very own specialty: the Rising Cards. In this trick, cards called for by the audience rose one by one from a deck held by the conjuror. It was an often-imitated trick, but, like many of these masterpieces, it was always best in the hands of its originator. At about this time, Thurston adopted the title "King of Cards."

Fortunately for Thurston, he had working for him at that time a young press agent named Billy Robinson, the man who was to later become a very famous magician himself under the stage name of Chung Ling Soo. Robinson arranged for Thurston to privately demonstrate his Rising Cards routine to Leon Herrmann, the nephew of Alexander Herrmann who had taken over the stage show when his much more famous uncle died. In the company

---

* This was the pen name of Angelo John Lewis (1839–1919), who wrote a number of excellent books on conjuring, still in print today.

Right: Like Kellar before him, Howard Thurston implied in his advertisements that imps assisted him in performing his miracles. Note the Kellar endorsement. Facing page: Tampa ran one of the Thurston road shows. Here is shown the puzzling Crushing trick in which it seems impossible for the young lady to survive the fearsome device pictured.

Press agents often greatly embarrassed Thurston, writing wild stories that said he had been trained in the black arts by Himalayan gurus. He denied and depreciated such tales, but had to live with them. Good stories are hard to deny.

Then, in 1907, he was made the offer he found impossible to refuse. Harry Kellar, long wishing to retire, saw in Thurston the perfect man to inherit his mantle. For a while, they worked together as Kellar broke in his

Thurston's famous Million Dollar Mystery produced any number of people, birds, and balloons from a small box. This trick was recently resurrected by Doug Henning under the title Things That Go Bump in the Night.

successor; they were often on the verge of dissolving the arrangement because of Kellar's penchant for perfection, in opposition to Thurston's casual acceptance of chipped paint and sloppy assistants.

In May of 1908, with a great publicity send-off, Thurston officially took over the combined Thurston-Kellar extravaganza, and for twenty-seven years he toured with it. The show changed each year to bring new and astonishing illusions to ever eager fans.

Among the most effective of those illusions was the Levitation of Princess Karnac. It was essentially the levitation first developed by J. N. Maskelyne, in a somewhat varied version, and is still a feature with today's leading performers. In his presentation, Thurston would dramatically intone:

> Rise, Fernanda, I command you to rise! Rise, as you rose in the Temple of Krisna one thousand years ago!

As the woman floated upward, the orchestra would play the "Meditation" from *Thaïs*, and two male assistants costumed in Hindu dress would kneel reverently at each side. As the prone figure slowly came to rest above the head of the magician, he continued:

> There she lies, asleep in space, suspended by nothing but the power of thought. There she can remain in peace for two hours, two weeks, two years. The slightest sound, the slightest whisper can disturb her sleep.

You can well believe that no sound was heard in the theater except for Thurston's voice and the orchestra playing softly.

Thurston never played the Far West, nor did he take his show into the southern United States. He found quite enough work touring the Northeast for a nine-month season, then took a rest while the props were repainted, rebuilt, and repaired, and new illusions were created at the workshop in Whitestone Landing, Long Island, to keep up with the demand for ever new miracles. That area of Whitestone not only served Thurston as a warehouse, but he also lived there, as did Horace Goldin; earlier Alexander Herrmann and Billy Robinson (Chung Ling Soo) had lived there, as well.

Howard Thurston's last full evening show played in 1931, after which he actually went into radio for a while. In 1934 he performed a special show for President Theodore Roosevelt at the White House, and in 1936 started out on a new vaudeville tour, but was felled by a stroke. Soon afterward, the man who—but for a strange twist of fate—almost became a preacher and a missionary, died, ever the man of mystery.

Howard Thurston inherited the Levitation presentation from Harry Kellar, and made it a feature of his act.

This Vanishing Horse illusion has been done by both Blackstones and by Siegfried & Roy, among others. In essentially the same trick, an elephant and a water buffalo have been used, too.

CHAPTER 17

THE TWO DANTES

DANTE I

The name "Dante" was almost sure to be adopted by a conjuror, and it has been held by more than one. Oscar Eliason, the first Dante, was born in 1869 to Mormon parents of Swedish descent living in Utah. He was one of nine children, and was intended to follow his father's trade of watchmaker. However, since he showed an early skill at conjuring and his father, Olaf, was a keen amateur, he began making local appearances in Salt Lake City. At the age of twenty-four Oscar was duplicating conjuring the "spirit" tricks of Anna Eva Fay (who had been working her act since 1874) and a "Dr." Waite, both successful impostors who had toured the area.

Oscar's poster at the time advertised "Eliason's Wonders," which included a mind-reading act and among which was a "Grand Spiritualistic Seance" described as

Being neither in defense of, or an attact [sic] on spiritulism [sic], but the phenomena still continue to bedevil the wits of all who see. An Entertainment Amusing and Instructive to Old and Young Alike.

On the same bill was Edmunda Eliason, Oscar's new wife, who was

ELECTRA, THE MAGNETIC WONDER
A Young Lady who Challenges the United Strength
of Six Powerful Men.

This was a copy of Annie May Abbott, known as the Little Georgia Magnet. The act consisted of the young lady resisting the best efforts of a group of men from the audience to lift her or push her out of place. Miss Abbott toured for many years with this interesting act, starting in the British Isles in 1891, then touring New Zealand, Australia, and India until her retirement in 1918. There were many, many imitators of her act.

The Eliasons traveled throughout the United States, as well as in Mexico, Cuba, and Canada. Picked up in Vancouver by an entrepreneur named Curtis they moved on to Honolulu and then New Zealand, where Eliason became Dante, a name he had picked out at the age of eleven and finally felt worthy of using. From New Zealand it was a short hop to Australia, where he achieved great acclaim.

Dante performed in court dress, with silk stockings and high-heeled slippers, not an unexpected costume for a conjuror of the day. His brother Franklin, six years his junior, assisted onstage along with Edmunda. Featured were the Bullet Catch and a Black Art number. As with many other artists of the day, Dante also did a replication of the Davenport Brothers' spirit-cabinet act.

The media, almost without exception, accepted and lauded the Dante show. He advertised heavily, liberally postering the towns he played, and broke records for duration of stay at the Palace in Sydney (101 performances).

A serious difficulty with his entrepreneur arose in 1899, with the two parties suing one another in all ways and in all directions. The result was that promoter Curtis left for America and returned to Australia with a troupe known as Hogan's Unbleached Coons, featuring a Black Dante, Curtis' obvious attempt at revenge. This artist performed several of Dante's more popular numbers, and the public flocked to see both for purposes of comparison.

Dante's show moved on, to tour from one end of the vast Australian continent to the other. A new minstrel group, Hudson's New Surprise Party, popped up to plague him with promotions for "The Black Dantes," and promises to not only perform some of the favorite tricks from the original's repertoire, but to also expose them to the audience. Imitators were everywhere, but the media gave them a very hard time. In defense of the genuine Dante, the governors of New Zealand and five Australian states gave permission for him to advertise that he performed under their official patronage.

The demand for his show was enormous. Dante sailed from Melbourne in November of 1899 after a hundred very successful appearances there, intending to play Queensland and then return to the United States via India or South Africa. It was not to be. During a hunting outing, the gun carried by his orchestra leader accidentally discharged and hit Oscar in the abdomen. Three days later Dante was dead, after uttering his last words: "Keep the show going, boys."

After a brief thirty years, this great artist was tragically stilled. Other magicians who followed him to Australia, notably Howard Thurston, worked in his shadow. Interesting enough, when Thurston in the 1920s engaged a young magician named Harry Jansen to perform his second show unit, he had him change his name to Dante. He was to become a very famous performer under that stage name.

Oscar's brother Frank, having been an active member of the troupe, took over the show under the Dante name, and until 1910 toured with moderate success. Edmunda stayed in Sydney, performing for several more years until she returned with her children to the United States and remarried.

The Dante gravesite at Waverley Cemetery, Sydney, is respectfully maintained by the Genies Magical Society of Parramatta.

DANTE II

Danish-born in 1883, Harry August Jansen was touring the United States at the age of twenty-one with a minor magic act. He was the one who took out the Thurston road show (from 1923 to 1932 in the United States and on a world tour) at the height of that magician's popularity. He is the naturalized American who is usually being referred to in the trade when the name "Dante" is used.

Thurston died while Dante was touring the show in Europe. Shortly after that, when he came to take out his own show, Dante reached back into his childhood and came up with an old nonsense expression that had been used when he played street games in Copenhagen; he called his show *Sim-Sala-Bim,* and the expression was used onstage when he invited applause from his audience.

His full-evening show was spectacular, even in an age when a lavish show was what audiences expected and usually got. His "Backstage Illusion," a featured number in his show, was designed—so he said—to give the audience an opportunity to catch him at one of his tricks. The stage was set so that it appeared in reverse, with an audience painted on the backdrop, and the performers facing away from the real audience. In effect, the live audience was "backstage" viewing the show from there. They saw a hidden assistant crouching on a secret platform behind a large box affair, which was shown—to the painted audience—to be empty. At a signal from Dante, the assistant would enter the box via a concealed panel, and the real audience was now smugly confident that it had seen the modus operandi of the trick. Then, to the total confusion of everyone, the person who burst out of the box turned out to be an entirely different one from the person who had

Dante had a very successful season in Sweden in 1931, aided by such colorful advertising.

The more famous of the two Dantes, Harry Jansen, provides a model image for a magician. His lavish stage show was titled Sim Sala Bim.

secretly entered the box. That person had, somewhere along the way, completely vanished!

Dante's chief assistant was Moi-Yo Miller, an Australian beauty queen who was a very important partner in the performance. Dante appeared in a 1938 motion picture, *Racket Busters*, playing himself, in *Bunco Squad*, and with Laurel and Hardy in *A-Haunting We Will Go* in 1942.

We have preserved on motion picture film at least some of the great magical artists of the past. Dante, Blackstone Sr., Roy Benson, Richiardi Jr., Channing Pollock, and Cardini—among many others—are to be seen in short film clips, while Dunninger and Houdini have entire movies and TV series in which their genius can be viewed. Only one known recording, from an old Edison wax cylinder, exists of Houdini's voice. That does not inspire awe; it seems to be a squeaky, thin voice that the Elusive American used to address his admirers. I prefer to believe that this recording is flawed. . . .

CHAPTER 18

THE BAMBERG FAMILY

The magical Bamberg family started, according to one version, in the early 1700s, with Jasper Bamberg of Leyden, Holland, using a magic lantern to impress investors in his business of seeking the Philosopher's Stone and other alchemical chimeras. Whether the subsequent Bambergs were descended from that rascal or not, we have the first really historically established entertainer in Eliaser Bamberg (1760–1833), who seems to have been more like what we would recognize as a conjuror. This man had had a leg amputated following a war injury, but apparently that only encouraged him to assiduously pursue a career in conjuring—rather than alchemy—and he was famous in his hometown for street conjuring, becoming known as *Le Diable Boiteux* (The Crippled Devil). His name appears as "A. L. Bamberg" on an 1823 Berlin playbill, which says he was a pupil of the Italian magician Pinetti. An 1831 almanac from Utrecht records that he was well known then.

The next generation saw David Leendert Bamberg (1786–1869) a favorite of Prince Fredrik of Holland, who frequently called upon his talents for light diversion. Soon after followed Tobias Bamberg, who is credited with having originated an interesting illusion routine called "Galatea," based upon the legend of the sculptor whose beautiful work turns into a living girl. That same legend was the basis for the theme used by Shaw in *Pygmalion* and for the musical *My Fair Lady*.

Next in the line was David Tobias Bamberg, known fondly in Holland as "Papa." But it was with the sixth generation, Tobias Leendert Bamberg, that the family business of magic took on international importance. This Bamberg, adopting an Oriental theme, became known as "Okito" (the letters of Tokio—Tokyo—rearranged). Okito's son, David, who chose the show name of Fu Manchu, made it six proven generations of the line. That meant that over a period of almost two hundred years, a Bamberg was always onstage somewhere in the world charming an audience.

Tobias was almost deaf due to a near drowning while skating as a boy in Holland. As a result, he never spoke a word onstage, preferring to perform his Oriental act in pantomime. His first wife was a French girl with an Iron Jaw act who hung from a trapeze holding on only with her teeth. Four months pregnant, she fell from the dome of a theater and was killed.

Okito broke in his first Japanese-style act in Berlin in 1893, when he was eighteen. It was immediately successful, but at the height of his fame, while working in England, he chose to elope with the daughter of the theater manager and abandoned the show. His new wife was also one of the stars of that same show, performing an act that was later called the Fata Morgana. It was a singing/dancing number with special lighting effects on a very elaborate costume. The theater manager was not at all happy about the elopement, since he lost two star acts and a daughter all in one night.

Okito chose to forget the name Tobias/Toby because his English wife said it was a name commonly given to pet dogs in her country, and she selected Theodore/Theo as more suitably dignified.

There came a time when Theo had to change—permanently—from Japanese costume to Chinese robes, in order that a major trick he designed would be more practical. He was thus a Dutchman with a pseudo-Japanese name dressed as a Chinese. No one seemed to care much about the contradictions, and the act was excellent.

Along the way his son, David, was born in England. On a stormy day in February of 1907, when the child was just three years old, the family was awaiting a boat train at Liverpool Street Station that was to take them to the port of Harwell, where they would board the S.S. *Berlin,* sailing to Amsterdam. As the train pulled in, they noticed that little David was missing. A frantic search discovered him in a shop looking over magazines, but by then the train had departed. Theo was furious, and vented his well-known temper on his wife and child. The next morning in the hotel room they'd taken to await the next train, Theo repented of his anger when he saw the newspaper. The S.S. *Berlin* had been lost during a storm in the English Channel, and there were no survivors.

The artist Okito was a great shadowgraphist,* and as such was hired in the United States by Howard Thurston to open the second half of his full-evening stage show. He also served Thurston as designer, mechanic, and carpenter, at which skills he was very adept. Magicians' props handmade by Theo are today highly prized by collectors. For a short time Okito worked

---

* Shadowgraphy is the art of forming figures with the hands and casting the shadow upon a viewing surface. A modern master of the art is Sonny Fontana of Venezuela.

side by side on the Thurston show with one of the stranger characters in the magic business, a stage mechanic named Guy Jarrett. This man was clever, inventive and valuable, but his blatant, abusive racism and generally unpleasant, abrasive attitude alienated him from the artists who could have benefited from his help. He lasted only one season with Thurston, and upon leaving was unsparing in his unfounded condemnation of the magician.

An amusing episode involving a magic prop that was handcrafted by Okito in his later years demonstrates the problems that can occur when a Western conjuror opts to adopt an Oriental theme. Edmund Spreer, the mechanical genius who was closely associated with both Okito and his son David (Fu Manchu), related that Okito was fond of photographing Oriental motifs and calligraphs for possible design use in the equipment he manufactured. In Hong Kong he shot many rolls of film, which gave him material for years afterward. One Chinese sign he found particularly attractive was used on a very elegant prop he made for a magician customer in the United States, and it was during its debut in that unfortunate gentleman's hands that a grievous error was discovered. This conjuror had reached the climax of the trick and had just opened the door of the boxlike affair to reveal a beautifully painted panel bearing the Chinese words so carefully copied by Okito. A group of Chinese spectators broke out in unexpected laughter, to the confusion of the conjuror, who had not expected that reaction to his efforts. Immediately following the show, the now subdued and serious

Above left: Okito, seen here in 1949, was one of the famous Dutch Bambergs. Above right: Fu Manchu's fabulous collection of over 300 authentic Chinese costumes was worth a small fortune, and always dazzled his audiences.

Above: Theo Bamberg (Okito) in 1893, showing his first stage setting and costume as a Japanese act. Several years later, this authentic Japanese-style costume was changed for a Chinese robe, which was used from then on. In this photo, the artist was eighteen years old. Left: In 1901, Okito posed with his assistant, Polising. Bumbling black-face lackies were popular at the time as comic characters onstage.

The Great Syko (David Bamberg/Fu Manchu) in 1917 at the age of thirteen, when he worked with Julius Zancig with the mind-reading act.

Asians visited backstage to inform the magus that his sign had admonished them, "Do not urinate in the alley."

Young David Bamberg made a great name for himself in magic, one that is still revered in South American countries and in Mexico. As a youngster he had worked an astonishing variety of jobs: as onstage assistant to his father; as a mentalist, at age thirteen, as part of the Zancig mind-reading team; as a shadowgraphist in variety shows; and later as a movie extra. He was only fifteen when he found himself alone in London, sent there to further his education. He accomplished that goal in a manner not intended by his parents, frequenting the interior of the Egyptian Hall theater, where the Maskelynes were host to so many major magic artists. It was a period of

*David Bamberg in
character as Fu
Manchu.*

maximum creativity in magic, and David took full advantage of it. Somehow, he survived very tough times and managed to get to the United States, then to South America.

When it came time for him to take his first big show on tour, David Bamberg also chose to adopt Oriental costumes, tricks, and mannerisms, as Okito had done. Both father and son were very highly successful with this theme. However, David always said that though he admired and fully appreciated the great artistry of his father, he learned more from and was more inspired by Thurston. Okito was aloof and dictatorial, seldom showing affection for his son. It is very difficult to understand how his parents could have allowed David to be out on his own, at such an early age, alone, without any support at all from home, while his father and mother were

In this rare photograph of Edmund Spreer as a performer, he is seen just weeks before his death, performing a water-bowl production used by Fu Manchu, the artist for whom Spreer designed and built so many fine illusions.

traveling with their show in foreign lands. He was often lonely and afraid, and he struggled for many years to support himself. Only years later, after David had fully proven himself as an artist, did his father accept him fully as a human being, and the last years of their association were very close.

While trying to get his own show together, David became part of the Great Raymond's show. Illusionist Raymond was very popular in Europe and Britain at that time. Edmund Spreer, the German mechanic who worked for Raymond, struck up a friendship with David when they met in Hamburg, and David took Spreer with him when he left Europe to strike out on his own. Spreer was a trusted assistant from then on, originating and constructing many brilliant tricks for his master.

David, as Fu Manchu, eventually took his show to Mexico and South

America, where he was to become so famous. Spreer designed and built a great number of effective stage props for him and was very much an integral part of the show for decades. He was not only a builder and mechanic, but served as chief assistant, troubleshooter, and stunt organizer. That was the day when employees were willing to serve an artist faithfully and knew with satisfaction that they were part of his success.

David had adopted the name "Fu Manchu" when a friend jokingly addressed a letter to him that way, and it served him well except when he tried to play countries where copyright laws prohibited the use of the name invented by writer Sax Rohmer. For that reason, he kept pretty well to South America and Mexico, where he worked for almost forty years.

Having seen Li-Ho Chang, a genuine Asian magician, attain great success in Latin America with a number of costume changes during his show, Fu began to change both setting and costumes for each of his own production numbers, and within a few years he had amassed a collection of over three hundred fine, authentic Oriental robes, some of them over two centuries old. His backdrops and curtains were hand-embroidered silk, and some weighed hundreds of pounds.

In 1935 Fu Manchu was featuring the trick that Dedi had used to fool the pharaoh, switching the heads of a black and a white duck. And he had Spreer design and build a nine-foot-tall aluminum robot, filled with machinery and equipped with doors that could be opened so that the audience could be shown every aspect of the insides. This monster walked about and answered secret questions that were asked of Fu while he was in the audience area of the theater. It was such a massive prop, however, that it could not be easily packed and transported, and it had to be junked. The principle behind the illusion, however, was new, and it was used in Fu's Pendulum trick.

This was a wonderful new version of the Sawing in Half trick, in which a huge razor-sharp pendulum slowly descended while swinging in a great arc, slicing a hapless lady like a shapely bologna. The inspiration, of course, was Edgar Allan Poe's story "The Pit and the Pendulum." The new principle he developed had the other magicians perplexed, and he even caught one of them—a prominent professional—on the darkened stage after his show had closed one evening, trying to discover the secret. It was a vain effort.

Fu Manchu, as David Bamberg, also went into radio in Mexico. He had his own show there for years, and soon after he also entered the film business, portraying his Fu Manchu character in such thrillers as *El Espectro de la Novia* (The Specter Bride) and *La Mujer Sin Cabeza* (The Headless Woman), none of which caused Cecil B. DeMille to lose sleep through worry. Though he had some excellent ideas for film themes and innovations, he was far ahead of his time. The Mexican film industry, which produced fully seventy-five percent of the Latin American product, was locked into certain formulas and refused to move in the new directions suggested by

*Li–Ho Chang began his conjuring career in his native Panama and toured the world with a full
stage show. He was an inspiration to Fu Manchu and other artists.*

The huge robot built by Edmund Spreer for the Fu Manchu show. It answered questions posed by the audience.

Left: Fu Manchu's marvelous Pit and the Pendulum version of the Sawing in Half trick used a clever new principle that amazed his spectators. Below left: The full stage setting for Fu Manchu's Chinese Lanterns number.

Bamberg. During his film career, David became a close friend of Orson Welles.

This fine illusionist was the last of his line to practice magic. During his long career, he broke attendance and length-of-stay records in several cities. He was creative, skilled, and hard-working, with the constant ups and downs that unfortunately plague so many people in show business. Fu Manchu was also extraordinarily skilled at shadowgraphy, an art he never tired of. His spectrum of experience in the entertainment business was wide, and it is exhibited in his autobiographical book, *Illusion Show,* which he wrote after his retirement.

Fear not. The pretty
lady will come to no
harm, though
threatened by the fear-
some Fu Manchu.

What really comes through in that story is that along with all the "glam-our" of foreign countries, meeting exotic people, and taking the applause from pleased customers, there is the labor of packing and making repairs, the breakdowns, the doubts, the failures, and the inevitable sweat. But a freezing night on a train can be forgotten when you get a standing ovation. You work with a raging fever because those people out front came here to see you. You awaken in the morning with orange smears of makeup on your pillow because you were so tired you forgot to clean up before you fell into bed. But you did feed the livestock and you put the canvas cover over the Sawing trick, because that's What You Do.

And you wouldn't surrender a moment of any of it.

CHAPTER 19

THE TWO BLACKSTONES

HARRY BLACKSTONE (père)

May you live as long as you want
And never want as long as you live
And live ten years longer than I
And I? Why, I shall never die!
—BLACKSTONE'S CLOSING SPEECH

I confess, the name "Blackstone" means more to me than any other in magic. For me, it represents all the glamour, excitement, mystery, and pure fun that constitute the art. When I first encountered that name, I entered the enchanted world in which I've lived ever since, to my great joy and continued fascination. That delightful giant elf who first smiled at me—personally, I was sure—from the stage of the Royal Alexandra Theatre so many years ago in Toronto changed my life in that instant. How sincerely I hope that I've proven myself worthy of his loving attention.

Henri Bouton was born in 1885, in the city of Chicago. He and his brother Peter did a "double" act as young magicians, and somewhere along the way Henri became Harry, perhaps inspired by the then popular magician Harry Kellar. "Harry Bouton & Company" was not altogether successful as a team, and the act became "Straight & Crooked Magic," with Harry being topped by brother Peter as a clown comedian. The act had become a single by 1915, with Peter tending to backstage matters.

For a while the name "Fredrik the Great" was used, due to the fortunate purchase of a large supply of fresh posters printed up with that name for a magician whose show suddenly folded. Harry once commented to me that

A formal portrait of Harry Blackstone, Sr.

he was lucky the printer hadn't sold him some posters advertising Barbasol. At that point, he said, he'd have taken whatever came along. But the German flavor of the name Fredrik was less than popular in a war-conscious world, and as the posters gave out, Fredrik faded away too. Then, as Harry Blackstone, he attained success, and the show toured the United States and Canada with a sizeable cast in tow.

Of course, it was the "big" tricks (magicians usually refer to these as "illusions," to differentiate them from smaller items) that made all the publicity or "flash" to attract the customers. The Blackstone "Indian Rope trick," for example, was heavily promoted on the billboards and in the ads. In actuality, it was a quick, relatively ineffective trick, far overshadowed by the master's specialties, such as the Floating Light Bulb and the Dancing Handkerchief. These two wonderful feats, still used successfully by the second generation of the Blackstone family, will win any audience by virtue of the personal

involvement of the performer. Blackstone's Vanishing Bird Cage, too, is a memorable part of Blackstone II's performance.

Brother Pete, so very much like Harry in appearance, was brought into service whenever a "double" was needed in the show. Otherwise he was busy doing carpentry, repairs, maintenance, and essential backstage work when not onstage as the chief male assistant.

The Blackstone show consisted of ten assistants in 1917, though he

Blackstone Senior and his crew in 1941. George Johnstone, still active as a popular trade-show performer, is the second man from the right, and his wife, Betty, is the drum majorette on the right. Note the strong resemblance between Harry, seated in the middle, and his brother Pete. You can find Pete. Mrs. Harry Blackstone, Billie, is on the extreme left.

advertised "A Cast of Thirty—Mostly Girls." No one seemed inclined to count heads, and everyone was happy.

But the business of show business changed, and Blackstone adapted. Vaudeville came and went, and the show was chopped from a full-evening extravaganza to a "circuit" unit. Then motion pictures moved into the vaudeville houses, and Harry sought out auditoriums and convention halls—and the remaining legitimate houses—that could accommodate the "big" show once more. With the coming of World War II, he formed up a USO camp show and worked for the troops under incredibly difficult conditions. When that outlet ceased to exist, Blackstone looked about for a way to get back into the theaters, but the era of the full-evening magic show was closing rapidly, as families stayed home to watch a strange electronic picture box that was to become the entertainer of us all.

There was considerable friction between Blackstone and Harry Houdini. The escape artist highly resented anyone performing anything that even vaguely resembled something in his act, and he was particularly possessive of any self-release effect. Blackstone successfully used the submerged-packing-crate escape as a publicity stunt just at the time that Houdini was at his peak of popularity, and Houdini never forgave him. The enmity between the two lasted until Houdini died, and Blackstone never had a kind word to say about him.

Howard Thurston and Harry Blackstone were fierce competitors too, though there never was any animosity between them. At Thurston's death in 1936, Blackstone attained a lot of new business by filling the vacancies that resulted.

I was fortunate enough to see the "full" show many times, just before it vanished forever. I was twelve years of age when I skipped school one Wednesday and took in the matinee at the Royal Alexandra Theatre. The great Harry Blackstone was there, and to my surprise, when he walked on-stage, I saw that he was a rather diminutive man (he'd looked huge on the posters!) with a shock of snow-white hair that stood out as if he were charged with a few thousand volts of static electricity. He had a minor speech impediment, a sort of lisp that he conquered by projecting his voice throughout the theater; the back row was well aware of what he was saying. He walked and stood like a giant, too. You *knew*, when he appeared before you, that this was a man of power and mystery. The short stature and defect of speech were forgotten in the radiance of his personality.

Though I knew next to nothing about conjuring at that point in my life, I was nonetheless confident that I could figure it all out. This magician wasn't going to get away with anything while I sat in the very front row of the second balcony, focused in on his every move!

Wrong. That elfin man hornswoggled me. He turned a box of chocolates into a live rabbit (which animal inappropriately went to an ungrateful monster child in the front row) and he summoned up a stack of real goldfish bowls—full of water and the expected inhabitants—from absolutely nowhere. He buzz-sawed a willing young lady into two neat halves, and later levitated her happily restored body into the air "between Heaven and Earth" while passing a metal hoop around her as she floated serenely in space. I was totally, irrevocably "hooked," and walked out of the Royal Alexandra Theatre determined that I was going to do that sort of thing myself someday.

Then the basic problem occurred to me. How could I possibly learn about all that stuff? Were there books on the subject? That weekend, I hurried to the Toronto Public Library and discovered *The Book of Magic*, by A. Frederick Collins. Within its pages were described some simple but excellent conjuring tricks, which I immediately set out to learn. Within a few months, I felt I had enough clever secrets mastered that I might be capable of beguiling Mr. Blackstone when he again arrived in Toronto. And, to my delight, I also found the Arcade Magic & Novelty Company, where Harry Smith and his wife, Sophie, dispensed apparatus and wisdom to aspiring magi; Harry

Blackstone feigns shock as his famous buzz-saw illusion divides a young lady into two neat halves. She was promptly restored to health and was seen on the next show.

volunteered to tutor me. The Smiths were to be almost solely responsible for my never having worked at a real job, aside from summer holiday employment. I blame it all on them.

When Blackstone time rolled around once more, I was ready. This time I sat in the front row at the Wednesday matinee. Again, I saw the miracles unfold before my eyes. But this time, as I watched this great artist, I became aware of another, unexpected fact: My perception of the performance was irrevocably changed. Now, understanding some of what was really taking place on that stage, I was lost in a different sort of admiration. I no longer experienced a chill as the lady rose into the air, but I appreciated the skill and showmanship that went into making this, not a mechanical marvel, but a theatrical triumph. Yes, I now knew where the fishbowls came from, but that was no longer important. What was important was the joy, the polish, and the competence that Harry Blackstone brought to his highly entertaining presentation of those mysteries. It was art. It was beautiful. And I wanted all the way in.

Nothing would stand in the way of my meeting the man himself. I went around backstage, and to my delight, there he was standing outside, his collar open and his tie dangling from his neck, taking a bit of air. I boldly approached and held out an index card I'd brought along, asking for his autograph. He looked at both sides of the card, then handed it back to me. "I have something even better!" he exclaimed, putting his hand around my shoulder. "Come with me!" And he led me into the holy of holies, backstage, past the equipment of his art, the gold-and-yellow boxes, packing cases with his name boldly stenciled on the sides, the folded embroidered foulards, even the wonderful fishbowls—all the apparatus that in his hands became enchanted.

It was still the day of grease-stick makeup, and dry Pan-Cake was unknown. The wonderful, distinctly "show biz" aroma of Leitner's product filled the tiny dressing room to which I was taken. From a trunk, Mr. Blackstone unrolled a real, honest-to-goodness full-color poster that showed him levitating a camel, along with a bevy of harem beauties. Briefly, I wondered why I'd not seen these items in the show—neither camel nor bevy—but I resolved to be forgiving of such a discrepancy. With a broad carpenter's pencil, Harry Blackstone scrawled his name on that poster, dedicated to me. My cup ran over.

We entered into a conversation, during which I made my career intentions quite plain to Mr. Blackstone, at great length. He suffered it all with commendable patience, shared a soft drink with me, and judiciously steered me to an exit so that the stage could be reset for the evening performance. Clutching my prize poster, I made for the tram to return home.

Disaster. On the tram, I put aside the autographed poster to make some notes about what I'd witnessed. I left the tram at my stop, and as it pulled away I realized that I'd left the poster on the seat. I was all of thirteen, and not supposed to cry, but I did. My parents never knew about it, nor did anyone else. It was years later, when I'd gotten to know Harry Blackstone rather well, that I told anyone about that calamity of my early youth, and it was Harry himself that I told.

There is one event in the Blackstone story that has been rather mangled in the retelling over the years. Though it sounds like a publicity agent's creation, it is not; it really happened. I am obliged to George Johnstone, who was a Blackstone assistant at that time, for a detailed description of the matter.

In Decatur, Illinois, on Saturday, September 2, 1942, the show was in the final stages of being set up onstage at the Lincoln Theater for the eleven o'clock matinee while films were showing to a packed house, mostly children. An usher was backstage sneaking a smoke—which was very improper under any circumstances—and he made an offhand remark that there was a fire in the basement of the drugstore next door. There was some concern from the Blackstone crew, but they were not alarmed until a fire marshal suddenly burst through the door and announced that the theater would have to be immediately evacuated. Chemicals stored in the next-door basement had caught fire and deadly fumes were beginning to seep into the building.

Harry was desperate. He paced back and forth in the dressing-room corridor in his shirt sleeves, wondering about the best way to get the audience out quickly and without panic. He made a quick decision, slipping into his dress coat. The film was just ending, and with a great fanfare he strode out in front of the curtain, flanked by the entire stage crew. "Boys and girls," he announced, "today I'm going to do the most spectacular trick *ever* seen, and it is so big that you will have to step outside to see it!" He instructed the children to quickly line up, row by row, and leave by the side doors, rather than out front, since sight of the fire trucks might bring about panic. Some of the adults said they preferred to sit where they were, but Blackstone was insistent that they, too, had to step outside to see this miracle.

In about fifteen minutes, the theater was safely empty, and Harry Blackstone had shown that in yet another crisis of decision, he'd been cool, calm, and efficient. He'd been well aware of the serious nature of the situation, having been through a previous fire himself, and as he knew, similar theater fires had resulted in numerous deaths because of panic among the patrons. Blackstone retired to his dressing room, as Johnstone tells it, where "he put his head down and had a good cry." Then, fully recovered, he joined the crew as they hurried back inside to save the props, which they took out into the loading area in the alley. Photographs taken at that time show a lad about nine years old sitting atop a stack of props. His name was Harry Blackstone, Jr.

The crew was assisted by Ted Banks, formerly the stage manager for the show, who had now been put on light duty because of a heart condition. Still, Ted lifted and carried along with the rest of them. Few are more dedicated than show people.

By now, clouds of thick black chemical smoke were billowing into the theater and out into the street, so that the entire area had to be cleared of spectators. It was six o'clock before the fire was out and the huge fans in the theater could be turned on to clear the air. The crew reset the show, and they were ready to perform the next day.

But there was a disaster that was perhaps due to the fire. As the time for Sunday's first show drew near, Ted Banks had not shown up to take his place. Half an hour before curtain time, his hotel was telephoned with a request that he be called. He did not answer, and when his room was entered, he was found dead of a heart attack. The show went on, with tears streaming down the faces of the master magician and his crew while they tried to conceal their grief at the loss. As Johnstone reports, there were "sobs emitting from behind curtains and from supposedly empty boxes." The tradition of "the show must go on" is not a superficial one.

Harry Blackstone in Decatur, Illinois, on Saturday, September 2, 1942, outside the Lincoln Theater. Beside him stands his stage manager, Ted Banks. They are watching the progress of the fire after having cleverly emptied the theater of its audience of youngsters.

As the years passed by, and I visited again with Harry Blackstone every time he came to Canada, we got to a first-name basis. He eventually moved to New York City, essentially in retirement by that time, and I was able to visit him often when, in 1951, I moved there myself. We exchanged many ideas,

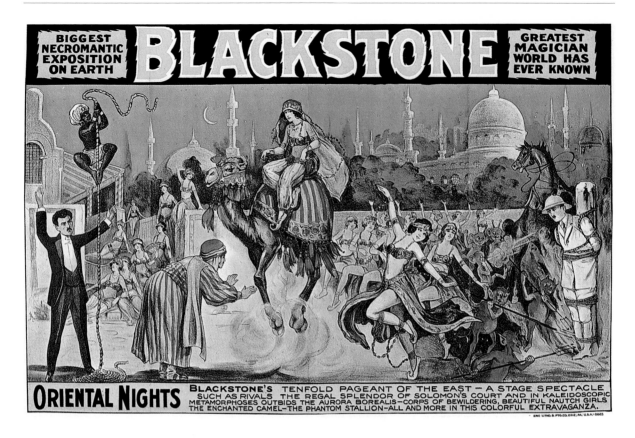

BIGGEST NECROMANTIC EXPOSITION ON EARTH

BLACKSTONE

GREATEST MAGICIAN WORLD HAS EVER KNOWN

ORIENTAL NIGHTS BLACKSTONE'S TENFOLD PAGEANT OF THE EAST — A STAGE SPECTACLE SUCH AS RIVALS THE REGAL SPLENDOR OF SOLOMON'S COURT AND IN KALEIDOSCOPIC METAMORPHOSES OUTBIDS THE AURORA BOREALIS—CORPS OF BEWILDERING, BEAUTIFUL NAUTCH GIRLS THE ENCHANTED CAMEL—THE PHANTOM STALLION—ALL AND MORE IN THIS COLORFUL EXTRAVAGANZA.

This lavish "Oriental Nights" poster represented the Blackstone show in rather fulsome fashion. If the camel, named Kaaba and nicknamed "The Spitter" by the crew, was replaced by a horse, no one seemed to mind very much.

I helped him with shows occasionally, and we shared our views of the world.

Then, one day in 1960, I received a call from a close friend of Harry telling me that I must encourage him to go to Los Angeles. The Ralph Edwards TV show, *This Is Your Life*, wanted to feature his life story, and since that show was always sprung as a surprise on the subject, they could not tell Harry why he'd been invited to go there. He didn't want to go. His asthma, which had been a constant burden to him all his life, did not encourage travel or stress. He was living in reasonable comfort in New York and his name alone brought him enough prestigious dates to enable him to coast along easily. A wealthy friend subsidized him, too, for in all the years that he had made top money as a performer, he'd not put anything away for his retirement.

When I spoke to him later that day at the Royalton Hotel, where he made his residence, I advised him that he could use a change, and after a few others of his friends, also in on the scheme, had similarly spoken to him, he finally packed up and went off to California "for a little while." The television show took place, and Blackstone decided to stay in Los Angeles. He moved into a small apartment not far from the famous Magic Castle, a private club for magicians in Hollywood. A room dedicated to Harry is one of the main attractions there.

About that time, I was doing an all-night radio talk show in New York for station WOR. One night in November 1965, I was broadcasting live when a chap from the newsroom laid a series of teletype dispatches on the desk before me. I glanced through them and came upon an item that began: "Harry Blackstone, famous stage and television illusionist, died today at his home . . ."

Harry had promised me and everyone else that he'd "*never* die!" and for me, he never did. Every time I have a success of any kind, I wish that he could know about it, and somehow, he's there. Harry Blackstone was, to me, the preeminent figure in the world of magic, the best damn magician who ever walked this earth, and a good, true friend and patron.

HARRY BLACKSTONE (fils)

I'm proud to know Harry Junior, who has splendidly kept the name and the glory of his illustrious father before the public. Blackstone *fils* quite wisely and properly dropped the "Jr." long ago, and is known to this generation in his own right. Of course those of us who have known both generations of the family cannot help comparing the two, and I will bravely attempt to do so now.

The present Blackstone is fortunate enough to have one of the most powerful stage presences in the business. His voice, unlike his father's, which had a sibilant defect, is deep, resonant, and enormously effective. Excellent stage deportment, modern and carefully selected dress, a judicious selection of performance material, and attention to detail have put today's Blackstone up front as a major star of magic. He retains the Floating Light Bulb, the Buzz Saw, the Dancing Handkerchief, and several more of his father's featured illusions which continue to delight audiences of all ages. Gay Blackstone, his lovely "chief assistant and mother of my children," as he likes to introduce her, labors on- and offstage to keep things running evenly.

Just recently I received a phone call from Harry at my home in Florida. He was to perform that evening at a local theater, and he invited me out to see the show. However, he warned me, it would be a somewhat truncated evening due to the fact that many of his costumes and properties had been held up in customs at the port of Manila, and he was having to fill the show with other items. That evening, I sat in fully satisfied amazement as Harry Blackstone and his cast thrilled a large audience who had no idea that they'd been shortchanged. His force of personality and his basic ability to entertain filled that theater, and the missing costumes, props, and tricks were not at all needed to provide all the excitement that his name promised that audience.

Offspring of famous and beloved people have a tough time living up to what the public expects of them. Each of the Bambergs labored under that bur-

Having come into his own as a master magician, Harry Blackstone II has dropped the "Jr." from his name. This generation of the Blackstone magi brings new glory to the art, and joy to today's audiences. Harry is all magic, all mystery, all entertainment. Can you imagine him in any other profession?

den, and survived handsomely. The present Blackstone has adopted the very best of modern technology and has used every bit of the hundreds of backstage hours he accumulated while traveling as a youngster in the business, to produce a very modern and effective spectacle that can hardly be equaled. Both Blackstones have been close friends of mine, a fact of which I am quite proud.

There may have been a time in history when the name Blackstone would bring to mind a famous jurist. I'm told there was such a person. Certainly, for the general public, that name now represents the magical family. It is hard to imagine any other possibility.

CHAPTER 20

SORCAR AND GOGIA PASHA OF INDIA

P. C. SORCAR

As was the case with so many of the great conjurors, the parents of Protul Chandra Sarcar (*sic*) did not want their son to take up magic as a profession, though it was already a family tradition. Born in 1912 in East Bengal, India, he did very well in his studies, and seemed likely to take up the engineering profession. But at age twenty-one, he opted to give up his formal education and enter conjuring.

This decision was all the more shocking to his parents because of the very low esteem in which magicians were held in India, a country then very conscious of caste and rank. There were no really "respectable" performers in the trade, which was almost always practiced in the streets, though with very great skill. Occasionally a "Jadu-wallah" would be invited inside a fine home to show his wares, but he entered and left by the side door, never to be treated as anything other than a minor servant. P. C. Sorcar (the slightly differently spelled name he now took) was to change all that.

The young Sorcar was ambitious and eventually attained a very high position in the magic community, to the point where he was invited to all parts of the globe to perform his colorful illusions. And along the way, he earned social acceptance in an India that was slowly abandoning its old ways. He called his show "Indrajal," which means "Magic." Live elephants, sumptuous costumes, a swarm of busy assistants and all sorts of exotic Oriental trappings made his show attractive to audiences who were eager to see this sorcerer from the mysterious land of India.

In 1956 he caused a sensation in England when he performed his Buzz Saw illusion on the BBC-TV show *Panorama*. Whether it was calculated or not, I cannot say, but just after the saw blade had zipped through the midriff of Dipty Dey, the lovely seventeen-year-old girl who was the subject of this startling illusion, the program ran out of time. Richard Dimbleby, the host, said good night to the viewers, and the switchboard immediately lit up like a Christmas tree. Anxious callers were assured that the girl had survived, and the newspapers had a grand time with the item.

The following year, pedestrians and motorists on New York's Broadway were startled to see a bicyclist making his way through traffic wearing a jeweled turban, silk robes, and slippers with turned-up toes. When they looked closer, they saw that he was blindfolded! The show business newspaper *Variety* noted the event: "Sorcar was 'legitimately' breaking the law. The magician was riding a bicycle blindfolded up Times Square." This was a publicity stunt to advertise Sorcar's upcoming appearance on an NBC-TV special program titled "Festival of Magic," hosted by Milbourne Christopher,* who performed his version of the Bullet Catch on that same show.

In Japan, the Tokyo Magic Circle elected Sorcar as their first non-Japanese honorary member. France, England, Belgium, and Germany followed with their own honors. But in 1955, he ran into trouble with opponents in Paris who, for some unknown reason, tried to close down his show, which nonetheless ran for eight consecutive weeks at the Théâtre de l'Étoile, then went on to Singapore and Australia.

At this time, Sorcar and the German magician Kalanag were engaged in a great blustery battle of words, each claiming the title "World's Greatest Magician." David Bamberg (Fu Manchu) commented on this foolishness in his book *The Illusion Show*:

> Their feud went on for years, until it became a "Custer's Last Stand" between two people—with a little Sicilian throat-slitting on the side. They never learned that there were many greats in magic but never a greatest. To use this title among fellow magicians is not only bombastic and in bad taste, but downright stupid.

My only personal encounter with Sorcar was in New York City during the 1962 World's Fair. I was working there on a magic show for the ubiquitous magician Mark Wilson when a bemused usher came backstage to inform me that I was being summoned to the front of the theater by "the world's greatest magician." I was astonished, believing that gentleman to already be backstage, but I made my way to the front to meet Sorcar and his son, Pradip. I was appropriately diffident and arranged for the two honored visitors to be accommodated in the very front row of the theater for the next

* Christopher had originally wanted Fu Manchu to star in the *Festival* show, but he was unavailable.

show, but rather regretted my courtesy when, from the stage, I heard Sorcar Senior proclaiming to the audience, quite plainly, that most of the illusions we presented onstage were his inventions. I did not trouble to see him out of the theater.

SORCAR JR.

On the death of Protul Chandra Sorcar in Japan in 1971, his very competent son, Pradip, took over the show. With even more exciting publicity stunts, Sorcar Jr. gained considerable attention from the press, though rising costs and shrinking facilities have now lessened the market for such a big show.

Pradip took advantage of tried-and-proven publicity stunts; on one occasion, he was sealed inside a locked canvas postal bag, placed in a locked, chained box, and dropped into the Bay of Bengal. Ninety seconds later, he popped to the surface and the box was recovered in the same condition as when it was submerged.

Pradip's spectacular show has played Japan (twenty-one times), the United States, the former Soviet bloc, the Near East, and Africa. He has developed and performed several new illusions and has written many books on magic.

Both Sorcars must be given full credit for having made the profession of conjuring acceptable to Indian society. They were instrumental in eliminating the prejudice that had followed magicians down through the ages in India, and they did it by persistence and example.

GOGIA PASHA

Gogia Pasha was an Indian from Dehra Dun, born Dhanraj Gogia. Originally trained as a physician, he assumed an "Egyptian" identity and with his large troupe, mostly family, he toured internationally.

I got to know him in Germany in 1950 while I was on tour there. A large demand for performers existed in postwar Germany, where Allied troops were stationed in great numbers. I took my small company—myself, Raymond and Pua,*—there and we traveled Germany, France, Denmark, and England.

Upon Pasha's arrival among the actors in Germany, he moved into a large apartment in Frankfurt, where the troop-entertainment business was centered. The rotund, full-bearded magician promptly announced to the entire show-biz community that he was throwing a feast of authentic Indian cooking for all who would contribute a certain number of Deutschmarks to

---

*Ray and Pua were Hawaiians who assisted me on this European tour. Pua now raises her family in New Jersey and Ray is a successful painter.

Indian magus Gogia Pasha made sure that there was no doubt about who was performing the Sword Suspension. He is about to remove two of those swords, leaving his assistant resting only upon the blade at her neck.

defray expenses. This was a great attraction to the artists, perhaps a bit wearied by then of schnitzel and kraut. On the appointed day, at the proper hour, we began arriving. Each visitor deposited the requested sum and was given a plate of victuals which, as I recall, was quite predominately curried rice of blistering flavor. Flushed revelers were soon putting aside their portions and leaving as gracefully as possible, which suited the logistics quite well in view of the great number of new arrivals who showed up as the afternoon wore on.

I was in residence just across the street, and with my two colleagues I retired to the lounge of the Nord Hotel and we began doing a bit of figuring. It soon became evident that Gogia had pulled off a pretty clever move. He'd given different times of arrival to different groups of guests, and with the steady flow of contributors he had enough sacks of rice and other basic Indian edibles to last that long winter.

Our theory was supported when the next morning an Australian showbiz couple with whom I'd worked in Singapore arrived at the hotel from the *Bahnhof* and found several actors sitting about in a heartburn daze nursing the German equivalent of Alka-Seltzer; the new arrivals cleverly guessed that Gogia Pasha was in town. It seems that he'd hit Sydney with the same scheme just two months earlier, and the show folks there were still breathing fire and popping digestive remedies.

There were much more compelling reasons to recall that this colorful turbaned gentleman had been through town. He left behind him an impressive reputation for the dazzling act he performed. Sari'd young ladies were levitated on the tips of huge scimitars and skewered by spears while jammed into wicker baskets. From Gogia's mouth issued any number of red billiard balls, followed by streams of ribbons and silk handkerchiefs. This was all punctuated by his visits to a tall brass vase that stood to one side of the stage all through his act, and that seemed never to be quite empty of water, though he tipped it up and drained it into a nearby tub every few minutes.

Swathed in bright silken robes festooned with gold chains and with his bristling black beard and turned-up mustache ever a-twitch, Gogia Pasha was every inch the colorful, romantic genie from the Arabian Nights tales. His broad smile and twinkling black eyes charmed and bamboozled his audiences in grand style, and I remember him well as a consummate performer. Nor shall I ever, ever, forget the curry. It is with me still.

Few of us can forget the image that the young Indian actor Sabu created in the motion picture *The Thief of Baghdad,* though a mixture of Indian, Arabian, and other Eastern themes was rather freely applied by the designers. The image that emerged satisfied for the cinema-going public their notion of where magic belonged. My own visits to Sri Lanka have exposed me to the provocative smells, sights, lighting, and general atmosphere that are part of that general culture, and I can certainly see in the temples, in the street magicians, and the other characters who flavor the place, how the very idea of magic is so readily evoked there in the Western mind.

CHAPTER 21

HOUDINI, THE ELUSIVE AMERICAN

So very much has been written about the life and exploits of Harry Houdini that to prepare a short summary is, for me, rather difficult. He is, in the public view, so close to being the representative magician that all others are compared to him. Ask anyone, on almost any continent, to name a magician, and Houdini's name will come up. George Bernard Shaw once commented that the three best-known names in history were "Jesus Christ," "Sherlock Holmes" and "Harry Houdini." We magicians all work in his shadow. Journalists refer to another performer "doing a Houdini" or they call a magician "a Houdini," while they would never think of saying that a pianist "did a Horowitz" or that a novelist is "a Hemingway."

Ehrich Weiss, the man who was to become Harry Houdini, was born March 24, 1874, in Budapest. He was one of ten children of a rather unsuccessful rabbi who moved his family off to the United States when Ehrich was just an infant. They took up residence in Appleton, Wisconsin, where Ehrich grew up. He was to later claim Appleton as his birthplace, as a convenience.

In his early childhood, he and his brother Theo went to a theater to see a spiritualist-type of act in which the performer was manacled and placed inside a cabinet, and manifestations took place that were ascribed to spirits. The Weiss brothers, even as young as they were, were not taken in by this flummery, and recognized that the performance was impossible unless the actor had freed himself in some way. At that moment, the idea of the "escape act" was born in the mind of Ehrich, and that fact was recorded in his very first diary.

Taken in London in 1901, this photograph shows Houdini fastened in handcuffs of both American and English origin, and one of his own padlock designs.

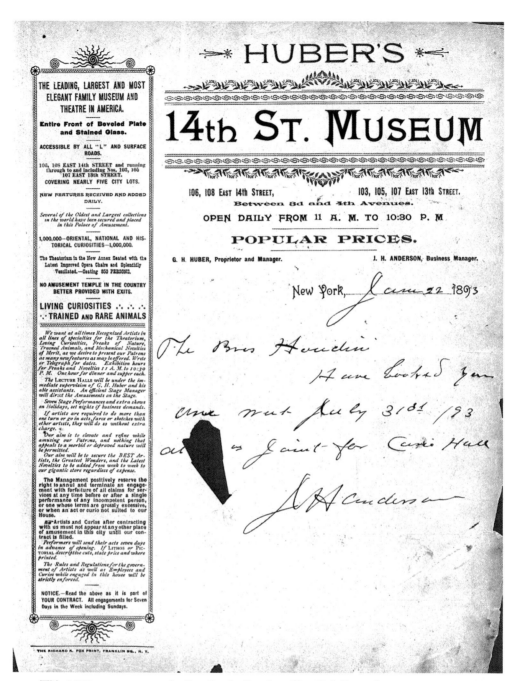

This 1893 contract was the first for the Brothers Houdini. It reads:

New York, June 22 1893

      The Bros Houdini

          Have booked you one week July 31st/93

          at _____ <u>00</u> Joint for Curio Hall

          J H Anderson

Houdini himself has cut out the dollar amount they were paid for the engagement. It was no doubt very little, and a cause of embarrassment for him. He was nineteen years old.

HUBER'S PALACE MUSEUM

106 EAST FOURTEENTH STREET, NEW YORK.

| A. MILLER, | WEEK COMMENCING JANUARY 21, 1895. | PUBLISHER |

EXECUTIVE STAFF.

GEORGE H. HUBER............Proprietor
J. H. ANDERSON................Manager
G. M. JANSER.............Superintendent
A. MARX ....Treasurer
F. E. FREEMAN..........Advertising Agent
GRANT LAFERTY.........,Stage Manager
PROF. HUDSON LANGDON......Lecturer
JOHN HILDEBRANDT.....Musical Director

PROGRAMME.

SUBJECT TO CHANGE WITHOUT NOTICE.

WEEK COMMENCING JAN. 21, 1895.

performance will begin with

THE TOOLEYS

Mr. and Mrs. in their Original Comedy Sketch.

Harry Moore,

America's Favorite Discriptive Singer.

BOBBY **THE DAILYS.** LOTTIE

New Original Changes
and Character Imitations.

The Favorite Little Serio Comic

Little Dot Davenport,

New Songs.

ALTERNATING TEAM,

Roberts and Row,

Musical Artists

k of the Favorite Vocal Comedian,

J. SHEEHAN,

performance will conclude with

Chinese Living Pictures.

CURIO HALL.

FIRST TIME IN THREE YEARS,

Count Ivan Orloff,

THE LIVING

TRANSPARENT

OSSIFIED MAN.

An Actual, Human Window Pane.

An Educated Hungarian Nobleman speaking five different languages. Bright, cheerful, Healthy, Hearty and Happy. Whose Limbs are Ossified as Hard as Stone and Transparent as Glass.

You Can See His Heart Beat!

You Can See His Blood Circulate!

His Nerves and Muscles plainly visible to the Eye. Medical Authorities Pronounce him

The Wonder of the Age

FOURTH FLOOR.

Our Menagerie

Monkeys, Birds and Animals from Every Clime Under the Sun. It will pay you to take a trip up stairs and see them. Remember it is free. No Extra Charge.

CURIO HALL.

By special request,

Prof. Stanton,

The world's greatest Hypnotic Expert, in his wonderful exhibition.

MLLE. EUGENIA GARRETTI

And her troupe of Educated Birds.

SIG. MUTTY,

Performing Monkeys.

The Houdinese

WONDER WORKERS.

UNO,

The Queen of all Snake Charmers.

Sixth successful week of

George Williams,

The Turtle Boy.

Carl Michaels.

In Feats of Strength.

Sig. Alburtis,

On the Tight Wire.

UNZIE,

The Australian Wonder.

The "Houdinese" (?) were back in Huber's Museum in New York City in 1895. Harry Houdini was not yet twenty-one years old and about to leave the Curio Hall circuit for England and the Big Time.

He left his Appleton home at age twelve to try his luck at carnival work, but soon returned, then joined his father in New York City to prepare for the arrival there of the rest of the Weisses. Those were mean, bitter times, during which Ehrich vowed to make things better for his family.

The young man was fond of exercise, running, lifting weights, and swimming, building his physique. He also developed gymnastic skills and learned to do some of the tricks of the circus and carnival artists. When he first began performing magic, he billed himself as a card manipulator, only dabbling as an escapist. At age seventeen, he took the name Houdini, borrowing from Eugène Robert-Houdin, about whom he'd read in books, and who had become his magician hero. His new first name, Harry, came from a contraction of Ehrich—"Ehry"—which was the pet name his mother always used for him. Starting with a friend as The Brothers Houdini, he began

Above left: Circa 1894, the newly married Houdinis were featuring their Metamorphosis illusion. Above right: Jonathan and Charlotte Pendragon have developed their own particular touch with spectacular effects for major stage shows all over the world. Their version of Houdini's Metamorphosis trick is the fastest in the business. The change is made in a fraction of a second.

playing local spots and was later joined by his real brother Theo when the friend opted for another choice of profession.

By 1893, the new Brothers Houdini team had developed their act to the point where they played the Chicago World's Fair. Soon they were back in New York again working at the famous Huber's Dime Museum on Fourteenth Street for near-starvation wages. The Museum featured the Lion-Faced Boy and a lady sword-swallower along with an astounding assemblage of freaks and oddities. The first contract of The Brothers Houdini with Huber's is a valuable part of this author's collection, and is reproduced here.

Numerous very minor engagements took them far and wide; then, when Harry married Beatrice Rahner, a member of a touring theatrical troupe, his bride replaced Theo in the act. Bess, as his wife was always known, worked all the shows with Harry as they did a mind-reading act and the usual magic tricks expected of conjurors of the day. When they were given the chance, they also performed, as their main number, the Metamorphosis. This was an amazing effect in which Harry was manacled, tied into a canvas bag, and placed into a locked trunk. Then the audience saw a three-second person switch when Bess pulled a curtain across the front of the trunk, and Harry suddenly emerged, free of all restraints. Bess was found inside the bag and the trunk. This spectacular number has since been performed by Joaquin Ayala, Siegfried & Roy, and many other magicians, but was brought to modern perfection by The Pendragons, a magical couple often seen by delighted audiences in Las Vegas.

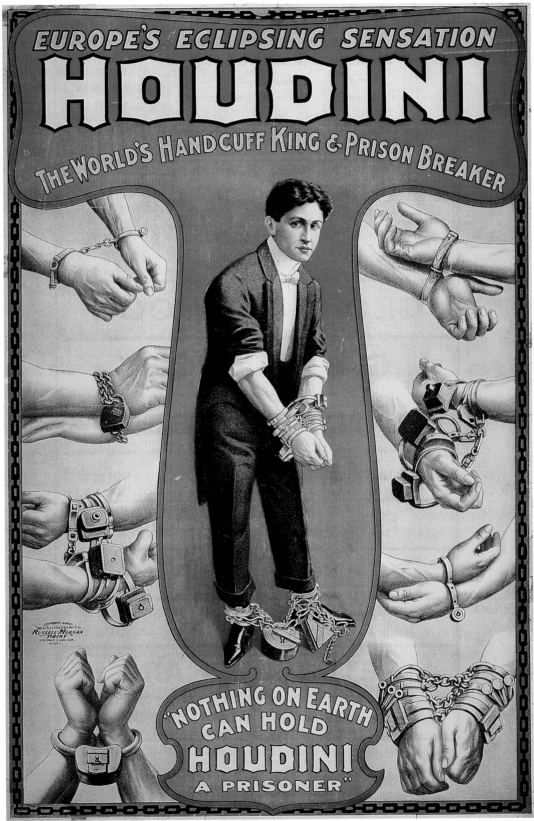

The Handcuff King believed in colorful, plentiful advertisements. This was one of many striking posters he used to throw out his challenge to the world.

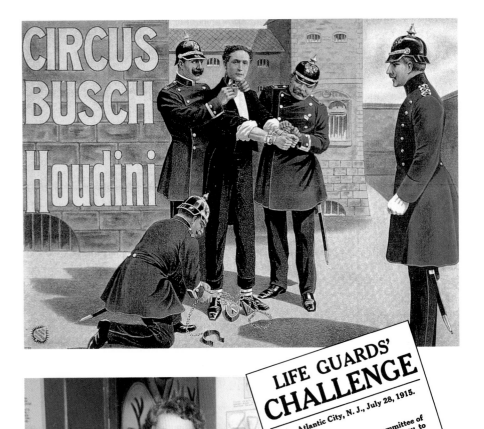

Left: Houdini, like all great artists of the day, was sought out by Germany's Circus Busch as a star attraction. He was an outstanding success in Germany and returned to the U.S.A. to great acclaim. Below left: Magician Char at the Butirskaya prison, where Harry Houdini performed his marvelous escape from irons and a prison van. Char holds the original irons in which the Elusive American was fastened. Below right: An example of the challenges that Houdini answered regularly.

LIFE GUARDS' CHALLENGE

Atlantic City, N. J., July 28, 1915.

HOUDINI

DEAR SIR:

We, the undersigned committee of Life Guards, hereby challenge you to release yourself from a Sea Bag restraint such as used on some of the Steamships and Sailing vessels to secure the murderous insane.

This restraint made from very heavy sail cloth encases the prisoner from neck down to and including the feet, arms crossed over the chest, and broad belting straps encircling the body all buckling behind the back.

The only condition in the test that we will put you to is, that you must make the attempt to escape in full view of the audience to prove you have no traps in the stage.

Awaiting your reply we beg to remain,

Faithfully yours,
WM. WEBBER,
WM. THOMAS,
M. NORWOOD JOHNSON
CORNELIUS DRISCOLL
Virginia Avenue Station,
Atlantic City Life Guards

HOUDINI ACCEPTS CHALLENGE

TEST TO TAKE PLACE ON THE STAGE OF

B. F. Keith's Theatre

ATLANTIC CITY

Friday Night, July 30, '15

Under the Condition that there must be No Danger of Strangulation from Straps Encircling his Neck.

work. The challenge was for the American to extricate himself from this device while onstage.

Concealed by a very small waist-high curtained cabinet onstage, Houdini began his task at 3:15 in the afternoon. After arduous struggling and several exits from the cabinet for breathers, the magician finally claimed victory at 4:25, to the enthusiastic cheers of his audience. During the process, he had literally cut his coat from his body with a knife held in his mouth, to relieve the heat he was enduring, and he was in a terrible state of exhaustion.

There are a number of details about the *Mirror* escape that give rise to certain speculations. Whatever happened to the blacksmith who had claimed the invention of the manacles? Surely he would have had something to say about the events of that evening, but we hear nothing from him. As for the cuffs themselves, there is no "invention" to be found, since their figure-eight configuration was already in use in the art at that time. The cuffs, which still exist in a private collection, are formidable indeed, but the locking mechanism is simply a set of concentric Brahma locks, quite standard for the day. Brahmas were very secure locks, but overly complicated and subject to failure. In addition, the key required for the *Mirror* cuffs is quite large and intricate. It is about six inches in length, and requires many turns to unfasten the lock.

Certainly, some uninformed accounts of how a key might have been smuggled to Houdini onstage are ridiculous. Author Will Goldston, who fancied himself a pioneering chronicler of Houdini and others, incorrectly said that a key was smuggled to the escapist in a glass of water brought to him by Bess. Another version says a key was transferred by a passionate kiss between Harry and Bess. The fact is that a duplicate key would have been impossible to make by any impression techniques or by any other means than the use of a machine shop, and that kiss would have had to be quite an involved, almost superhuman feat, considering the size of the key.

I strongly suspect that the following is what took place: Well in advance of the performance, Harry Houdini, with the cooperation of the *Daily Illustrated Mirror,* agreed that a special set of handcuffs would be made, and that the *Mirror* reporter would challenge him with the cuffs on behalf of the newspaper. There is no reason to suspect a faked challenge. Assuming that he would be able to manage the manacles in his usual fashion, Houdini instead found that he would not be permitted to examine the cuffs in advance of the performance, and was in big trouble when confronted with the mechanism onstage. He *had* to be successful, and perhaps Bess reasoned with the reporter that if her husband was defeated the Mirror had sponsored an event that was distasteful to all concerned, and a victory by Houdini was essentially a "win" for everyone. In any case, I can *assure* you that the *Mirror* handcuffs were not opened with anything but the key. Your own imagination might produce the most likely scenario.

Though Houdini and another prominent magician of the day, The Great Raymond, were said to have had a longstanding enmity that was evidenced on one occasion by an actual fistfight between the two, Raymond was chairman of a gala dinner held by the Magicians Club of London at the posh Savoy Hotel in 1920 to honor the American escape artist. It was attended by all the leading figures of magic who were then in the city. Feuds between magicians were not at all uncommon, with claims of infractions of copyright, theft of routines and themes, duplication of equipment, and other no-nos that theatrical folks respect. In a high-pressure business like this, it's to be expected.

Houdini's really serious feuds were with the spiritualists and other psychic phonies of his day. Late in his life, after his beloved mother had died, he took on with great zeal the task of showing how the spiritualist fakers of his day were victimizing the bereaved. Though he naïvely believed that merely by duplicating the spiritualists' physical tricks and/or preventing them from doing the tricks, he could prove his case, even the U.S. Congress denied him the satisfaction of getting legislation passed to protect the public against what he saw as a hazard to them. Then, as today, there are politicians who are either falsely convinced of their powers of discernment, or are too interested in being reelected, to do much about the fakers.

One particularly important foe of Houdini's was Margery Crandon, the wife of a wealthy dentist in Boston. She had a reputation for bringing about the usual floating trumpets, thumping tables, and other manifestations of the séance room. A very attractive blonde, Margery had charmed all the scientists who came to test her powers but who had no idea at all of how to go about it properly. The worst evidence against her came about when she produced wax molds of "spirit hands," which she said were formed when a ghost had plunged his ectoplasmic hand into a pail of melted paraffin, removed it, and then dematerialized from within the layer of congealed wax. This left a sort of waxen glove behind. Houdini was easily able to show that these "gloves" could be made by perfectly ordinary means. Margery's career took a sudden reverse when she produced a series of prints in dental wax that she said came from the phantom thumbs of her dead brother, Walter. The prints were discovered to belong to her very-much-living dentist, who had apparently cooperated in perpetrating this part of her hoax. In spite of this very powerful proof of her chicanery, Margery's fans, of course, persisted in their belief, though more responsible investigators now dismissed her claims.

Margery outlived Houdini by many years but died a crazed alcoholic who was still trying to put her shattered career back together after her meteoric success had been so effectively slowed by Houdini. In my opinion, Margery rather won the encounter with Houdini, a confrontation which was not well designed or carried out and which only cast heavy doubt on her claims.

In his efforts to stay on top professionally, The Elusive American staged such powerful publicity stunts as vanishing an elephant at New York's Hippodrome. His excursions into magic, however, were never as effective as his escape stunts. Compared with almost any of the leading magicians, Houdini was not a great conjuror. That is the considered opinion of professionals who witnessed his performances. David Bamberg (Fu Manchu) recorded in his memoirs that as a boy, he had been shown brilliant card work by Harry Houdini, who was a frequent guest at his family home, but he also said that when Houdini tried an all-magic presentation at New York's Globe Theater it was "lousy."

Yet audiences were thrilled by the man himself, because he was a great *showman* and he was a calculatedly endearing person. That was his secret. I recall that Fred Keating, a leading theater and cabaret conjuror who had witnessed Houdini's act many times, told me:

> The band played, of all things, the "Pomp and Circumstance" march when Houdini walked onto the stage. It was corny, but the audience ate it up. He was short and stocky, a little bow-legged, dressed in rather baggy clothes, but smiling as if his face would break. He walked onto the stage rolling up his sleeves, and you could almost hear him saying, "I can beat up any man in the house." It was a triumph of audacity over skill, because during the magic part of his act he fumbled with the Flight of Time* trick, and the timing was never right. He did some ordinary card flourishes, and if he dropped a card he looked at it on the floor as if it was the card's fault, not his. But when he got down to the escape act, whether it was being tied up in a chair with yards of rope, or wriggling out of his straitjacket, he was a master, bouncing around and sweating like a wrestler. The audience didn't much care about the inept magic. They wanted to see the little guy beat the big guys.

That last sentence is a good observation, and I think it was the big secret of the exceptional success of Houdini's escape act. Here was a little man beset by two or more burly men from the audience who had set about to bind him or otherwise restrain him, and he always managed to win. There had to be strong identification by the audience with the escape artist, and even those who challenged him found themselves rooting for him to beat the odds once more.

He was the supreme egotist. Walter Gibson, who ghost-wrote Houdini's books for him and traveled with the show for some time, would tell how,

---

*A trick in which ringing alarm clocks were taken and thrown into the air one at a time, where they vanished and then reappeared one by one across the stage.

Proving that the Houdinis were not adverse to a little hanky-panky early in their careers, this 1896 theater program from Grand Rapids, Michigan, is shown exactly as it appeared in the scrapbook kept by Houdini, the "X's" in pencil having been made by him. Bessie Houdini played the part of Mamie Riley in the minstrel show and had a solo spot as a featured singer as well. Opening the second half, Harry and Bessie did some "Psycrometic Letter Reading and Fooling with the Spirits." It will be seen just how much of the bill was occupied with projector novelties at that period in the history of entertainment.

long after she had retired from active participation in the stage show, Bess Houdini would pace about backstage, calling attention to her husband's over frequent use of "I" and "me" as he addressed the audience. It appears that Bess never quite got over her husband's success, which no longer required her presence onstage.

His egocentric bias is understandable enough. The amount of newspaper publicity he obtained, the attention lavished on him by both the public and the profession, the enormous draw he was everywhere he appeared had to force him into a higher hat size. Some have described him as unbearable, always expecting to be the subject of the conversation, never failing to be the foremost figure of any group photograph, and thrusting himself into every situation in order to take center stage. But that was one of the major reasons

for his extraordinary success; he was in the business of selling the product known as Harry Houdini.

In the Houdini Hall of Fame Museum in Niagara Falls, Canada, there is one item that indicates to me, better than any other artifact, the nature of Houdini's attitude toward himself. It is a Keith Orpheum Theater program that used his favorite photo, a confident pose with his arms folded. The printer set in type the words "HARRY HOUDINI" beneath the photo. With a broad, angry stroke of the pen, the magician has crossed out that line, and inscribed beside it: "*Houdini.* That's enough!" It was, as he wrote, quite enough.

The two most sensational escapes that Houdini originated were the Milk Can and the Chinese Water Torture Cell. The former consisted of a steel can shaped like a farmer's milk can, but big enough so that Houdini could fit inside in a semi-doubled position. The can was tapered toward the bottom, so that it would not be said that the upper part was merely a sleeve arrangement that lifted off. Also, of course, the can held Houdini just as comfortably with the taper, and a good percentage of the total volume and thus the weight of the filled can was thereby eliminated. In performance, the device was filled with water, Houdini entered (dressed in a bathing suit), and the

Above left: The Houdinis, Harry and Bess. Above right: Unlike the time Houdini reassembled the Tony Pastor program to put himself at the coveted closing-first-act position, when he played the Keith-Orpheum circuit in the 1920s that position was his by contract. He featured his very strongest number, the Chinese Water Torture Cell, which had nothing at all to do with torture and wasn't in any way Chinese.

lid was slammed on and locked in place with padlocks. A covering tentlike affair dropped over all of this, and moments later the magician strode forth, the covering was pulled away, and the sealed, locked can was seen behind him. It was still full of water.

The Torture Cell was somewhat different, and was not introduced by Houdini until 1912, when he was thirty-eight years old and a recognized superstar. The Cell was a huge rectangular box almost the size of a short-ened telephone booth, made of heavy sections of mahogany with a transparent plate-glass front. There was a lid that hinged apart like stocks, with two cutouts for Houdini's ankles. A steel cage was located inside the Cell. The performer was secured into the lid by the ankles, and the lid was fastened with a padlock. He was then hoisted upside-down above the water-filled Cell and was lowered into the water. The lid was secured to the Cell by built-in locks on each side. The theater orchestra then launched into a sonorous rendition of "Asleep in the Deep," a favorite repertoire piece of bassos, and the audience leaned forward in their seats, eyes fixed upon the concealing curtain. Around the Cell stood stagehands armed with axes, instructed to smash the glass front if something went wrong.

Minutes after the canopy had been lowered over it all, Houdini made his appearance, dripping wet, before the cheering audience. This number was first seen at Circus Busch in Germany, and was a sensation from its first appearance. The apparatus was constructed in England, probably by James Collins, one of Houdini's trusted assistants. The Cell remained as the major attraction of Houdini's act for the rest of his days.*

Late in his career, Harry Houdini decided to enter the motion-picture business. Films were squeezing live entertainment out of the theaters, and he evidently hoped to segue his vaudeville fame into movie stardom. That hope was not realized. His ego dictated that he write, direct, produce, and star in his own films, and he was not proficient at all those crafts. Embarrassing films like *The Grim Game, The Man from Beyond, The Master Mystery,* and a turgid serial, *Terror Island,* remain as warnings to all who would adopt expertise beyond their reach.

Abandoning the movies at age fifty-two, Houdini planned new wonders for his stage show, one of which was a Buried Alive stunt in which he would

---

*Both devices, the Milk Can and the Torture Cell, are preserved at the Houdini Hall of Fame Museum in Niagara Falls, Canada. (The Water Torture Cell is the property of Mr. Sid Radner, and on loan to the museum.) More than one of each was manufactured; those at the museum are the actual working devices last used by Houdini. How those major props came to be exhibited is a story in itself. The Houdini will was quite specific about what was to be done with his props after his death. In a postmortem display of ego, he had left instructions for his executors to burn all his theater props. That was not done, since brother Theo preserved and used the milk can, the handcuffs, and the other specialized equipment for several years after Harry died, though not with the same skill and never with the same impact. Theo was doomed to continue as "the brother of Houdini" and as a second-rate performer always in the shadow of the great performer, a shadow in which he'd been born. He used the stage name "Hardeen."

CIRCUS
CORTY-ALTHOFF
BREMEN, Grünen Kamp.

Täglich abends 8¼ Uhr: **Gr. brillante Vorstellung**
In jeder Vorstellung:

HOUDINI

5000 Mark

zahlt Houdini demjenigen der ihm nachweisen kann, daß er bei seiner Entfesselung in der Folter-Wasser-Zelle Luft bekommt.

5000 Mark

zahlt Houdini demjenigen der ihm nachweisen kann, daß er bei seiner Entfesselung in der Folter-Wasser-Zelle Luft bekommt.

5000 Mark

zahlt Houdini demjenigen, der ihm nachweisen kann, daß er bei seiner Entfesselung
in der Folter-Wasser-Zelle Luft bekommt.

Above: The most sensational trick ever presented by Houdini was the Chinese Water Torture Cell, a death-defying effect that he performed right up to his death in 1926 at the age of fifty-two. Right: Harry Houdini denied he'd ever heard of Major Zamora, the Triple-Jointed Dwarf who would escape from chains and ropes and also manage to enter and leave a gigantic ale bottle. But in this 1874 poster, here he is sandwiched between the Ossified Girl and Major Zamora himself. Harry fibbed.

GLOBE MUSEUM
298—BOWERY—298
BET. HOUSTON & BLEECKER STREETS
MEEHAN & WILSON, - - Proprietors and Managers
PROF. GEORGE GRAHAM. - - - - Lecturer

10c The Old and Popular Family Resort AT POPULAR PRICES. **10c**

WEEK COMMENCING
MONDAY, APR. 16, '94
CURIO HALL No. 1.
Infinitely Interesting, Intelligently Instructive.

Engagement for a short time only of the
WONDERFUL

OSSIFIED GIRL
MISS EMMA SHALER
A beautiful young lady, 26 years old, weighing 49 3-4 lbs., gradually, but surely turning into one solid mass of bone.
☞ **DO NOT MISS SEEING HER!!** ☜

FIRST APPEARANCE OF THE
PEERLESS PRINCE OF PRESTIDIGITATEURES
PROF. HOUDINI
Introducing a Series of Incomprehensible Experiments in Sleight of Hand, Modern Necromancy and High Class Magic.

LAST WEEK OF THE
GREAT SUCCESS
MAJOR ZAMORA

The Celebrated
TRIPLE-JOINTED DWARF
With His Wonderful
BOTTLE OF BASS' PALE ALE

Return of the Young and Beautiful
VERMONT GIANTESS
BIG ALICE
5 feet 11 1-2 inches in Height and Weighs 601 lbs. She is the Handsomest Fat Woman in the World.

THE MEDICO-ELECTRIC BATTERY Free to all Visitors
CURIO HALL No. 2 Prof. Blocks' Cosmoramic Views, Mme. Zilla, the Queen of Palmistry. Original London PUNCH AND JUDY, to Please the Young Folks.

AND ✳ COUNTLESS ✳ OTHER ✳ NOVELTIES
FIRST-CLASS DRAMATIC AND SPECIALTY ENTERTAINMENT EVERY HOUR.
ALL PERSONS occupying seats at the last DRAMATIC PERFORMANCE AT NIGHT can remain for the Olly and Afterpiece, which commences immediately after the Drama is over WITHOUT EXTRA CHARGE

e Theatre is presented almost a continuous Stage Performance consisting of Drama and Specialties from 1 to 10 P. M.

ADMISSION 10 Cts.

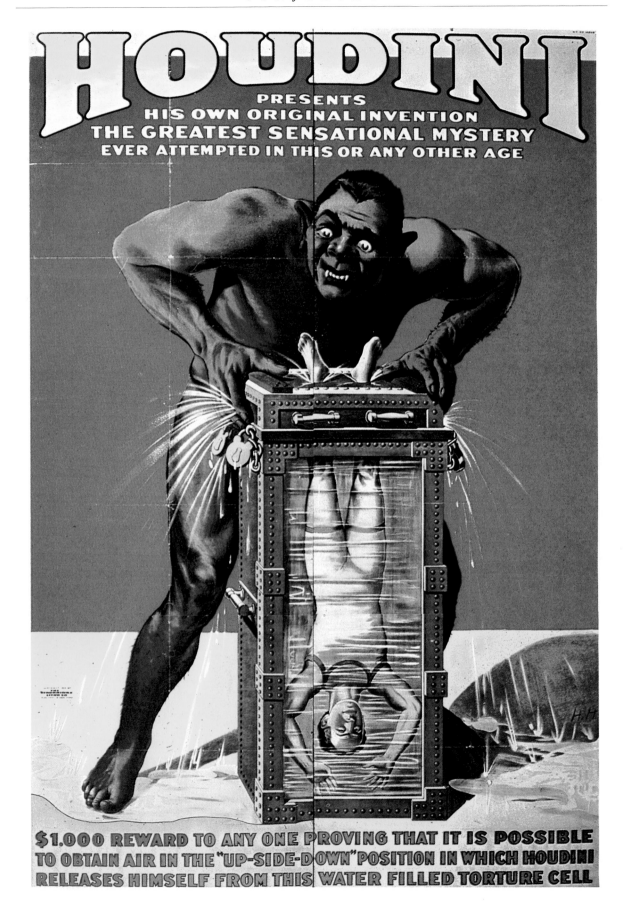

BURIED ALIVE!
EGYPTIAN FAKIRS OUTDONE

Master Mystifier
HOUDINI
THE GREATEST NECROMANCER OF THE AGE—PERHAPS OF ALL TIMES
The Literary Digest

Left: This is the poster prepared by Harry Houdini to advertise his Buried Alive stunt, planned for the 1927 season. His untimely death in October 1926 meant that he never performed the trick. Facing page: The Chinese Water Torture Cell was a featured act with Harry Houdini for many years. Contrary to what Hollywood would have you believe, he did not die as a result of it.

be locked into a bronze coffin and entombed in a ton of earth in a large tank onstage. A minor sensation had been created by an "Eastern yogi" named Rahman Bey, who could not speak any Eastern languages and was suspected of being from Flatbush rather than the other side of the world. Bey demonstrated that he could be buried alive for short periods of time—up to ten minutes—and Houdini topped that feat by being sealed into a metal coffin and surviving for an hour and thirty-three minutes underwater in the pool of the Shelton Hotel in New York City in 1926. Now, stunned by the tremendous interest this stunt aroused in the public, he prepared to bring a version of that feat to the stage.

The posters and advertising copy for the Buried Alive stunt were already

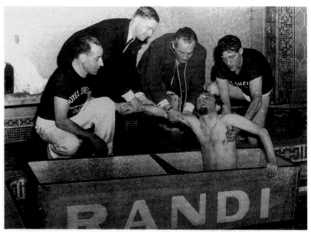

Above left: Harry Houdini prepares to be sealed into a galvanized-iron "coffin" at the Shelton Hotel in New York City, in 1926, not long before his death. He established a survival record of 1 hour, 31 minutes. Above right: The Amazing Randi in 1955 as he broke Houdini's record for survival in a sealed coffin. At the Shelton Hotel pool in New York, where Houdini had established his record of 1 hour, 33 minutes, Randi added 11 minutes to the record.

prepared early in 1926, when Houdini was playing the Princess Theatre in Montreal, Canada. Following the matinee show, two students from McGill University visited him in his tiny dressing room and interviewed him for the school paper. Asked if he could, as he had claimed, withstand a blow to his stomach, Houdini answered that he could, and was preparing to stand up to demonstrate when one of the students, an amateur boxer, struck him in the solar plexus. Unprepared, the magician fell back, badly hurt. His ego made him stand up and take another blow to prove his point, but he had been more gravely injured than he could have known. He barely made it through the closing show and took a train for Detroit, where upon arrival he was immediately taken to Grace Hospital with a high fever. It was found that his appendix had been ruptured and peritonitis had set in.

Despite what doctors could do for him, such a massive infection in those days was almost certain to be fatal. Ten days later, on Halloween, Harry Houdini turned to his wife, Bess, and told her, "I think this thing is going to get me." He died in her arms.

The body of Houdini was shipped to New York in the coffin he'd intended to use for the Buried Alive stunt. He was buried at Brooklyn's Macpelah Cemetery beside his mother and other family members. Though the gravestone says "Here lie the remains of Harry Houdini and his beloved wife Bess," in actuality Bess was later buried elsewhere, refused admission to the plot because of her religion. Macpelah Cemetery is restricted to the Jewish faith. Bess was Catholic.

Though the Houdini Hall of Fame Museum holds a great number of the playbills, photos, films, equipment, and memorabilia of Harry Houdini, still available to be seen and wondered over by the public, something is missing; there are elements of the man that cannot be displayed in a museum, pre-

Harry Houdini in one of his favorite photographs, at the height of his fame. He holds a copy of his book The Unmasking of Robert-Houdin.

served under glass, or examined in an album. The personality, the demeanor, the smile, and the other intangibles vanished along with the man himself. We can only wonder at those wonders.

CHAPTER 22

THE RICHIARDIS

Four generations of magicians stage-named Richiardi have now thrilled international audiences. Peru gave us all four, beginning with Izquierdo, who was born in 1885 and never left South America. We know little of his act. Ricardo, the next in line, was known as The Great Richiardi. He worked in Africa, Asia, and Europe as well as in South America, finally coming to the United States in 1936. He featured especially gory magic, chopping off heads and buzz-sawing through folks in a very grisly fashion. Spectators were invited to troop across the stage and see the severed body and the gaping wound before the assistant was restored once more. Women fainted and strong men faltered.

Ricardo Richiardi was killed in an auto accident in the state of Georgia while on tour with a tent show. His son Aldo was only fourteen years old, and before taking up the profession of his father and grandfather as the third of the line, he attended military school for two years, then studied singing and dancing for another four years, and he was ready. He adopted the stage name "Richiardi Jr." and began his career in magic.

He was one of the most colorful, energetic, and dynamic artists ever seen in the profession. Moving like a matador, demanding split-second timing from his assistants, Richiardi Jr. overpowered any stage just by stepping onto it. Fast, vigorous music accompanied a whirlwind of action. He put new life into old routines and in 1949 in New York he was bringing in a gross of some $40,000 a week, putting him among the top three moneymakers on Broadway that season.

Aldo had a particularly effective presentation of a standard illusion first presented by Robert-Houdin: the Etherial Suspension. One variety of that trick involves standing the subject between two brooms. One broom is

176

removed, and the subject is lifted to a horizontal position with the single broom standing upright beneath an arm. Richiardi Jr. moved through that sequence like a flamenco dancer, bringing excitement and color to what could have been just a clever puzzle.

A characteristic of his performance was that he *never* handed over a prop to an assistant or merely placed it aside; he *threw* it somewhere. That "somewhere" was usually where an assistant was standing waiting for it, but many a time that assistant had to make an unchoreographed jeté to catch it. On one occasion Aldo was tossing swords to his son, Ricardo, when one blade went into a spot where it was invisible against the lights for just a second to the catcher. It came down, point first, and literally pinned Ricardo to the stage through the leg. He limped about the stage for the rest of the week, but the show did go on.

It was Richiardi Jr.'s strong presentation that first inspired Doug Henning to become a conjuror and set the pace for David Copperfield's very effective dramatic style.

Much of Richiardi's success was due to the same kind of theatrical blood-letting that had served his father so well. Using an overhead buzz saw and with a strong odor of ether filling the theater, Richiardi sliced a girl into two and then also invited his audience to line up and file by the mutilated corpse of his pretty assistant. Only when all had been thus satiated and had returned to their seats would he bring her back to life to take bows.

He wowed 'em in the Orient as well as in Britain and Europe, with such other miracles as vanishing a girl from a chair* and having her reappear in a box that had been empty only a moment before. When he returned to the United States in 1971, I was privileged to share the bill with him at Madison Square Garden's Felt Forum for several weeks, doing my escape act. I began to understand what drove him. He suffered from diabetes, which, with his strenuous life-style, produced "highs" and "lows" with frightening irregularity. He swung from exuberance to depression, and it was all we could do to understand his moods. He was screaming threats at one moment and embracing the offended party the next. Through it all shone his great artistry.

In 1985, a complication of his ailment caused serious infections of the extremities to set in, and after necessary major amputations were performed, he seemed to give up. He died soon after.

Another member of the cast at that Felt Forum show was a German act named Omar Pasha. This was a Black Art number, very well done, and shortly after the actor closed in New York, he returned to his home in Wiesbaden, where he died. Aldo's son Ricardo, who worked with Omar Pasha on the Felt Forum show, has developed a similar act to great acclaim. He is the fourth generation of a very justly proud family.

* This was the chair trick originated by Bautier de Kolta.

CHAPTER 23

THE MANDRAKES

There are two quite different Mandrakes to be dealt with here. One is the comic strip hero "Mandrake the Magician." The strip was both written and drawn by Lee Falk, who also created one of the most enduring comic characters, the Phantom. Later, Mandrake was drawn by Phil Davis. The two-dimensional magus was seen in newspapers all over the world starting in 1934, after which the character entered the comic-book field and even the movies. Always impeccably dressed in silk top hat and tails, the comic character Mandrake "gestured hypnotically" and made all manner of miracles seem to occur for his befuddled spectators, usually as a means of defeating dastardly criminals.

In 1911, the live Leon Mandrake (his real name is not revealed) was born in British Columbia; at the early age of eleven he first walked onto the stage of the Edison Theater in New Westminster as a magician after learning the rudiments of the art from library books. Soon after, he was performing a sword-box trick at the Pacific National Exhibition, using more easily-available broomsticks in place of the swords. Unable to find a girl willing to trust her life to such a young performer, he talked the boy next door into wearing a rag-mop wig and announced that this was "Princess Thora." The local kids were not deceived, and revealed the secret. "That ain't Princess Thora," they shouted, "that's only Jackie Giles!" We have no record of whether Mr. Giles ever overcame this childhood trauma.

By age sixteen, Leon and his stepbrother Carl Jackson had joined a show that toured western Canada and the United States. When the show broke up 1500 miles away in Winnipeg, the two kids worked their way back home. Two years later, Leon was performing in the United States as both a

MANDRAKE
by **LEE FALK**
and
PHIL DAVIS

magician and a ventriloquist, using the name "Mandrake" for the former and "Leon" for the latter. By 1935 he had a two-hour stage show using seventeen assistants and two buses full of people and equipment.

It appears that cartoonist Lee Falk had come up with the name Mandrake independently, basing it upon the claimed miraculous powers of the poisonous plant of the same name. Phil Davis, the eventual artist of the cartoon strip, even changed the look of his character somewhat to match Leon's appearance after the two met. It was an excellent symbiosis, each entity enhancing the other.

Mandrake and his first wife and assistant (professionally named Narda, after the comic strip character) parted in 1946. He met Velvet, a former assistant to magician Harry Blackstone, and she became his second wife and the mother of Lon Mandrake, who is a science teacher also working today as a mentalist in British Columbia.

With the decline of interest in the full stage show, Leon Mandrake scaled down his illusions to fit a cabaret format. By 1956, he had settled in Portland, Oregon, with a television show called *Alexander the Great*, in which he performed mentalism. Claude Alexander, "The Man Who Knows" (1880–1954) had a great influence on Leon, who purchased the props and costumes of Alexander, as well as the rights to the name.

An extensive tour of the Pacific Islands followed, then a return to Canada and a tour of the Orient. In the 1970s, the college tours were big business, and Mandrake and Velvet got on the circuit, which they worked until 1980. Leon Mandrake retired in 1984.

*Anyone got a hairpin?
Strictly a posed picture.
Well, everyone has to do
something in their spare
time.*

because perhaps I had already released the trigger, in which case I was effectively dead. But the re-locking bar had not slammed into place, and I'd not heard the handle turn, which would have been the result of a correct combination having been dialed. I realized that the manager was in a panic, unable to coordinate and useless to us at that moment.

Fortunately Moses knew what to do, for I was slowly passing out and was not offering any useful suggestions. He asked who it was who opened that safe every morning, and a young woman stepped forward to perform that task in those desperate seconds that remained of my consciousness. A few scrapes and clicks, and the handle was turned. The door cracked open. As I fell forward out of my confinement, Moses caught me and I heard a loud *clunk* as a steel bar rotated out of the side of the safe door and engaged only thin air rather than the door edge. A clattering sound announced that the lock-box panel, held in place by my forehead until the door opened, had fallen free to hit the floor.

Well, I looked pretty silly in the newspaper the next morning. The headline said something like "ESCAPE ARTIST DOESN'T." In the fervor of youth, I *insisted* on proving my skill, and a rather meager article the following day said that with a reporter present I'd escaped from another safe, one not equipped with a relocking device. Be assured that when I tried that stunt again, I carefully checked out the safe before I entered it. . . .

DEAN GUNNARSON

A Canadian escape artist born in Winnipeg and raised in San Antonio, Texas, Dean came upon a book about Houdini when he was just nine years old. He was soon asking his school chums to tie him up with jump ropes and developing ways to free himself. Two years later, he returned to Canada, and with his brother Todd, Dean was in business as an entertainer at birthday parties.

He graduated from jump ropes to straitjackets, appearing before any

The Brothers Zachs consisted of George Zachs, the escape artist, assisted by his brother. They borrowed heavily on the success of Harry Houdini's act.

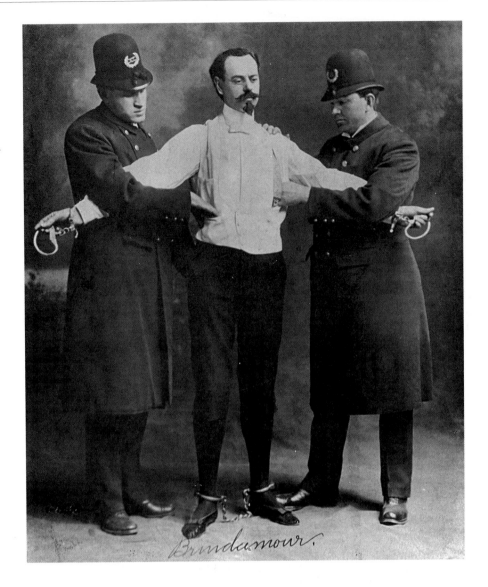

Brindamour (George Brown) was active as an escape artist at the turn of the century. Here he is being searched by two policemen while being manacled.

audience that would sit still long enough for him to effect his escape. Jumping back and forth between Canada and the United States, the two brothers soon became known for their dramatic and heart-thumping routines. Dean duplicated two of Houdini's most famous escapes for a 1987 TV special called *The Search for Houdini;* then, in California, he was manacled by the Anaheim Police Department and locked into a shark cage at the "20,000 Leagues Under the Sea" display at Disneyland and filmed live underwater for a nationwide TV audience that watched him make the daring escape. In Puerto Rico he was chained and nailed into a packing case and tossed into the nearby ocean, and back home in Canada he got himself sealed into a wine barrel and dunked in the Niagara River as well.

In 1991, Dean Gunnarson was chosen to mark the 500th episode of a famous Japanese TV show, "Naruhodo! The World" ("Seeing the World"). For this show, he jumped from an airplane at 13,000 feet above a skydiving field in New York State while wrapped in a straitjacket that covered his parachute. To add the Gunnarson touch, he asked that his hands be fastened with two pairs of handcuffs as well. That fall should have taken him forty-six seconds, without a parachute, before he crashed to the ground. Forty seconds after he left the aircraft, Dean was pulling the ripcord and all of Japan let out a great breath.

Dean is dedicated to good causes, and devotes much of his time to raising money for the Rainbow Society, the Cancer Foundation, and the Variety Club. He is also interested in young performers and spends time helping them get started in magic. Like his idol Houdini, he is a teetotaler and a very happily married man. Also like Houdini, he has his brother by his side at all times as a trusted and able assistant.

At twenty-seven years of age, this brilliant artist is just getting started. So, keep looking up when you hear that Dean Gunnarson's in town anywhere in the world. You can expect to see him hanging up somewhere—or streaking to earth—struggling to free himself from yet another challenge.

BERNARDI

As a child, Bernhard Eskilsen entertained his friends in Denmark with hand puppets; it was an indication of his future life before the public. At seventeen, he went to sea, and excelled at an amusement in which his fellow-sailors would truss him up and challenge him to escape. When his ship visited Ålborg, Denmark, his shore party encountered a traveling "King of Escapes" who offered 100 kroner to anyone who could tie him so that he could not escape within ten minutes; Bernhard took that money easily. A year later, out of work in the town of Randers, he decided to try his hand at offering the same challenge, and was spotted by a circus director named Giovanni Belli, who offered him a job with his show.

But instead of being an immediate star, young Eskilsen found himself cleaning up after the horses, doing a clown number, and serving as a general errand boy for the circus artists. Wanting to step out of that rank, he began learning the art of contortion. A few years later, in 1927, he was able to leave Belli's circus and accept a contract with the Tivoli Gröna Lund ("Green Grove") amusement park in Stockholm doing a combination contortion-and-escape act under the name of Bernardi. He sold postcard photos of himself in ridiculous deformations, and began to do rather well financially.

He had read about the fabulous success of Harry Houdini (who had just died) in America and the United Kingdom, and decided to concentrate on escape artistry. He married, and his wife, dressed as a page boy, served as his assistant. On a cold winter day in 1928, he set up a press conference at a riverbank, and announced he would be shackled, tied into a sack, and thrown into the icy water. The local police rushed in and made an official

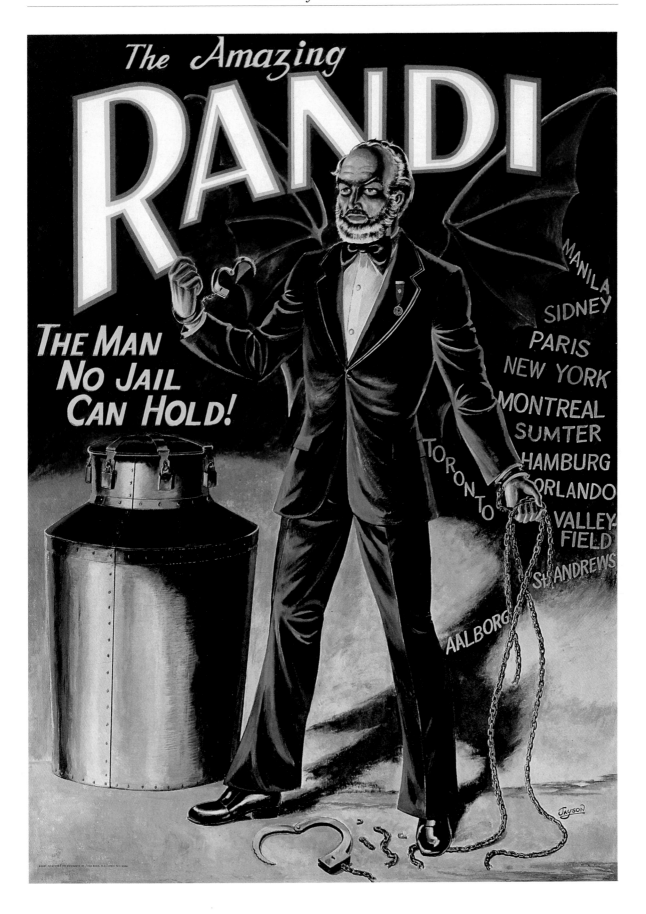

fuss, declaring that suicide was against the law in Sweden. However, some five thousand people had gathered to see the feat, and the police decided to stand back. Into the dark waters went Bernardi, and just thirty-two seconds later he emerged victorious. The press was delirious, and the fame of the daredevil was established.

Bernardi made improvements to this effective but dangerous publicity stunt, which he now began doing with the sack sprinkled with gasoline and set on fire.

In the spring of 1929, facing up to such challenges as a new type of handcuffs the Swedish police were then using, Bernardi was doing so well at Tivoli that he could afford to buy a lion, which he worked into the act by making it serve as an apparent threat to the escapist when he was thrown, fully bound, into its cage. That animal purchase was followed by many others, giving him a small zoo in a short time.

Then he lost everything in a fire. The menagerie and his props were gone, and he was bankrupt. His wife, Hildy, apparently decided that she should move on, and there was a divorce.* Things looked bleak indeed for Bernardi.

The ever-inventive artist developed a new twist that brought him much success. He became the impresario for a mysterious chap called "Mr. Bosco, the Man with the Mask," who, as it happened, also did an escape act, but only while masked. Bernardi promoted Bosco assiduously, asking huge prices for him that he himself had never earned. It was advertised that the ever-masked Bosco traveled from town to town in a packing case along with the rest of the props, and that brought out crowds just to see the baggage wagon unpacked upon arrival at the train station. They witnessed Bosco emerging from a huge box. It was a grand publicity stunt. Manager Bernardi, of course, traveled first-class in the proper coach.

In 1937, the hoax collapsed when Bernardi decided to get married once more. At the ceremony, he revealed that Bosco and Bernardi were one and the same person. The crowds were all the more pleased at this great surprise, and the show prospered. The train station scenes had of course been carefully staged and carried out.

In the wartime season of 1940, there were accusations that Bernardi was a spy, and there were many problems, not the least being that an escape artist might encourage the notion of liberation beyond what neighboring countries could tolerate. Characteristically, in 1942 he came up with a "living sculpture" presentation and toured Hungary, Rumania, and Yugoslavia with it. The spring of 1944 found Bernardi back at his escapes, now performing for a circus in Denmark, which carried him through 1945.

On April 22, 1946, Bernardi prepared for the opening of the new show season at Rønne, Denmark, by setting up the publicity stunt he'd already

*See "Miss Hilden" later in this chapter.

performed so many times before with such great success. In front of an out-door audience of thousands, and more than a dozen press representatives, he and his assistants readied the chains, the manacles, and the weighted, gaso-line-soaked canvas sack in which he would be confined before being thrown into the water at the riverside. This time, cautious police officers in atten-dance insisted that a safety line be fastened to the escape artist's wrist in case the stunt backfired. Reluctantly, Bernardi agreed to this precaution.

With the sack ablaze in a roaring tower of flame, he was thrown into the water and sank from sight immediately before the eyes of the excited crowd. Minutes passed by, rather than the thirty seconds or so that it usually took for him to appear triumphantly at the surface. Worried assistants asked the police to quickly haul in the safety line, and when it came in tangled in the empty sack, without Bernardi attached, there was some consternation, though most of the crowd were sure that this was just another dramatic twist to the famous act that had always worked before.

Then, as Bernardi at last made his appearance at the surface of the river, swimming to the pier, a great cry of excitement went up from all present, followed by a sudden silence as he abruptly stopped and quickly sank from sight again. Divers were in the water instantly, but it was too late. The great Bernardi was dead when he was brought up only a moment later.

The coroner ruled it was not the performance itself that took the life of the escape artist. He had been working all along with a heart problem; that had produced a clot, which traveled to his brain and killed him in a matter of seconds. His stunt had only aggravated a condition that would eventually have taken his life in any case. Perhaps, given a choice, the artist might have preferred to thus pass from the scene in this moment of glory.

Swedish escape artist Bernardi died doing this trick, chained up and tossed into the sea. Here he is seen being manacled by the local police.

MISS HILDEN

The wife of Bernardi was the German escape artist Hildegard Neureiter, who dressed as a page boy when assisting her husband. She even stepped in to replace him on the show as the performer when he was indisposed.

In 1929, right after the disastrous fire that temporarily bankrupted the Bernardi show, "Hildy" left the marriage and worked for a while as a waitress, saving every coin to purchase stage equipment and costumes. That end accomplished, she took up billing herself as "Escape Queen Miss Hilden," aiming to be the first serious woman escape artist. She was quite successful, doing truly dangerous and exciting stunts such as being fastened in steel chains and suspended above the stage to free herself.

Miss Hilden married an agent named Wähl and developed a new and spectacular act which took place in a huge aquarium device. She was wrapped in chains and a straitjacket, tied into a sack, and set on fire before being thrown into the tank. The audience watched in fascination through the side of the tank as she freed herself underwater. Under the name Hilden-Wähl, the "Sensation of Sensations" performed for the troops during wartime; she gave her last performance in 1945, the year before her first husband, Bernardi, died so tragically. She divorced agent Wähl, remarried, and as Hildegard Ohlsson now lives in retirement in Malmö, Sweden.

LAURICE

Proud of a family history in the conjuring profession, young Laurice travels from his home in New York to all parts of the world in response to demands from his sponsors. Several engagements in Japan and Aruba and frequent U.S. television appearances have earned him major international clients.

The Amazing Randi hangs over Niagara Falls after wriggling out of a straitjacket, seen falling into the maelstrom below on a cold January day. This was filmed for the Canadian TV production World of Wizards.

In April of 1991, to celebrate the 117th anniversary of Houdini's birth, Laurice was fastened in handcuffs, leg irons, and chains, then stuffed into a padlocked, nailed packing case. The men who made the box, union carpenters from New Jersey, were appalled. "I made it as solid as can be. I don't know how he's going to get out of it. I'm kind of worried," said one of them.

Sturdily made of 2-by-4's and 1-by-8 planks, the box withstood careful examination from the thirty-five press representatives who stood by in amazement. The padlocks, all eight of them, were supplied by a New York locksmith who was equally concerned.

The huge box, holes drilled in the sides to allow it to sink, was lowered into New York's East River. Within a minute, Laurice was seen at the surface of the cold (41°F) water

The Master of Impossibilities, Laurice emerges from the East River atop the steel safe that had imprisoned him moments before.

gasping for breath in a feat that recalled Houdini's greatest escapes. But when Houdini did this kind of work, he had one less risk: the incredibly polluted water of that river.

On another occasion, Laurice was locked into a safe that had also been drilled with holes to admit the water into which it was plunged, and when the fearsome device was raised from the depths moments later, the escape artist was found standing triumphantly on top of his watery prison, freed of shackles and waving to the assembled press.

Laurice continues to support his claim to the title, The Master of Impossibilities.

CHAPTER 25

THE MANIPULATORS

CARDINI

When a young Welsh magician named Richard Valentine Pitchford took a clerk's position at the magic counter of Gamage's department store in London, it was to learn the fine art of meeting and entertaining customers. Soon after, he went traveling around the U.K. and Europe with a "manipulation" act, practicing constantly to develop his own very distinctive style. At first, he decided to use his middle name as his stage name, but it was to little acclaim. A further change to "Professor Thomas" was equally unnoticed. Then he became "Val Raymond" and found that that, too, was not quite the ticket. Finally, in Australia, he settled on "Cardini," and under that name he was from then on a smashing success in vaudeville and nightclubs.

As a result of a World War II injury, Cardini suffered from a memory loss, but was otherwise little impaired. His meticulously crafted act underwent many changes before it was perfected, and though many imitators soon emerged to take advantage of his approach, few survived very long.

Impeccably costumed in tails and top hat, carrying a walking stick, and with a monocle jammed into his right eye, Cardini was seemingly totally confused and just a little tipsy. He lurched about his stage finding fans of playing cards at his gloved fingertips and cigarettes—lighted ones—almost anywhere he reached. (With better awareness today, the alcoholic-haze and tobacco themes are becoming increasingly less popular with magicians, I'm happy to report, though a few youngsters still find glamorous connotations in the use of the substances as theatrical props. Countless American performers have used the manipulation of cigarettes as the basis for an act, as did David Nixon and David Berglas in the U.K. in past years.)

Assisted by his charming wife, Swan, costumed as a page boy, Cardini

The artistic manipulation of Cardini set the standard for others. Assisted by his wife, Swan, he portrayed a tipsy Englishman to whom miracles occurred.

created a very high standard for a generation of magicians. He had mastered the technical aspects of his sleight of hand to the point where it no longer occupied his attention, which was turned entirely to his mime and timing skills. When billiard balls dropped from his hands in apparently endless numbers, and began multiplying and changing colors between his fingers, no one appeared more surprised than he himself. The monocle dropped from its place frequently as Cardini's eyes widened in astonishment at his own talents.

Hardly any modern manipulator of playing cards or other magical props can fail to credit Cardini for his innovations. Though I am personally convinced that there are several young performers today who are in every way equal to and even superior to Cardini technically, he was the one who put their specialty in focus for the public. He was the first, in so many ways.

CHANNING POLLOCK

Facing page: Carter the Great worked most of the time in the Orient, though he personally harbored great dislike for all Asians.

All "dove workers" in the business today can thank Channing Pollock for providing them with a living. This absolutely flawless performer not only set the standard in the business, but also originated many of the "moves" and effects used today by magicians all over the world. When the suave, tail-suited Channing first reached up to his lapel and unraveled his red carnation into a large silk handkerchief, tied it into a knot, and then materialized a live dove in each hand simultaneously, eager young artists were set into a frenzy to solve and master this wonder.

An Italian film that featured part of his act (shot in a U.K. nightclub) was surreptitiously copied on eight-millimeter film in dark theaters by ambitious magicians. Imitators came and went, some surviving even though the master was still around because they put their own innovations into their acts; but most found it impossible to approach Pollock's performance, and they quietly abandoned the attempt.

Not only birds appeared at Pollock's fingertips. Playing cards by the dozens showered down on his stage, fans of cards popping into existence and fluttering away only to be immediately replaced by more. Both his card manipulation and his dove work have perhaps only been equaled today by Lance Burton, who admits his debt to the master. He says of his mentor, "When I was a little boy, I wanted to be Channing Pollock. I still want to be Channing. I'll go on record as saying Channing Pollock is the coolest guy on the planet."

On one of the annual Magic Circle shows at the Scala Theatre in London many years ago, I had the distinct misfortune of following Channing Pollock's number. Not only that, but I had props to set on a stage that took a long time to clear because of the hundreds of magically materialized playing cards that had to be swept up, and the curtain calls Pollock took before the stage was finally "dark" and free to receive my props. It was an unenviable situation to face, walking out to greet an audience so blown away by Channing's tour de force that they could not quite recover. It was like following God.

Channing Pollock ruled the fifties in "small"* magic. His cool, aristocratic, almost detached manner would have been, in a lesser performer, an arrogant attitude; with him, it was natural and perfectly acceptable. The care that he showed toward his birds was an example to all the magicians, and his general effect on the trade was enormous, particularly in the way employers of talent sat up and took much more notice of conjurors after Channing came to their attention. When he left the stage to a quiet retirement in California, he left behind him a heritage of technical excellence and superb design. He is a living legend in our art.

*As opposed to large illusion-boxes.

CHAPTER 26

THE MENTALISTS

One class of conjuring retains, in the minds of a portion of the public, the status it enjoyed in medieval times. Tricks done apparently with the mind alone are still given a strange "unproven-but-not-disproved" status by many persons, and by some others they are accepted without question as genuine. Because these feats don't seem to be "tricks," and there is a great hunger to accept strange powers of mind given to or learned by certain individuals, many mentalists find that they have a difficult time leaving their audiences with the message that they have just witnessed a form of entertainment, rather than a supernatural demonstration; some others do not even try to dispel notions of occult forces, and even encourage them.

My personal conviction is that any performer owes his audience a fair statement. It may be difficult to believe, but ethical conjurors do not lie to their audiences! They allow spectators to assume untruths; they mislead them; they even represent (by inference) that a piece of equipment is unprepared, when it might well contain a pretty lady about to be produced for the edification of an admiring crowd.

Let me give you an example: Suppose that I have just noticed an antique ship's compass sitting in your living room. Admiring it, I tell you that I can influence the compass to behave in a peculiar manner. I ask you to place the instrument on a table, and I approach the table, calling attention to the fact that the compass needle is, as expected, pointing in a northerly direction. I seat myself at the table, clench my fists, lean forward toward the table and tell the compass to deflect. It does, the needle suddenly wobbling about and

swinging to point due south, after which it regains its normal function and once more slowly swings around to point north!

A supernatural feat? Not at all. And did I lie to you? No, I did not. I was carrying a simple magnet with me, part of a child's toy. It was taped inside the front of my shirt. Seizing my opportunity, I set about creating the circumstances under which you would be interested in seeing a demonstration.

Then, by simply leaning in toward the compass as I sat before it, I caused the amazing deflection.

However, if I had volunteered to tell you that I did not use a magnet to do this trick, or had claimed that it was done by some supernatural means, that would have been unethical. In the same way, when you hear a magician telling you that the person he has chosen from the audience is not a confederate, you should be able to depend on that to be true. If you are told that no camera tricks are being used in a television presentation, you should be able to believe it. This is nothing more than truth in advertising.

Now I must tell you that the exact scene described above happened to me about a year ago in the New York home of a publisher. When he reads this, he will agree that I didn't lie to him, but I sure got him a bit bewildered! Here's what I did: I looked up recent information on him, and found that he had been profiled in a magazine piece several months before my visit. A photograph of him in that magazine had shown the ship's compass in his living room. I'd noted this information, then went along to meet him fully equipped for this "impromptu" demonstration equipped with the concealed magnet. It was that simple.

Many magicians have, at one time in their careers, practiced the "fortune-telling" game to make a living. Well before he became Fu Manchu, David Bamberg learned the mind-reading act of the Zancigs and was instructed by a carnival worker named Professor Seward how to do the "cold-reading" process. In the 1920s, while still a teenager, he worked as Professor Zaza, palm reader ("mitt-reader" in the argot), at Atlantic City's Rendezvous Park, and in his memoirs he expressed his guilt:

> On Saturdays and Sundays, when the sucker trains came in from Philadelphia, I would read as many as a hundred mitts a day at fifty-cents per mitt for my share. I coined money and managed to save over a thousand dollars. I gave a stock reading and learned to "fish" in a short while, which was the art of getting them to give me information without realizing it. But it was monotonous work and I got fed up with everyone's gripes and bleats and broken hearts. Even if one could predict the truth, they wouldn't want to hear it. All they wanted was good news. I tried to kid myself for a time that I was doing some good when I would tell some poor working woman with a half a dozen kids "that a great change" was coming into her miserable life but deep down I thought it was a revolting racket. I finally quit and hoped that I would never have to do it again.

I myself almost fell into the snare. When I was eighteen years old, I performed a prediction trick for a Toronto newspaper for publicity purposes. It appeared that I'd been able to foresee, three days in advance, the final score of the World Series published in the headlines of their paper, and the resultant write-up was flattering indeed. It resulted in an engagement at a local bar-and-grill establishment, which provided me with a weekly salary that was adequate though not sumptuous. The newspaper article got on the wire services, too, and attracted the attention of a man from Florida, who showed up unannounced at the door of the home where I was boarding. Obviously a believer in such powers, he offered to pay me a handsome sum every week if I would only agree to give him, via telephone, regular information about what horses would be winners at certain Florida tracks. Though I told him in no uncertain terms that what I'd done was merely a publicity stunt, he could not be discouraged, and began coming to my place of employment to persuade me to enter into business with him. At that time, I was recovering from a serious back injury and was wrapped in a plaster body cast. My heavy hospital bills were pursuing me, and the temptation to accede to the man's plan was almost too much. I can understand how the easy money comes so readily to those with no scruples.

This specialty branch of conjuring—mentalism—is something I studied in great depth early in my magic career, and I believe it to be a very captivating form of entertainment, if not abused. Though I eventually turned to the escape aspect of magic, I've never lost my interest in the artists who bamboozle their audiences with subtleties which appear to be ESP, psychokinesis, prophecy, or some other mental power. May they all treat their audiences with respect.

CONTE ALESSANDRO DI CAGLIOSTRO

Cagliostro was one of the most infamous characters of the great drama that was the French Revolution. His story belongs here only because he set the stage for the advent of mentalism, by creating an atmosphere that made incredible claims seem acceptable, at least to the gullible. Said to have been born in 1743 at Palermo, Sicily, as Guiseppe Balsamo (an assertion that has been seriously questioned), he liked to claim that he was a gypsy, which he might well have been. Since so much of his career was described by himself, it is well to treat it all with some caution. However, some aspects have been well established.

He began his fabulous career with a few forgeries of theater tickets and a falsified will; then he robbed his uncle, and was accused of a murder. At this point he happened upon a marvelous and much safer way of earning money: pretending that he was able to locate gold and buried treasure for paying clients. The man who was to become Cagliostro would show gullible customers sites where he said he sensed concealed assets.

(Some sixty years later in New York State, one Joseph Smith, who was to become founder of the Mormon church, worked the same racket, perhaps inspired by the success of Cagliostro. Though Smith was charged and convicted in court with being "a disorderly person and an imposter," having claimed to be able to divine "hidden treasures in the bowels of the earth," it appears that Cagliostro was only forced to flee Sicily as a result of his impostures.)

Marrying very well in Naples, Cagliostro went into the eternal-youth business in 1780 at Strasburg. He and his equally crooked wife traveled Europe, selling age-regression potions to wealthy clients and claiming that his wife, then twenty, was actually sixty years old. He himself told willing dupes that he had witnessed the crucifixion of Christ, but appeared much younger as a result of his magical elixir.

Paris went wild over him, with Cardinal de Rohan, not noted for his discernment, a prominent fan of the Sicilian faker. Cagliostro related fanciful stories about his conversations with angels, lurid accounts of his childhood discoveries of his powers, and descriptions of gigantic cities in remote parts of the earth. There were, of course, always a number of people ready to listen to him and believe him. For them he promised to locate gold and jewels, taking a fee, then moving on to other locations before having to make good on his promises.

The fake count lived in high luxury, with estates all through Europe filled with treasures of every sort. He was consulted by statesmen and philosophers, many of whom declared him to be genuine and possessed of real magical powers. Very much in the manner later subsequently adopted by Madame Blavatsky, founder of Theosophy, Cagliostro demonstrated physical marvels, such as writing that appeared on slips of paper which seemed to materialize from thin air, penned by spirits or beings from other planets.

It was, very much like the present day, an age of credulity. Saint-Amand, in his biography of Marie Antoinette, says of this period:

> The mania for the supernatural, the rage for the marvelous, prevailed in the last years of the eighteenth century, which had wantonly derided every sacred thing. Never were the Rosicrucians, the adepts, sorcerers and prophets so numerous and so respected. Serious and educated men, magistrates, courtiers, declared themselves eye-witnesses of alleged miracles.

In Paris, in 1785, Cagliostro became involved in the famous Affair of the Diamond Necklace,* a scandalous event that is thought by some historians to have precipitated the French Revolution. He was brought to trial along with his dupe Cardinal de Rohan. Though he defended himself cleverly and

---

*While the people of Paris were starving, Marie Antoinette was said to have squandered the national budget on an expensive piece of jewelry.

effectively against those charges, he was imprisoned in the Bastille for other reasons. Eventually released after nine months, he was ordered to leave France. He went to England, where it seems he was no longer as welcome as before, and he was locked up in Fleet Street prison. Fleeing through Europe and once more back in Rome, he was denounced by his wife to the Holy Inquisition, charged with heresy, and condemned to death; but old fans intervened. The sentence was commuted by the pope and Cagliostro was imprisoned at the San Leo prison in Urbino until his death in 1795.

The elder Alexander Dumas' *Memoirs of a Physician* and Goethe's *Grand Cophta* are based upon events in Cagliostro's incredible life.

Cagliostro obviously employed various optical and chemical methods, along with some basic sleight-of-hand, to produce small tricks as convincing evidence of his powers. His name was even evoked by Robert-Houdin to add luster to one of that master's more spectacular feats, and modern conjurors delight in naming certain of their tricks after the Sicilian charlatan who so effectively fleeced his world for so many years.

When Cagliostro died, so, effectively, died a belief in genuine sorcery, though it peeps from out of its grave occasionally even today. The era of the admitted trickster dawned, in which audiences were no longer asked to believe that those who performed mysterious demonstrations did so with divine or demonic assistance. The real, honest conjuror stepped from the wings of the stage and took a bow for his skill, originality, and dedication.

AXEL HELLSTRÖM

In a demonstration that can be considered as close to "real" mentalism as anything else ever attempted, a mentalist will often offer to find an object somewhere in his audience after it's been hidden with him out of the room. One method of doing this is known as muscle reading. This was developed to a high art by several artists, but when the Swedish mentalist Axel Hellström displayed his talents at a gathering of very impressed magicians in 1928, he gave his name to the art. From that time on it has been known as "Hellströmism." In the 1950s the Hungarian Franz Polgar originated the stunt of having his paycheck for the performance thus hidden, and if he failed to locate it, he forfeited the payment. Though the method is somewhat different, this act has since been copied by mentalist Kreskin, most of whose show was taken from the work of Joseph Dunninger.

A modern practitioner of Hellströmism is Lev Schneider, a Russian immigrant to the United States who speaks little English. His ability to locate a hidden object merely by following closely a person who is aware of its location, is just short of supernatural. Even magicians who know fully the techniques he uses are puzzled by his sensitivity. I have never ceased to marvel at his ability, which must appear, to the layman, to be genuine telepathy.

Mentalist Hellström was fond of telling all that he had baffled Thurston with his mind-reading act. "The Man with the Sixth Sense" certainly set the pattern for others who followed him.

On one occasion, Alex Hellström performed a marvelous publicity stunt in which he worked with magician Harry Blackstone. He managed to find—by one means or another—a carved cigar-store Indian that had been stolen. Harry told me about that event years ago, but would never discuss the details. Hmm.

*John Randall Brown
was probably the first
American artist to pop-
ularize the "muscle
reading" act of
Hellström, and taught
Washington Irving
Bishop the method.
Bishop became a
leading performer with
the technique.*

WASHINGTON IRVING BISHOP

An American mountebank who learned his trade as an assistant to John Randall Brown, a newspaperman who specialized in muscle reading as perfected by Hellström, Bishop flourished in the 1880s. He started his career working with the famous spiritualist Anna Eva Fay, first functioning as her manager. Then, in 1876, he chose to expose her methods in the New York *Daily Graphic* newspaper, and at that point began doing his own show. At first, he denied the existence of any paranormal powers; then he apparently decided that the easier path was with the fakers, and he became a "real" psychic overnight.

Bishop is credited with originating the "blindfold drive" trick (1885) in which the performer is able to navigate in a vehicle while his eyes are covered. Bishop used a horse and carriage, while modern practitioners depend upon an automobile.

One of Bishop's favorite routines, copied from Brown, was to have a fictitious murderer, a weapon, and a victim chosen from among the audience members while he was out of the area. Upon his return he would identify all three. He performed this and other mysteries in the United States and in Britain, with great success. In Britain he made great but spurious claims of wealth, even turning over the proceeds of several performances (less "expenses") to charitable causes. His pretensions of riches were part of his pose, apparently to attract huge fees for specialized projects in which he tried to become involved.

It was also in Britain, however, that he lost a £10,000 lawsuit brought against him by the famous conjuror J. N. Maskelyne, who objected to his claims of genuine psychic power. Bishop left England to escape having to pay the penalty.

The mentalist Bishop was fond of claiming that he'd been tested by scientists, but when the conditions for the tests were not of his own making, he failed. When challenged to do specific feats that he claimed he could do with regularity, he switched tests or the conditions for the tests, and only then succeeded. His claim was that he did not understand his own powers, but when a newspaper editor named Charles Howard Montague learned to do Bishop's act, successfully duplicating a drawing done by one of his audience, he declared

Mr. Bishop would have us infer that he does not know how he does it. I know how I do it, and I am rather of the opinion that his self-consciousness* is not a great way behind my own. It is very difficult for me to believe that so expert a student of the sensations of other people should be so poor a pupil in his own case.

Bishop chided Montague for failing to recognize that "Almighty God" had given him his abilities, but Montague was unfazed, proceeding to perform the Bishop act for many large audiences, always denying that any supernatural forces were at work.

After numerous marriages and bouts with alcohol and drugs and almost every excess available to him, Bishop's death in New York at age forty-three had a certain macabre mystery about it, since he had said that he was subject to cataleptic fits and might thus be buried alive if not carefully examined after his apparent death. A dramatic "swoon" following his stage performance was not uncommon for him, and he claimed that several times he'd come close to being sliced up by doctors about to perform autopsies on his still-living body. His mother, a rather overdramatic, raving woman who, some years earlier, had thrown herself into her husband's grave as he was being lowered to his final rest, made wild accusations about her son's having been autopsied while not yet dead, but nothing was proven. The event pro-

---

* He means, self-awareness.

vided journalists with marvelous stories for decades, and is still occasionally resurrected.

HENRY SLADE

"Dr." Slade was a spiritualist faker who could produce apparently spirit-written messages on school slates that had been washed and then sealed together, face to face. The trick was a simple one, but it fooled several scientists, including an Austrian astrophysicist named Zöllner, who even wrote a book, *Transcendental Physics*, based upon his observations of Slade's tricks and his firm belief that they were *not* tricks.

J. N. Maskelyne appeared as a witness against Slade in England in 1876 and was easily able to demonstrate to the satisfaction of the court that his slate writing was brought about by fraud. Slade was convicted and sentenced to three months at hard labor, but a technical error in the way the charge was worded caused a mistrial, and Slade left England hurriedly before a new trial could get under way. He never returned to the British Isles.

In Europe and in America, Slade was a great success until repeated exposures brought about his downfall. He finally signed a definitive confession of his fakery, faded from view, and at last died in a sanatorium in Michigan.

ERIK VAN HANUSSEN

It is a strange paradox that a magician pretends to control the destinies of men, but cannot control his own.

—James Ellis

Herschel Steinschneider was born in 1889 in Vienna, the son of Siegfried Steinschneider, an Austrian-Jewish traveling comedian. As a boy of fourteen, he traveled with his father, learning the tricks of the variety artists and circus performers. Soon he was performing mentalism, specializing in making objects move, apparently by mind power.

At the age of twenty-one, he made an abrupt change of direction. He became chief reporter for a newspaper called *Der Blitz*, which had a reputation among the public of making its money by blackmailing celebrities. Apparently Herschel was suited to this kind of work. Then along came World War I.

He was drafted into the army and used his mentalist talents to entertain the troops, eventually becoming a minor officer. He also took up dowsing—finding water, buried treasure, and other things with a forked stick—an "art" that has been shown to be entirely imaginary, though it is generally accepted

Van Hanussen, psychic pretender, was featured with Circus Busch in 1919 with his "gifted medium." Such bizarre—and effective—advertising was common with this artist.

as fact in the world of the paranormal. He even entertained the kaiser, which of course helped his reputation enormously.

Out of the army in 1917, he took the professional name "Erik Van Hanussen" (sometimes written "*Jan* Hanussen") and joined a small circus. In Kraków he published a booklet titled, "Worauf beruht das?" ("What Is This Based On?") which dealt with subjects like telepathy and clairvoyance and in the spirit of an exposé labeled them all as frauds. In 1920 he wrote and published (in Vienna) a second booklet, "Das Gedankenlesen" ("Thought Reading"), for the second time in print calling the idea of telepathy, clairvoyance, and mind-reading a swindle.

Then, amazingly, he did an about-face and threw himself into that very business, now treating it as if it were genuine; he claimed clairvoyant and telepathic powers. The Austrian police labeled him a swindler, but before they could proceed further, Van Hanussen went off to Czechoslovakia, which he now chose to claim was his homeland, but he was no more welcome there, soon being charged with using trickery and taking money under false pretenses.

By 1929 he was in hot water again and found himself in court, charged with fraud, but the case against him was dismissed for lack of evidence. His own version of that episode in his life was somewhat different from the facts; asked about it later in his career, he said that he had appeared in court as a sworn expert witness for the state.

The newly emerged mentalist moved into the cabaret scene, and then

Erik Jan Hanussen

to the Ge
ernment.
twelve ho
strate his

Also, h
arm Brun
leaners, o
terminate
a suit tha
own histc
Hanussen

The Re
Nazi plan.
seer's visic
Hanussen
he was sec

On Apr
a shallow ;
twelve tim
passed an ;
law "for th
and comm
even thoug
passed!)

Who ga
though pap
by Count v
and were n

Even in
others as tl
attracted at
one was tal
fascinate; tʲ
his life, tho

Erik Van H
always in da
that he cou.
supply of si
than a centu
dreadful fall
juror. But, ι

began giving public shows at major theaters. He had expensive full-color posters printed up and was soon playing to packed houses. The price of admission was almost double the regular price of a variety show, and Van Hanussen also gave very costly personal readings for his customers. On stage, he was a striking figure in stark white makeup and a tail suit.

He went off to Berlin, and within a few months he had captured that troubled city with his tricks. He played a long run at the Scala Theater and was a celebrity. The news media built him into a major psychic figure, though from the descriptions given, the tricks he was performing were obviously derived right from extant sources.

At about this time he was introduced to a Count von Helldorf, a powerful member of the newly formed Nazi party, and the two men began using one another. Helldorf borrowed large amounts of money from the psychic, who had lots to lend, and Van Hanussen got political favors from the count. Though he had to convert from Judaism to Protestantism in order the join the party, Van Hanussen did so willingly.

He became Adolf Hitler's favorite *Hellseher* (clairvoyant), and served the Nazis as one of their most vehement and savage anti-Semitic propagandists, even turning out a weekly newspaper for the party which trumpeted that theme. Once, when a minor astrologer named Möcke dared to point out

German psychic pretender Van Hanussen used this dramatic poster to advertise his highly paid appearances in Berlin just before World War II. He came to a bad end.

French conjuror Robin was the first to show the illusion effect that later, in a somewhat different version, became known as Pepper's Ghost. Here he is seen at the Salle de Robin in Piccadilly, London, in 1851 performing a Second Sight act. Objects handed to him were identified by his assistant, seated and blindfolded.

performers, he was using his abilities to convince his clients that he was really a supernatural being.

JULIUS ZANCIG

The Zancigs were a married Danish couple who performed a two-person act that was basically an advanced development of Robert-Houdin's Second Sight act. Agnes was a hunchback with black, piercing eyes; Julius was tall and darkly handsome. They billed the act as "Two Minds with but a Single Thought," which was a clever dodge that did not, strictly speaking, claim telepathy.

In their time, the Zancigs caused as much excitement and controversy in the press and among scientists and the public as any claimed psychic matter has ever enjoyed. A major British newspaper publisher, Lord Northcliffe,

used the power of his *Daily Mail* to influence opinion in favor of telepathy, which he believed took place between Julius and Agnes. He was totally convinced that they possessed mysterious psychic powers.

As with most such two-person acts, the "receiver" (Agnes) would sit on the stage, blindfolded, while the "sender" (Julius) wandered about the theater accepting objects, written words, and small documents from members of the audience. Agnes would describe, apparently by telepathy, the appearance of the objects and details from the written material handled by Julius. A great deal of training, study, and practice was necessary in order to do this act, which of course had nothing to do with ESP of any sort.

Sir Oliver Lodge, a very prominent British scientist, and Sir Arthur Conan Doyle, the equally famous creator of the fictional Sherlock Holmes, witnessed the Zancig team in operation, and declared them genuine because they had no idea of how the trick might have been worked. These two gentlemen also believed in the popular spirit mediums of their day, for essentially the same reason.

Just as the Zancigs were at the top of their form, Agnes died. Julius was genuinely attached to her, and felt profound grief at losing the mate who had spent so many long years developing the very difficult and sophisticated

Above left: Sir Arthur Conan Doyle, who believed everything he could not solve was supernatural, was convinced that Julius Zancig, seen here with his second wife, Ada, had genuine telepathic powers. Above right: Julius Zancig in 1926, late in his career. He set the standard for two-person mental acts, still being performed today.

methods by which they communicated. He eventually remarried, this time to a Brooklyn schoolteacher named Ada. She was a confirmed spiritualist, and though she managed to learn the rudiments of the act, she was extremely shy and ashamed to face the audience with a blatantly fake act. For that reason, she performed with her head down and in a barely audible voice.

Seeing that Ada was unsuitable as a partner, Julius sought for another, and found Paul Vucci, a young man who was eventually to become an outstanding sleight-of-hand nightclub performer under the name "Paul Rosini." Though Paul (who was called Henry in the act) was very proficient as a partner, the problem was that he was just draft age in 1917, and was about to become Uncle Sam's involuntary partner. Julius was fortunate enough to happen upon a thirteen-year-old youth named David Bamberg, who dropped into the position neatly for a while, under the name, Syko. His story is told in Chapter 18, which includes the life of the famous Fu Manchu.

Eventually, Ada went back into service with Julius, but in his later years he, too, apparently began to accept spiritualism and spent much time at séances. Public enthusiasm for the Zancigs faded, and the act was soon working at carnivals and in cheap tent shows. To the dismay of his colleagues, Julius dedicated more and more of his time to belief in "real" psychic claims, and finally died in very impoverished circumstances in 1929.

There were others who used the same methods as the Zancigs with great success. In their heyday during the 1940s, Lesley and Sydney Piddington had England thoroughly convinced that they were able to read one another's minds. Aside from their great skill, the fact that they were able to make use of radio exposure (in 1949) was a strong reason for their success. At a period when the ESP was being referred to as mental radio, the Piddingtons were regarded by many as probably able to converse by telepathy. They were careful to disavow any such idea.

There were interesting variations of the basic act. The team of Mercedes and Mlle. Stantone headlined vaudeville with an act in which Mlle. Stantone, seated onstage at a piano, was able to play any tune whispered to her partner in the audience. Similarly, the Svengali Trio used the musical theme in such an act from 1900 to 1925, playing the United States and Europe. An American act, Liz and Tom Tucker, were equally successful with this sort of performance until quite recently, appearing on television to the acclaim of both press and public.

MAX MAVEN

If a voice can make an actor, Max Maven has it made. That, combined with his fearless hairstyle and makeup, distinguishes him from most other mentalists of today. Perhaps only Joe Dunninger, as a mentalist, comes close to him in making such effective use of his image.

Max Maven specializes in mentalism, and has performed his wonders internationally. He is especially well known to Japanese audiences, and has been a consultant and designer for major artists in the field.

When not employed as an advisor and designer by leading performers such as David Copperfield, Harry Blackstone, and Mark Wilson, Max is usually in Japan arranging TV specials, since he speaks that language fluently. He has hosted eight television specials in Japan.

He is a prolific writer within the trade, and he turned out an informative one-hour videotape, *Max Maven's Mind Games*, for MCA, which is available to the public in video rental stores.

Max is a performer who stands on the edge of both worlds, reality and fantasy. It is not difficult to find your sense of actuality fleeing when he manages, somehow, to pluck a thought from you that you were sure you held securely. And, who knows, maybe Max himself wonders if it can really be done. . . .

ANNEMANN

Theodore Annemann was born Theodore John Squires, in 1907 in New York State. Working first as a railway clerk, he got into show business as a tenor singer and then assisted a magician doing a dove act. Finally finding his place as a mentalist, he became famous in the trade for originating and refining many of the standard tricks still done today by performers, and he produced what remains the most authoritative and rich source of material for mentalists, a limited-access magazine called *The Jinx*.

A brilliant inventor and performer, he was noted for his version of the Bullet Catch and for stunning mental effects that put him among the all-time greats of that genre. He had a great gimmick which many who met him remember well. When he shook your hand, you were startled at the

Even professional magicians will be surprised to see Theo Annemann in this very early photograph, which hints at the considerable charisma that he was to generate as a mentalist.

very cold feel of his hand in yours. That was achieved by Ted having kept his hand in his jacket pocket, where a small rubber bag of ice was concealed.

Annemann died mysteriously in 1942, by his own hand, two weeks before his first planned indoor performance of his famous Bullet Catch.

KUDA BUX

A Kashmiri with dark, deep-set eyes and heavy eyebrows, Kuda Bux was known as the Man with the X-Ray Eyes. He earned this title by means of his blindfold act. While such an act is and was commonly done by many mentalists, Bux had a version involving large wads of cotton placed over bread dough that filled his eye sockets; the whole thing was then bound in place with multiple layers of bandages until his head appeared to be a huge ball of cloth. He would then drive a car, duplicate handwriting or drawings, and even fire a rifle at targets indicated by a volunteer. Once, like P. C. Sorcar, he bicycled on New York's Broadway while blindfolded, a dangerous feat even when fully sighted.

Kuda Bux first attracted international attention in 1935 by performing one of the most famous "fakir" stunts, walking on burning embers. He did a carefully observed firewalk in England and subsequently duplicated the performance in the United States, outside Radio City Music Hall. It was a stunt that he was familiar with from his early days in India and Pakistan, since it was frequently executed as part of religious ceremonies in that region. Though it has now been demonstrated—by physicist Dr. Bernard

Above left: It seemed impossible for Kuda Bux to drive a car, copy handwriting, and shoot a rifle while blindfolded in this way, but he did all of those things. Above right: The eyes of Pakistani Kuda Bux looked as if they could indeed penetrate any barriers to support his claim of being "The Man With The X-Ray Eyes."

Leikind of California—to be a perfectly ordinary (but not intuitively obvious) phenomenon, one popular and very successful New Age "guru" in the United States continues to use it as a purported example of supernatural power or "mind control" to convince customers that impossible things can happen to them.

Ironically enough, in the last years of his life Kuda Bux suffered a gradual loss of his eyesight due to glaucoma. Though his performance methods were and are well understood in the trade, he has been made into one of the Unexplained Mysteries so needed by the paranormalists to bolster their beliefs.

"DR." STANLEY JAKS

Stanley was a gentle soul, a consummate performer who came from Germany via Switzerland to the United States and soon became known as a mentalist. He developed one feat that was a showstopper: He invited a member of the audience to inscribe a signature on the bottom section of a long horizontal blackboard, then managed to duplicate it from above, curve for curve, *in reverse*, while blindfolded.

His approach to mentalism was scholarly, deliberate, and elegant. He had first specialized in close-up sleight-of-hand performance early in his career, so that mental tricks that required great dexterity were easily mastered by the "doctor." Some of his best tricks were so basically simple in theme and method that they deceived magicians who thought they could figure them out and found they couldn't.

Jaks was seen in very posh nightspots like the Savoy Plaza in New York, and he traveled widely in response to great demand for his talents at exclusive bookings for very select audiences.

HARRY LORAYNE

The history of mentalism provides us with a great number of memory artists, from Petrus de Ravenna (active at the close of the fifteenth century in Italy), who was thought to be using diabolical forces to be able to demonstrate his prodigious memory, to today's Harry Lorayne, an energetic gentleman who amazes audiences with his ability to memorize long numbers and even to call off the names and hometowns of all the people in an audience after having met them only once. Harry is also the inventor of some of the most astonishing and (forgive me, Harry!) complicated card-trick routines ever put on paper, and is much in demand at magicians' conferences as a lecturer and instructor. His memory system is marketed through books and tape courses.

Joseph Dunninger, the great mentalist, at the height of his fame. He was known as the Master Mind of Mental Radio.

DUNNINGER

It proves difficult to write about someone you've known well. Your subjectivity suffers, and you don't know whether you've really presented a true picture of the character you've chosen to describe. That's how I find it with Joe Dunninger.

Born the son of a tailor on New York's Lower East Side in 1892, Joe was interested in magic as a boy. Among the many acts he went to see at that time, he was impressed by a two-person mind-reading routine performed by Mr. and Mrs. John T. Fay. John was the son of Anna Eva Fay, a spiritualist who was very popular in vaudeville in the late 1800s and attracted the interest of Harry Houdini. John's wife was Anna Norman. After John's death by

Fourteenth Street Theatre.
art 74

WEEK COMMENCING Monday, March 12th.

Special Matinee on Friday and Saturday at 2:30 for
Ladies Only. No Gentleman Admitted.
Matinee on Sunday at 3:00 for Everyone.

Evening Prices. 25c & 50c. Matinee Prices, all Seats 25c.

ANNA EVA FAY.

⌐ PROGRAMME. ⌐

SPECIAL NOTICE.
Read carefully. Everything done is the result of natural causes.

SPECIAL EXPLANATION TO THE PUBLIC.

MISS FAY wishes it distinctly understood that the results produced,
especially in the "Somnolency" and "Materialization," are wierd and bewildering, but the forces and means employed, although at present not
thoroughly understood by the mass of people, are perfectly natural, and may,
at some future day, be utilized by scientific workers.

PART FIRST,
**Anna Eva Fay will introduce many Novel Features in her peculiar line of
Cabinet Experiments.**

MISS FAY having appeared for nine consecutive months at the Queen's
Concert Rooms, London, and later for three weeks at the Crystal Palace.
For three months Miss Fay was the guests of Prof. Wm. Crooks, F. R. S.,
No. 20 Mornington Road, W. C. During that time Prof. Crooks built the
Galvanometer, an electrical machine to test physical demonstration.

During Parts First and Third, in which Miss Fay appears, and during which she is at such
a high mental strain, it is necessary for her to have a complete release from the same some-
time during the performance, consequently the following will be introduced in

PART SECOND.

MR. WETHEREL RHOADS'
ROYAL ENGLISH MANNIKINS
Harry D'Esta,   Wm. W. Rhoads,   L'Mai D'Esta,   Manipulators.

No intermission between Part Second and
PART THIRD.
The entertainment will close by placing Miss Fay in a Hypnotic Condition and she will
give her weird and startling vistons of what she sees and hears in Hypnotic Dreamland by

"SOMNOLENCY."

SPECIAL NOTICE—Miss Fay receives hundreds of letters and is obliged to employ two
secretaries to assist in her correspondence. Letters regarding "Somnolency" will not be
answered unless they contain an envelope properly addressed and stamped for the reply; even
then no reply will be sent to letters deemed silly or unimportant. Even when the above conditions are complied with it may be several days before a reply can be sent. Don't write
unless it is important. Letters are answered as a matter of courtesy. Send all communications
to the PLANTER'S HOTEL. No one received in person at the hotel.

MISS FAY "DREAM BOOK"

In the hands of the publisher now, is a book that Miss Fay has
compiled from years of experience interpreting all dreams, which are
alphabetically arranged, with full directions as to how to put yourself
in a somnambulist state to receive the benefit of your living nights.

BYRON'S QUOTATION.
"WE LIVE BY NIGHT, AND NOT BY DAY."

When you write your letter to Miss Fay to the Planter's Hotel,
enclose twentyfive cents for one of these books.

C. Schreiner Printing Co., 810-12 N. 15th St.

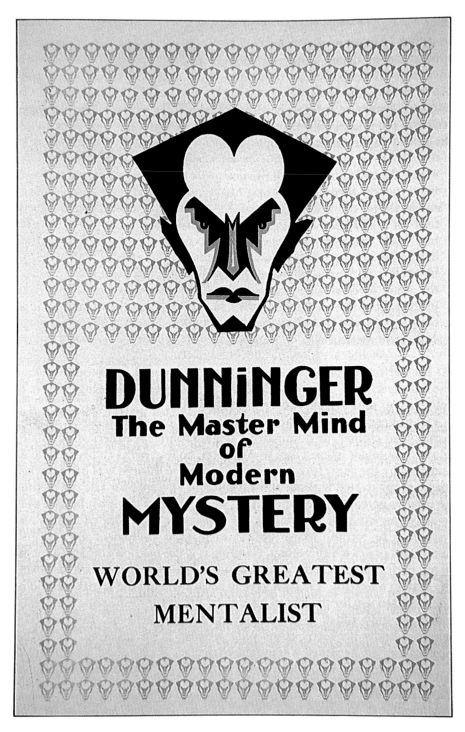

DUNNINGER
The Master Mind
of
Modern
MYSTERY

WORLD'S GREATEST

MENTALIST

Facing page: In her advertising—this example is from late in her career—Anna Eva Fay seems to be getting off the hook by telling clients that what she does is "perfectly natural." Nonetheless, she was widely believed to have genuine psychic powers. Left: The Master Mind of Mental Radio, Joseph Dunninger, reigned as the greatest mentalist in the world, heard on radio nationwide and seen by millions via television. He was an innovator and a prodigious performer, who set the standard for all mentalists and is widely imitated today.

suicide, Mrs. Fay was billed as "The High Priestess of Mystery," and went on with the act, eventually headlining shows in 1908–1910.

However, unlike the "double" act done by the Fays, Dunninger's was a one-person act, never using any assistants—or at least not so that anyone ever knew about it. He was very careful to assure his audiences that he worked entirely alone, and published a carefully worded but quite genuine offer of $10,000 to anyone who could prove that he used paid confederates.

No one ever collected, though many tried, and for a very good reason: He never used any.

Becoming a very highly paid and fully booked mentalist at posh affairs all over the United States (though he had an overpowering fear of flying, and traveled almost exclusively by train all of his life) Dunninger made most of his early fortune before income-tax laws went into effect in this country, and he invested heavily in Oriental artifacts, eventually amassing the largest collection of rare Tibetan art in the United States outside of a specialized museum in Staten Island, New York. His home in New Jersey was filled, wall to wall, with sculptures, wall hangings, exotic rugs, dozens of carved crystals, and gold figures of deities. In the basement was a mass of material from the Houdini home, most of which he sold to the Houdini Hall of Fame Museum.

On one occasion when I was visiting him, he asked me to climb up on a chair and obtain one of his many scrapbooks for him from atop a cabinet. In doing so, I uncovered a dusty domed metal chest studded with rounded red and blue stones, and I asked him about it. He told me to bring it down to the table, warning me that it was "very heavy." It was, and I lowered it to the table with great care, wondering what was in it to make it so weighty. Joe flicked aside the catch and lifted the lid; there was nothing inside the chest! "It's heavy," he said, "because it's solid gold. And those"—he pointed to the marble-sized stones—"are star rubies and star sapphires. Here, get the light over your shoulder." As I did so, Joe scrubbed off some accumulated dust with a paper napkin. In each stone there was a bright star-shaped reflection. I was appropriately impressed.

For all his elegant, commanding onstage mannerisms—including a strange pseudo-Oxford-accent affectation—Joe shed it all when he sat down to discuss his favorite topic: conjuring. That interest was a semisecret one, for The Amazing Dunninger was known to the public as a mentalist, "The Master Mind of Mental Radio." He appeared on radio starting in 1943, and on television frequently in the fifties and sixties performing the most astonishing series of stunts that were ever devised by anyone. The list of persons he used in these presentations reads like a *Who's Who.* Jack Dempsey, Bob Dunn, Harry Truman, the Duke of Windsor, or Babe Ruth—it seemed as if Joe Dunninger could reach into anyone's mind at will.

On one occasion, Dunninger had the postmaster general of the United States in position at the main post office in New York City. On his live TV presentation, he asked that official to reach into the thousands of letters going by him on a conveyor belt, and to choose just one. A few minutes of "concentration" and Dunninger wrote down on a large pad of paper what he believed the address was on that letter. You guessed it. When the postmaster read out the address, it was the same as that appearing on Dunninger's pad.

I was all of fifteen when I went to a Wednesday matinee at the Casino Theatre in Toronto to see the man in action. I'd heard him on radio, sponsored by Bigelow Carpets, and I had to see whether he could really do what was claimed. Dr. Joseph Banks Rhine's book *Extrasensory Perception* had claimed my attention, and I believed what I read there, that telepathy had been proven by scientific research. If so, maybe this fellow Dunninger really was a walking example of ESP at work. I had to find out.

Joe Dunninger made a convert that afternoon. No, he didn't persuade me that ESP was real; he did show me that he could convince others of it. It was to be some time before I learned just where Dr. Rhine had gone awry in his conclusions about paranormal powers, and just how naïve many scientists were—and still are—about such matters. But at that point my meeting Dunninger in person was many years away. It was enough that I'd seen him in action, at two consecutive shows, and even been onstage with him as a volunteer.

Yes, I was one of those who trotted up to the stage when Joe asked for "persons who have never met me nor spoken to me—total strangers only, if you please." I sat as instructed, I watched carefully, and I saw a genius at work manipulating all of us who had agreed to be subjects for his "experiments in thought reading." He was magnificent. He gently directed us to do exactly as he wished, while allowing us to believe that we were in control. He orchestrated our responses and managed us with firm authority. And we loved all of it.

With a certain amount of savvy about mentalists' techniques, I was not hard put, sitting on that stage, to detect the methods that were being used by Joe Dunninger. If I'd had to *prove* that he did any specific thing, I'd have been in trouble. But then he approached me, fixed me with a fierce stare, and asked me, "Young man, are you a conjuror?" When I answered that I was, I was asked to return to my seat in the audience, so that "folks won't think that we're in cahoots!"

I was floored, almost literally. I wasn't wearing any giveaway rabbit-in-hat badges, nor did I have a deck of cards sticking out of my pocket. Yet this marvel had *known* that I was a magician, albeit an amateur! How?

That answer was arrived at when I'd had my second viewing of the show, after sitting through the movie that came between. When the answer came, it was accompanied by a very new view of what my art really was. It was no longer just a matter of routines and secret moves; it was a system of imposing my personality on my audience and making them do things *my* way. Joe Dunninger taught me more that day than any other book or person ever taught me. And later, when I got to know Joe well personally, I made sure to tell him about it.

Joseph Dunninger maintained an enigmatic image all of his life. He never quite said that he read minds, but he didn't say that he didn't, or couldn't.

Publicly, he stayed away from magicians and seemed apart from their interests; personally, he loved to talk tricks and to root around in magic shops, particularly that of Al Flosso, his lifetime friend and confidant. Al was one of magic's great characters, who had grown up with the Marx Brothers and with Dunninger. Al was hardly a sophisticated person, but he was loved and respected by everyone in the business, and he could do things with coins and playing cards that made your eyes water with envy.

Dunninger's final series of programs for ABC-TV, recorded in 1971, were never broadcast. By that time he was suffering from Parkinson's Disease and could not summon up the strength of presentation he'd previously displayed.

Joe had, as they say, a way with words. Though he always disclaimed any supernatural powers, he could leave an audience with absolutely no other explanation of what they'd seen. When asked for an answer on the enigma, he had several answers. "Any child of twelve could do what I do," he might say, "—with thirty years practice!" Or, "I'm not a mind reader, I'm a thought reader. If a man comes up to me an' hits me in the eye, I don't have to be a mind-reader to know his thoughts; he dislikes me." As John Fisher has said about Dunninger,

> Perhaps more important was a simpler claim: "I look upon myself as an entertainer." Unlike so many psychic performers, he never abused that position.

Joe often included in his publicity material a quote from Thomas Edison of which he was very proud: "Never have I witnessed anything as mystifying or seemingly impossible."

When Joe came down with his final illness, it was the end of the booming voice and the great dominant personality. He became a tiny, quiet man with an inner glow that was not quite extinguished. I was with him shortly before he died, knowing that I'd never see him alive again. His last words to me, delivered from his wheelchair with a mischievous smile, were "I *was* pretty good, wasn't I?"

Oh yes, Joe. Oh yes.

URI GELLER

In 1972, the American media were busily running accounts of an Israeli mentalist who had astonished not a few scientists by bending spoons and keys and performing a number of other, more standard tricks of the conjuring repertoire, including reading the contents of sealed envelopes. Reaching

Uri Geller and Robert Steiner, national president, 1988–89, of the Society of American Magicians. Bob has stated that Mr. Geller does magic tricks well known to those who study magic.

back as far as the sixteenth century, the handsome young former fashion model borrowed and improved upon such basic tricks as Blindfold Driving and the Obedient Compass, along with a relatively current novelty in which a scrap of metal foil held by a spectator becomes too hot to hold, seemingly through the mental powers of the performer.

In Israel, where the public had not been quite as susceptible as in America, he had been accused of doing tricks when he had promised to do genuine psychic feats; the court assessed costs and the price of the tickets was refunded.

But it was the newest marvel that he later performed—seeming to bend and break metal objects by mind power—that made all the news. That, it seemed, was original with Geller, unlike the other standard routines.

Insisting that his demonstrations were the real thing, Uri Geller traveled the world with his story of having been given his powers through a distant planet called Hoova in another star system, and a UFO called *IS* or "Intelligence in the Sky." The unsteadier portion of the public ate up all this stuff, which sounded very much like bad science fiction, flocking to Geller's performances and making him unquestionably the most charismatic and successful mentalist in history.

The magicians, with very few exceptions, were quick to solve Mr. Geller's numbers. In 1985, Australian conjuror Ben Harris published a definitive book on metal-bending methods, and in Norway, magician-author Jan Crosby amplified that to include the watch trick* and an analysis of the bent-spoon records. In Sweden, *Trollare och Andra Underhållare* ("Magicians

---

*In which a spectator's watch placed face down on his hand is made to advance.

and Other Entertainers") a history of magic by author Christer Nilsson expressed no doubts about the nature of Geller's performances. Writing on the requisites for an effective approach to conjuring, Nilsson said:

> Certainly the first and last point to be made is that the *quality* of a performance is what decides whether it is good or bad. No one nowadays takes a magic trick as a fact; no one believes in black magic. Even though some commercial texts state the opposite, we know that Uri Geller is just another illusionist, nothing more.

But there *was* more to Uri Geller than just his unquestioned skill; he had the charm and charisma to convert admirers into worshippers. The portion of the public who believed him to be a real wizard were so fervent in their belief that they would defend their convictions even when confronted with incontrovertible evidence that he used conjuring methods. Scientist and science fiction author Arthur C. Clarke, who was at one time said by Geller supporters to have been convinced by his tricks, said of such tenacity of belief:

> One thing, however, remains to be explained—the Geller effect. By *this* I mean the ability of one able though perhaps not outstanding magician (though only his peers can judge that) to make such an extraordinary impact on the world, and to convince thousands of otherwise level-headed people that he is genuine, or at any rate, worthy of serious consideration.

Dr. Clarke's observation is well drawn. Even the U.S. scientists who first encountered Mr. Geller were aware of his conjuring tendencies. Parapsychologists Hal Puthoff and Russell Targ clearly knew, in one instance at least, that Geller was showing them a magician's trick. They described it in their book *Mind Reach,* where they said that they "had every confidence that Uri could do that trick [the blindfold drive] as well as any of the dozens of other magicians who do it."

Geller claims that he is now paid large sums of money ($1 million, nonrefundable, just to try) by mining companies to use his psychic abilities for finding gold and oil, sometimes only waving his hands over a map to do so. He celebrates the fact that he has become a multimillionaire twenty-five times over from finding oil this way, though he declines to identify his clients. "It's nice to have money, because you don't have to worry about paying bills and mortgages. . . ." he says.

As an entertainer, a conjuror, and a mentalist, Uri Geller is one of the most convincing and perhaps one of the richest, of them all. But he is a conjuror, not a supernatural being.

DAVID BERGLAS

This artist, the youngest person ever admitted to the rank of MIMC (Member of the Inner Magic Circle), is now president of this very prestigious magicians' club of London. He was at one time a performer of general magic—one of his most remarkable illusions was the suspension of a lady in midair with her head resting on the back of a folding chair—but he now specializes in mentalism.

I was particularly impressed by David's trick in which he tears up an entire newspaper into scraps, then allows members of the audience to instruct him which scraps to keep and which to discard, finally getting down to one bit of paper, and selecting a sentence from that fragment. It turns out to be the sentence he has previously written on a card in a sealed envelope!

When a huge wooden table begins waltzing around the stage under David's direction while being touched by a group of folks from the audience, one could almost believe in spirits!

GLENN FALKENSTEIN AND FRANCES WILLARD

The daughter of Willard the Wizard (1896–1970), a well-known and much-loved magician, Frances was the living projectile in her father's famous Cannon illusion as a child. She says:

> My earliest recollections were as a pigtailed girl of six holding a candle in the wings. That was my first duty as a magician's assistant. I stood in the wings in a white and gold satin military costume, waiting to carry the candle out to my father while he performed. . . .

In 1958, as a teenager, she first performed with the Wizard one of his most mind-boggling routines, an idea that originated with the Davenport Brothers back in 1855: Willard's version of the Spirit Cabinet. Today, it is an important part of Glenn and Frances' act.

In this baffling performance, Frances is seated at an upright post inside a curtained cabinet, and audience members tie her hands behind her with strips of white cloth, then nail the cloth strips firmly to the post. Her neck is secured to the post in the same fashion. In spite of her restraints, after the front curtain is closed Frances causes objects inside the cabinet to fly about, but when Glenn whips back that curtain, she is still tied in position, apparently unconscious. A gentleman spectator, asked to join her inside, ends up with a bucket over his head; his coat has been removed. More than that, when the pair are revealed to the audience, Frances is seen to be wearing his

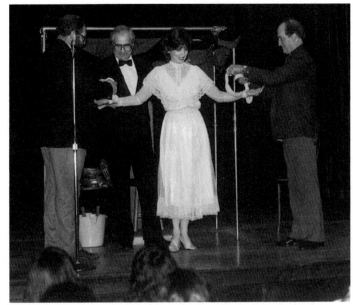

Above left: Glenn Falkenstein and Frances Willard are a popular mentalist team often seen at the Hollywood Magic Castle and industrial shows.

Above right: Glenn Falkenstein directs, while Frances Willard's wrists are firmly tied by two spectators, using strips of cloth. Their presentation of the Spirit Cabinet is exactly like that of Frances' father, Willard the Wizard.

coat, but is also firmly tied! It's about as close to a real miracle as you're going to get.

Glenn Falkenstein, at one time a speech therapist (he has a degree in education), used to have his own radio show as a mentalist. He refuses to claim any psychic powers, though he does things that might easily convince anyone that he is a supernatural wonder. Glenn's specialty, the Eyeless Vision act, is a knockout. He seems to be able to see through half-dollars applied over his eyes with eight lengths of adhesive tape and covered by a real, opaque, steel mask.

Glenn is not only Frances' partner in mentalism, but also her husband. In another routine that emulates the Zancigs and the Piddingtons, the two perform a mind-reading routine that has audiences laughing and puzzling over the apparent telepathy that they are exhibiting. In 1991, Glenn and Frances received the prestigious Dunninger Award from the Psychic Entertainers Association for their "outstanding professionalism and proficiency in the performance of mentalism."

They close their show, whether they're in Las Vegas, at the famous Magic Castle in Hollywood—where they are one of the most popular attractions—or at a trade show, by cautioning the audience:

> We don't foster a belief in spiritualism or the occult. This demonstration was meant for entertainment, and entertainment only.

And, like all good mentalism, it's *great* entertainment.

STEVE SHAW

Steve was born in England and raised in South Africa, and has made the United States his home for many years. His handling of the popular spoon-bending act is superior to any other I've ever seen, a result of much dedicated work on this amusing demonstration. In 1980, along with Michael Edwards, Steve was invited by a famous and well-funded parapsychological laboratory to be tested and examined for psychic powers. At that time, neither of the boys was known as a mentalist or magician, though both had performed locally in their respective towns. The parapsychologists easily accepted them as genuine psychics and until the hoax was voluntarily exposed in 1983 by the boys themselves, the scientists were sure they had proven the existence of supernatural forces.

Project Alpha, as the matter became known, was designed to show that

Mentalist Steve Shaw has developed a touch with the Spoon Bending trick that is just a shade short of supernatural. Steve's one of the Alpha Kids who bamboozled a pair of parapsychologists a few years ago into believing they were really psychic.

scientists are easily deceived and that they usually have inadequate knowledge of conjuring techniques. It was a great success and has resulted in some parapsychologists being more careful about their conclusions.

Though Mike Edwards got a real, honest job and now only performs occasionally in magic, Steve Shaw has gone on to become a ranking professional. He has been buried alive on network television and escaped from six feet down in the ground. In 1984 he performed another Buried Alive stunt, being dug up after three days. He has developed many new angles to standard methods of the mentalists, and as a result has traveled internationally with his act.

ALEXANDER

Billed in 1900 as "The Man Who Knows," Claude Alexander did a regular Oriental-style magic act in the first half of his stage show, but regardless of the high quality of his conjuring, the audience was impatiently waiting for his question-answering second half.

Dressed in a turban and Oriental robes, Alexander asked that questions be written out by his audience on slips of paper, which were then folded up. The slips were collected and spread out before the artist. He held each to his forehead, appeared to divine what the question was, and then provided an appropriately veiled and provocative answer. In spite of the obvious fact that he was a conjuror and trickster, the audience ate up his every word and wanted more. This constitutes both a tribute to his skill and an indication of the great lack of judgment on the part of the spectators.

In 1931, just three years before Alexander's death, young Leon Mandrake purchased his costumes and props and in 1951 obtained the rights to the name and the act.

Mentalism is unique in conjuring in that it is perceived as something that *might* be done by genuine means. The need for some artists to at least encourage that belief is reflected in the existence of The Psychic Entertainers Association, an organization perhaps closer to what conjurors' societies used to be before the turn of the century. It is carefully organized and conducted to maintain a closely limited membership of those who would rather have their skills be suspected to be paranormal. And, who knows, some of those involved may actually believe they can invoke Dark Powers and call upon genuine psychic gifts. Not many, I hope.

CHAPTER 27

THE PICKPOCKETS

One of the specialties entered into by some few conjurors is the pickpocket act. Although the usual methods of the traditional prestidigitator are used, it takes a somewhat different skill to take objects from the pockets and person of a spectator. One part of that skill is to successfully misdirect the attention of the victim.

Many regular magicians have dropped the occasional "dip" stunt into their acts, but we are dealing here with specialists who make the art the major content of their performances.

DOMINIQUE

In 1948, at age sixteen, a Parisian named Dominique Risbourg was doing card manipulations as a professional magician, along with some ventriloquism, but then changed his direction entirely by switching over to pocket picking as an act. Now a popular artist and star at Las Vegas casinos and such famous clubs as the Paris Lido, Dominique (he has used just his first name as a professional) has become known as "The Man with 300,000 Suspenders," from the fact that he estimates he has removed that number of them from the trousers of unsuspecting gentlemen in his audiences. A prominent feature of his act is the Electric Chair number in which a seated audience member leaps up when he seems to have experienced an electric shock. This trick was first developed by English conjuror David Devant, and has been brought to a finely tuned and hilarious routine by Dominique.

Now living outside Paris, where he indulges in his passion for gardening, Dominique returns to the stage whenever he feels the urge—or runs out of suspenders.

DR. GIOVANNI

Dr. Giovanni, born in Budapest as Adolph Herczog just before the turn of the century, was first an acrobat, then a magician. Settling into what was to become his specialty, he claimed the title "King of the Pickpockets." He was a substantial gentleman, and used to advertise that he traveled with "300 kilos of baggage" but that most of the weight was his own body.

I saw him in Tokyo and in Montreal, and it was always exciting to see his brilliant performance. He was assisted by the fact that he overdid his accent, claiming to be amused by his inability to express himself clearly. This allowed him to laugh uproariously at his own predicament, while he draped himself all over his onstage volunteer from the audience, whose pockets were meanwhile being emptied by the seemingly overcome performer. The misdirection was impressive.

During his busy career, the Doctor was asked to perform for President Franklin D. Roosevelt, George VI of England, and Winston Churchill, among others. When I saw him in Japan, he was so popular that he was working *three* clubs at once, and a schedule was published in the newspapers telling his fans where and at what hour he could be seen in the various areas of Tokyo! He would sprint from one club to the other, and the shows were timed to coincide with his availability.

Giovanni always traveled with his entire family in attendance, along with appropriate tutors. He used the title "Doctor" quite honestly, since he had been trained in the medical profession as a young man. Surely, he was brilliant at removing imbedded wallets.

THE BORRA FAMILY

In my estimation, the absolute King of the Pickpockets has to be the man known professionally as Borra. For years, I'd heard rather colorful accounts from other magicians about his incredible skill as a pocket picker, and I'd taken them all with a large grain of salt. When, in 1990, I finally caught the act in Helsinki, I was able to discard my skepticism once and for all.

At the age of fifteen, Borislav Milojkovic was assigned to watch for shoplifters and pickpockets in the family's variety store in Belgrade. The rather specialized education that he received from that employment led him to change any plans he might have had to pursue a conventional trade, and brought about a change of name as well. He joined a local circus, became Borra, King of Pickpockets, and entered into a life of honest crime. He startled his distracted volunteers by deftly extracting wallets, papers, and cash from their pockets and removing their wristwatches without so much as ruffling their sleeves. He was billed then as "The Thief of Baghdad."

Now a citizen of Austria (since 1948), Borra was first professionally "dis-

covered" by Bertram Mills, a prominent English circus owner who signed him up immediately after seeing his act. Since then, he has appeared in countless theaters, salons, and convention halls around the world and has been seen on almost as many television shows from Finland to the United States. He is one of the almost mythical figures of the magical art, always discussed and used as a standard against which other pickpockets are compared.

"My father wanted me to enter the family business," says Borra, "but I told him that what I was doing was absolutely unique, and I went my own way." That decision created an entire family of dedicated thieves. But Borra has learned something about stealing. "One thing I discovered is that it's not difficult to take something away; it's much more difficult to put it back!"

This artist has his own philosophy about the basic drive he experiences. "Sigmund Freud said that there's a criminal down deep in every person. Perhaps I, too, am a kleptomaniac, but I get a double satisfaction: When I take, I give back, and that makes me happy. When I can do that, I don't have to really steal."

Borra speaks fourteen languages, but he doesn't include Finnish and Iranian among them. "I can only do my act and hold simple conversations in those tongues," he says modestly, "so I can't say that I really know the languages."

When he really feels ambitious, this remarkable artist will do the "big" act. Beginning with a series of clever manipulations of billiard balls and other objects, in a manner that would be expected of any standard magic performer, he will suddenly begin removing valuables of various kinds from his pockets and returning them to startled members of the audience who can swear that he never came near them. Actually, if they thought about it, they might remember that a rather odd-looking, fumbling, unsteady, elderly-appearing usher had shown them to their seats, and they might realize that the usher had been Borra himself, in disguise! Their valuables had been taken at that time, without them even suspecting that the King of Pickpockets was the one leading them down the aisle.

When Borra opts to perform in a simpler manner, he begins with the usual sleight-of-hand demonstration; then he wanders into the audience to carefully select three persons, whom he seats upon the stage. These subjects then lose just about everything in their pockets, as well as their neckties, belts, and even suspenders. Of course, their watches are in Borra's pockets before they even take their seats onstage. When one spectator finally makes his way back into the audience, he finds that his glasses have been taken from him *while he was wearing them* and that Borra himself is now wearing them. The expression on that man's face, as he realizes how he has been duped, is something to see.

What Borra refers to as his present "semiretirement" brings him away from his comfortable life as a gentleman farmer in Graz, Austria, to tour for as many as eight months of the year. The man who says, "I have pocket picking in my blood" finds it difficult to stay off the stage and away from the applause. He cannot resist being back at work, to the continuing delight of his enthusiastic fans.

The King of Pickpockets also busies himself away from home as a consultant to police departments and agencies such as Scotland Yard and Interpol, for which he acts as an advisor on card cheats and—of course—pocket pickers. He has over two hundred diplomas, certificates, and letters that express the gratitude of those he has instructed in the art of detecting fraud. He is an honorary member of Interpol and an Honorary Master Detective of the Zurich police force; in Bern, Switzerland, he has been extended a most

peculiar privilege: Should Bori-
slav Borra ever be arrested in that jurisdiction, he can demand
a private cell.

There are two Borra brothers who are also doing the act. Borra II is
Dragisa Borra, an older brother, and Borra III is Vojislav, two years younger
than Borislav. Then there's Charly Borra, the son of Borra I—that's
Borislav, in case you got lost along the way. In all, four Borras are robbing
innocent citizens, to the delight of their audiences all over the world.

In the United States, pickpocket Ricki Dunn, who began his professional
career as a fire eater, is currently prominent as a club performer, billed as
"America's Funniest Pickpocket." Bob Arno is seen in Las Vegas. In the
1960s U.K. artist Vick Perry was a very popular international performer of
the nimble-fingered art. Denmark's Tommy Willy Jörgen Iverson performed as Gentleman Jack in Europe in the sixties and seventies, then
retired from professional thievery in 1980. His prize student, Kenny Queen,
carries on the trade. Sweden's Svedino, Gérard Majax in France, Mark Raf-
fles, and Mac Freddy are regularly found dipping into the pockets of European audiences.

Above left: Borra directs the attention of an audience member to his wallet . . . Above center: Having mean-while removed the spec-tator's glasses without being detected, Borra now returns his wallet to him, while looking at that spectator through his own glasses! Above right: The spectator checks his wallet once more as he prepares to return to his seat, still unaware that Borra is wearing his glasses!

CHAPTER 28

THE CHILDREN'S ENTERTAINERS AND THE STREET WORKERS

Entertaining children is a specialized art. Entertaining children with magic is very, very much a specialized art. I regret to say that not many young magical artists today go in for this branch of magic, which demands much patience and experience. Most of us professionals earned our first fees working at birthday parties, then moved on to entertaining adults, leaving the kids to others. There is a very rich market for the conjuror in children's entertainment, which is largely ignored.

'Twas not always so, for when I was young, parents looked up magicians in the phone book, where some bravely advertised that they were kids' performers. One was a bouncy little man with a big booming voice who taught me most of what I knew in magic before I came to know the community of magicians in my hometown of Toronto.

JOHNNY GIORDEMAINE

This diminutive wizard from Malta arrived in Toronto as an immigrant when he was very young. He trained as an electrician and worked at that trade for ten years with the telephone company. Then he suffered a severe electric shock during his work and was almost paralyzed, losing his power of speech and much of his coordination. Determined to overcome this disability, Johnny subscribed to the Tarbell Course, a correspondence system for learning magic. It was such effective therapy that he soon regained all his capabilities, and then some. He was soon one of the finest manipulators in the business.

Johnny Giordemaine changed direction and became a professional conjuror. He toured Europe and the United States and in 1933 returned to Canada to become the first magician there to ever appear on television, a closed-circuit arrangement in the T. Eaton Company, a local store. I was just ten years old when I first met him on a Saturday morning at Eaton's store in Toronto, where he functioned as the resident magician. It was the beginning of a series of endless Saturday morning visits during which he made time in between customers to instruct the few kids who came by for that treat.

Johnny and I were the same height. In fact, all the kids were as tall as Johnny, a bundle of energy and enthusiasm who made children's entertainment his specialty. He would always get a great reaction from his audience as he finished some especially good trick, took his bows, and then announced brightly, "You know, I've been doing this ever since I was small!"

Aside from being incredibly facile with his manipulation of oversize billiard balls (he could hold *five* of them in one of his tiny hands!), Johnny Giordemaine was quick, frenetic, and full of self-amazed expressions that greatly pleased his small fans. He was a popular, ever-busy artist who pretty well was Mr. Magic for my generation and locality.

Well after I had entered my teens, I would accompany Johnny to some of his shows, just to watch him in action and learn a bit more about handling difficult audiences. On one such pilgrimage to a small farming community, we met the One in Charge (that's who you always asked for immediately on arrival) and were solemnly led to the backstage area, where Johnny was shown a handsome wooden wheelbarrow, painted gold! Without hesitation, the little wizard began setting his props into the barrow, but the moment the One in Charge was out of earshot, Johnny began laughing heartily. He explained to me that the year before, when he appeared at this affair, he had broken one leg of his magic table and had to request another. None could be found on such short notice, and in desperation, he had seized upon a wheelbarrow to serve as his table. Yes, the entertainment committee, believing that Johnny always worked out of a wheelbarrow, had prettied one up for him for this year! And yes, he did the show just as they expected him to.

For the long hours that Johnny Giordemaine spent behind his counter in the department store patiently coaching us kids in the art that a few of us actually opted to follow in later years, I hope he was well rewarded. Of course he was.

ALI BONGO

Arabs of the world, unite! There is an Englishman who sports a monstrous turban and ridiculous shoes with turned-up toes, and who for his burlesque of an Arabian wizard should be put to every imaginable Persian pain and

Ali Bongo is the consummate jester of England, seen frequently on television and in theaters entertaining children and adults alike with his show, The Shriek of Araby. *He also acts as advisor to other stars of magic like Paul Daniels, designing new tricks and routines for them.*

Turkish torture. Except for the fact that children all over the United Kingdom adore his madness, that is.

Ali Bongo, to use his professional name, was born in India and is the premier children's magical entertainer in England. His very wide exposure on television has made him a familiar figure there, and the highly eccentric costume and movements are designed to attract the kids' attention and keep it. His show, *The Shriek of Araby,* is pursued by Ali whenever he is not being sought out and kept busy by the top professional magicians as a technical advisor, for he is highly informed on the illusion business.

One advantage of highly exaggerated makeup is that it allows the performer to vanish by simply washing up. Ali can thus escape the mobs of urchins who would otherwise follow him down the street wherever he went. Long may he delight us.

THE STREET WORKERS

In Greek and Roman times, there were magicians in the streets, bringing oohs and ahs from their customers and passing the hat, or bonnet, or helmet for contributions. Around 1420, Englishman John Rikil was one of the famous street buskers of Henry V's reign. A Mr. Brandon entertained the subjects of Henry VIII from 1521 to 1535, and Thomas Stanley did the same for those of Mary I in 1554. In the late 1800s the streets of Paris, served as a stage for the "Zouave," and with the 1900s came Claudius Odin. In the British Isles, a hairpin of a man named Carlton worked in 1895; Solly

Left: This early German engraving shows how the Cups & Balls performance was so much a part of conjuring repertoires of the day. The magician is plucking a ball from the spectator's nose. Below left: Loyal James flings a straitjacket skyward after wriggling out of it, to the delight of his outdoor audience. When not street-performing, Loyal is often seen with his wife Debbi (AbracaDebra), his son, Loyal, and daughter, Maja. He has worked with Vincent Price and Tony Curtis on television, and has toured in the Orient as an escape artist. He has also held world records for being sealed in an ice tomb and for lying on a bed of nails. Says James of his street performances, "The sun and the moon are my spotlights."

A street performer in London's Leicester Square shows an Asian visitor an old Oriental trick.

Busker Frank Smith, known as the Gypsy Man, trusses up his young assistant, Lee Corcoran, in a burlap sack and chains.

Lee is laid out in the afternoon sun while Frank makes the rounds, collecting coins from anxious spectators.

The collection is complete; Lee is free in a matter of seconds and ready to start again. Lee's grandfather, John Eagle, is in the Guinness Book of World Records *as a strongman.*

Mack and Tom Reid followed in 1900, and Wilf Higgins in 1907. At that time, William Charles Payne reigned in London as Professor Du Payne, The Prince of Street Magicians, and the fabulous Cardini, before he came indoors as the suave befuddled drunk, was seen in the streets in 1919.

The current revival has featured Philippe Petit, the wirewalker who was to startle New Yorkers and the world by leaving the streets where he performed as a magician, juggler, and acrobat to walk between the Twin Towers of the World Trade Center in 1966. A fine artist named Jeff Sheridan has been working in New York City from 1967. Harry Anderson, now so well known for his part in TV's *Night Court*, worked the streets of San Francisco in the seventies. Mal Cross, he of the ferocious mustache and wild costume, Bill McQueen with his fast hands, and young Mike Rubenstein are currently seen on the pavements of American cities. Citizens of Budapest enjoy the charm of Alex (Sándor Horváth) and reward him generously for his skill.

Street working is the ultimate crucible, the sternest test and the greatest challenge for the magician. Great respect is due the artist who chooses to pit his wit and skill against an audience that can move about freely, defeat his attempt to control their viewpoint, arrive or leave at any point, and insolently insult and challenge his earnest efforts. Winning over that sort of audience is difficult at best and sometimes thankless. Often, the hat is empty and so is the stomach of the conjuror, and frequently that is not his fault at all. These are brave guys indeed.

Above left: This charming gentleman was demonstrating and selling simple magic tricks in the streets of Paris, 1947. I captured the moment before the box of matches snapped shut. Above right: Hungarian magician Alex works in Budapest, where the law still frowns on street performers, much to the dismay of the tourists.

Street performer Alipio
directs his audience's
attention skyward. The
control of a spectator's
attention that can be
attained by a skilled
conjuror is no better
illustrated than in this
photo, taken in a square
in Brussels, Belgium.

ALIPIO

Gather 'round. To my mind, this man is the archetypal street performer, and he will serve, willy-nilly, in that function. He possesses all the cunning, charm, and fascination that are displayed by the many others I've seen, most of them nameless and wandering gypsies. He is the mountebank, the charlatan, the Pied Piper who I fear may be vanishing from our streets.

Another magician, my friend Gilles-Maurice de Schryver, introduced me to Spanish-born Alipio in the Great Square of Brussels, where he was holding an audience in thrall. His control of the crowd, the utter delight with which the children reacted, and the astonishment of the adults all attested to his skill as an open-air artist. A small, slender man in shirtsleeves, he could have functioned in the streets of medieval Belgium with exactly the same effect, though with somewhat more chance of being burned at the stake.

Alipio's philosophy about street work is interesting. He believes that this kind of conjuring pays ten times less, and is ten times as hard as any other sort, but he wouldn't change his direction for any reason. The advantages, to him, are enormous: He can choose his audiences, and he can choose whether or not to work. Since the work is seasonal, five months of the year he labors hard under the sky, then spends the rest of the year creating new ideas and routines. He says:

> My concept of the street magician is this: you arrive in a city you
> don't know, where people speak a language that you don't speak, without any magic props, wearing only the costume. You leave the train or
> airplane with *one* coin in your pocket and two or three weeks later you

Another example of the total control Alipio has over his audience's attention. All eyes are on the playing card that flutters down from nowhere. They are all wondering, will it be the one selected a moment ago by the young spectator? But of course it will!

go home with your own magic props on a first-class ticket, not a dollar or a franc in debt, and a lot of money left over.

I need hardly tell you that Alipio delights in long hours of coffee and conversation with magicians who buttonhole him for after-hours conferences. Unless a café closes its doors on such a group, they will gab and prestidigitate through the dawn, eager to demonstrate or to witness some subtlety of hand or mind that will enrich their experience of the magical art. Balled-up paper napkins and scruffy playing cards are manipulated repeatedly to illustrate a point, and arguments over the merit or lack of merit of some turn of the wrist will occupy much heated discussion time. They are golden hours indeed, to the aficionado. To see Alipio at one of those sessions is a treat.

Alipio also juggles, sells tops and yo-yos, and turns all his talents to making a living in the open air. Like the other street workers, he's an honest, happy soul who owns his own business, has a small overhead, pays his debts, and leaves his customers happy. What else can a man ask for?

CHAPTER 29

FAR EASTERN WONDERS, THEN AND NOW

An account of magic in early China is told in the illustrated book *Xin Xi Gu Yue Tu* and tells of two typical tricks of conjurors in the T'ang dynasty about A.D. 750. They are "Spouting Fire" and "Eating a Knife." Both are illustrated here. The book relates that when the latter trick was done "the knife enters the mouth in six parts." Whether that means in six consecutive stages or in six pieces is not made clear. A trick said to be of Korean origin, "Hiding in the Jar," was said to also be popular at that time. In this presentation, there were two large empty jars on two separate tables. A person was seen to enter one jar and then emerge from the other. In modern conjuring parlance, this would be known as a transposition. We are told that an Indian trick, "Lying on the Sword," which is not described, was also to be frequently seen in the T'ang period. This reference is probably to the Sword Suspension trick in which the "suspendee" is lying in the air on the tip of a scimitar.

As early as the Ming dynasty (1368–1644) Chinese conjurors were doing the same Decapitation trick as that described in 1584 by English writer Reginald Scot in *The Discouerie of Witchcraft*. The Chinese called the trick head-growing (the best translation!), and a Master Du was reported to have performed the following routine. He placed his own son on a bench, apparently cut off his head with a broadsword, and covered the two parts with a cloth. He then took up a collection from the onlookers before circling around the body several times and restoring the boy to life.

The story is also told that one day Master Du was performing his marvel

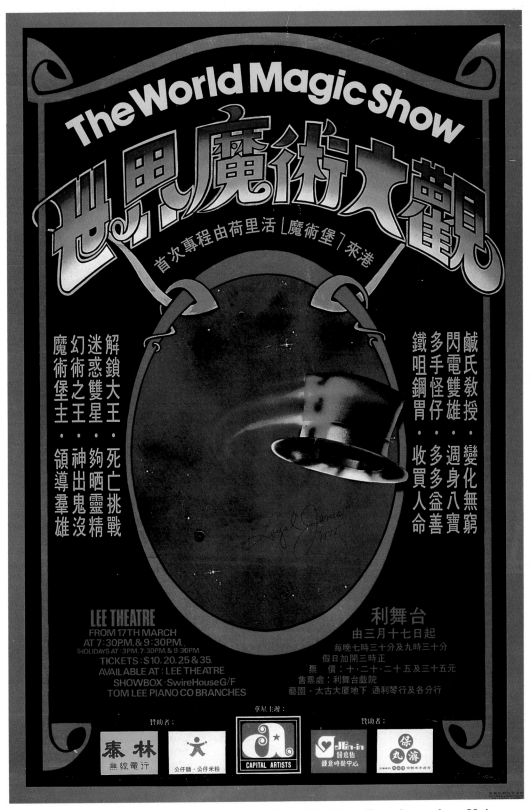

Loyal James is advertised in this poster used for a 1976 Hong Kong theater show. He is "The Man Who Cheats Death." Other stars on this show were Peter Pit, Peter De Paula, and illusionist Chuck Jones.

信西古乐图细部：卧剑

Above left: Illustration from Xin Xi Gu Yue Tu *showing T'ang Dynasty artists performing the "Spouting Fire" and "Eating a Knife" tricks. Above right: This somewhat unrealistic illustration gives an idea of the "Resting on a Sword Point" trick that has been a popular illusion in the repertoire of Oriental magicians for many centuries now.*

when a passing monk laughed at the wrong moment. Du was thus unable to make the restoration as planned, and he pleaded with the audience to punish the monk so that things could proceed as usual. Obtaining no response, Du "planted a calabash and it grew up right away." Once more asking the monk to apologize and receiving a refusal, Master Du replied, "Well, you force me to do this," whereupon he struck the calabash off the vine with the sword, and the monk's head fell to the ground. The boy, I'm happy to report, survived nicely. How is that I miss witnessing these marvels?

The story of Master Du's problem seems to combine the Mango Tree trick and the Decapitation into one garbled and doubtful story. I'd like to speak to the monk, please. . . .

Historians of magic have always credited the Japanese magician Kuma (also known as Kim Yen Soo) with the invention of an excellent illusion involving two large cylinders, one nested inside the other. Kuma lived from 1884 to 1963, and I had the privilege of seeing him perform in 1944. However, it appears that Kuma was only perpetuating a routine that rather predated him. A painting some five hundred years older depicts a trick that is described thus:

The conjuror manipulates two empty tubes with his hands. He takes from them vegetables, fruits, cups, bowls and even a full evening meal. More surprisingly, he at last takes out a jar full of wine, but the jar is so

Left: Kuma was apprenticed to a magician in Japan at age five and made his debut at eight. He moved to the U.S.A. in 1904, then was known as Kim Yen Soo, and insisted, during World War II, that he was Korean. Among magicians, he is credited as the inventor of a trick now known as the Kuma Tubes, but this shows up in fourteenth-century Ming dynasty records as being old, even then. Right: These Chinese magicians are performing an earlier version of the Kuma Tubes trick that Kim Yen Soo perfected. From two nested cylinders, repeatedly shown empty, a large quantity of silk ribbons and kerchiefs are produced, followed by a jar of water which is too large for either of the tubes to fit over!

big that the tube cannot then cover it! This is the well-known Magic Tubes trick. . . . Often, living animals are taken from the tube, even monkeys. . . . The conjuror takes rice from the tube, several times more rice than the tube could possibly hold, then puts all the rice back into the tube, and the rice just disappears. This is known as, "The Rice Back to the Barn."

In 1830 we find a record that the first company of Chinese "jugglers" arrived in Britain. Remember that juggling, conjuring, and acrobatics are all part of the same school, in the Oriental classification. The troupe advertised that they were from "the Court of Pekin" and performed at Saville House, No. 1, Leicester Square. They introduced the Linking Rings trick, which used eight steel rings that linked and unlinked in amazing configurations. This is one of the very oldest tricks in recorded history, and was so effective that it was copied in 1834 by the English conjuror Jacobs, who also "borrowed" a few other Oriental tricks. This Court of Pekin troupe also did fire eating and the production of ribbons from the mouth, both common, basic tricks of Oriental conjurors. The program described one of their numbers thus:

> From under a green carpet, on which the performers walk, and where it appears impossible that anything can be concealed, an immense Flower Pot is produced, and afterwards a large Basin is exhibited (as if by magic) full of Water. . . . A great quantity of shreds of white paper is cut small and put in a basin of water and covered up, which on removing the cover is discovered to be a perfect string of Red Paper of nearly a hundred yards.

The East Indian Needle trick, already seen in Britain by that time, consisted of the performer swallowing a number of sewing needles and a length

Above left: Young Japanese artist Mahka Tendo manages to startle his Western colleagues by performing minor miracles that defy tradition. His work with cards is second to none, and he has become a favorite at magicians' conventions all over the world.

of thread, drinking a glass of water, and then coughing up the long sequence of needles threaded at intervals.

(The most impressive performance of this startling trick that I have *ever* seen—among many, many performances I've witnessed over the years—was by Teller of the Penn & Teller team. I do not think that performance can be improved upon.)

In 1854 Tuck Quy and troupe came to London via Peking, Hong Kong, San Francisco, and New York, where they were seen by John Henry Anderson (the Great Wizard of the North), who sent them to England. They played in Liverpool, then went on to the Drury Lane Theatre in London, but since their tricks were much the same as those of the other Oriental troupes that had already been through that area, they caused little excitement.

That was one of the problems. Oriental magic, until very recently, did not change at all. Even today, the street performers of the Orient each do the same predictable though clever routines. You've seen one, you've seen 'em all. Only with the entry of the Japanese in the last fifteen years has there been a great change in the Oriental approach to the art. Young Japanese performers, in particular, have shown originality, dedication, and skill of a most impressive magnitude. They have stepped out of the mold in which their ancestors were cast, and brought striking new techniques and fresh ideas into existence.

Early on, there really was no great difference between Indian and Chinese performers, except for their basic costumes. Though the tricks now often include very westernized items, there is still little difference. Early Indian conjurors might perform the Mango Tree trick, in which a seed is covered with a cloth, and each time it is uncovered a bigger and bigger plant is discovered, culminating in a fully grown shrub bearing real mangoes. For their contribution, the Chinese team might be doing the same trick with a melon seed, ending up with a number of ripe melons. Both groups would be doing the Basket trick, wherein an assistant is placed in a wicker basket through which swords and spears are stuck at every imaginable angle, with the result that the assistant still emerges intact. But the Chinese might use a lacquered box for the purpose. Today, Mexico's Joaquin Ayala regularly does the Basket trick for Las Vegas audiences; he uses flaming torches, showing that the tried-and-true routines are still earning reputations for the practitioners.

In 1867, the Reverend Justus Doolittle, a missionary in China for many years, published *The Social Life of the Chinese*, a book in which he described as common entertainments the ever popular Linking Rings trick, growing a melon from seed, any number of dismembering-a-boy routines, the East Indian Needle trick, sword swallowing and fire eating. Of course the usual incredible juggling feats and heart-stopping acrobatics were also reported.

In that same year, the first Japanese troupe landed in Britain. Their repertoire was mostly balancing, but the Butterfly Trick, in which the colorful insects, torn from tissue paper, were made to fly about the stage propelled by rapidly manipulated paper fans, was also featured. Later, the Royal Tycoon Troupe of Japan appeared at the Egyptian Hall, long before Maskelyne & Cooke ever got there. In 1928, the Ko Ten Ichi (also Ychi), Ten-Ichi and Ten-Ji troupes, who had first begun arriving in Britain in 1908, were still attracting audiences. They featured the Thumb Tie, a trick in which the performer's thumbs were tightly bound together with cord, and yet hoops could be caught over the arms and the conjuror otherwise showed that he could free himself, though upon examination he would be found immediately retied. Manuscripts describing how to perform the Thumb Tie have been on sale in magic shops ever since.

Japanese conjurors specialized in a fountain effect, too. They walked about the stage touching tables, persons, and spots on the floor, from which water then spouted. They appeared to pick up a jet of water and place it anywhere on the stage. The American Dante featured this in his big stage show at the beginning of this century. The trick can still occasionally be seen in modern Japanese performances, and in 1988 I saw it done in Beijing by a Chinese acrobatic and magic group.

St. George's Hall in 1921, while Maskelyne and Devant were there, hosted Lingha-Singh, described as a "Hindoo." Long Tack Sam, a popular Chinese magic star, appeared at the London Coliseum in 1922 with his color-

A colorful poster for the Ko Ten Ychi Troupe, showing their performance of the Fountains trick. The artist has a poor idea of how water behaves, and everyone appears quite dry.

Above: An ad from the 1912 catalog of Oaks the Magician selling the description of how to perform the Ten Ichi Thumb Tie trick. Right: Butterflies cut from tissue paper were made to flutter realistically about the stage by Japanese artists. "Paper Magic" is one of the traditional divisions of magic, along with Fire, Water, and Silk magic.

fully costumed cast, doing the traditional water-bowl productions and live-stock tricks. Han Ping Chien featured the Linking Rings, Cups & Balls, paper tearing and restoring, and bowl production.

Lu Chang Fu was a magician who worked mainly in Germany and in England in the 1930s. He displayed his skill at the Miser's Dream, the But-terfly trick, the Needle trick, and his own version of the Floating Ball. He was known for his presentation of Sands of the Desert, in which various brightly colored sands were mixed together by stirring them into a large clear glass bowl of water, then separated out again by the magician merely reaching into the water and taking up a fistful of *dry* sand of any color called for. It was a charming example of Oriental conjuring, also performed in the 1950s by American Fred Keating and brought back to attention by the Canadian magician Doug Henning in the 1960s.

Though the influence of Western magic, as such, only began to take effect in China about 1915, it was taken up with great enthusiasm, particularly in Shanghai. That city, with its interesting mix of cultures from both East and West, is considered the center of conjuring in China today, and many pro-fessional performers make their homes there. One of the leading native per-formers is Mo Wu Qi, considered a pioneer of the art. He has managed to incorporate Western ideas into the traditional Chinese performance.

Another is Ke Tian Ying, who is active translating Western manuscripts and books on magic into Chinese.

Born in 1889 in Panama, Li-Ho Chang was one of the major magicians to perform in South America and around the world with a huge show. He entered the profession in a strange way. At age twenty-two, he was a conductor on a small train that ran the one-hour trip between Panama City and Colón. He'd never had any interest in magic, but when a visiting magician arrived in Colón and began commuting daily to Panama City on the train, Chang became acquainted with him and was invited to see the show. Chang lived in Panama City, but frequently would stay overnight in Colón after a late show, and his interest in magic was kindled.

Chang said that once, in Africa, he performed his Black Art act in which luminous skeletons danced on a darkened stage. When the lights went up to the expected applause, silence reigned. The theater was empty.

He was a poor manager of his money, and though he was a millionaire—in U.S. dollars—four times during his career, there were occasions such as the one in Paris when he had to sell his typewriter in order to eat. His full show, which he toured until 1955 when he closed it in Spain, was titled *"Una Noche en el Palacio Encantado de Pekin"* ("A Night in the Enchanted Palace of Peking"). He was an inspiration to David Bamberg (Fu Manchu).

The present Oriental contributions to conjuring are fast becoming evident in the Western repertoire. While Occidental magicians have always relied on a number of tricks and ideas of Oriental origin (Rice Bowls, Chinese Linking Rings, and so on) those are of ancient vintage. Today, spectacular recent innovations in manipulative technique are challenging Western performers to keep up with their Oriental colleagues.

Young performers from Japan are causing a great sensation in the field. The Napoleons—Koishi and Ueki—are a comedy magic duo very well known in that country from their frequent TV appearances and their own TV series. They are perhaps best described as the Japanese version of Penn & Teller, and are frequently seen at magic conventions around the world. Tomohiro Maeda, a new face in magic, has specialized in "table magic" and works full time at this difficult branch of the art. He is said to be the first full time professional Japanese specialist in this type of magic. With spectators seated across from him and at his very elbows in the Tycoon Club of Tokyo, he does wonderful sleight of hand and confounds them all.

Shintaro Fujiyama of Japan is a master of both traditional and modern magic. His handling of knotting and unknotting silks has to be seen to be believed. I recall that in a lecture he gave to professional magicians in the United States, he described silk handkerchiefs as "feminine" and ropes as "masculine." As only an Oriental artist could, he then demonstrated how one ties knots in each of the two materials, gently with the silks and firmly with the ropes. It was a lesson that the more astute of his listeners found

Above left: Shintaro Fujiyama, besides his wonderful manipulations with silk kerchiefs and ropes, features large illusions in his show. Here he is assisted by Tomiko. Above right: Fukai & Kimika, relying heavily on traditional Japanese props and costumes adapted to modern tastes, pluck an endless number of parasols out of thin air and fill the stage with them. Left: Russian conjuror Kio, surrounded by the circus performers, severs a woman in two with a saw.

Above left: The Magic Napoleons are refreshingly funny, original, and highly entertaining artists who are very well known as television hosts and club entertainers in Japan. Above right: Young Tomohiro Maeda of Japan specializes in close-up sleight-of-hand marvels, particularly with playing cards.

quite compelling, and such nuances are the reason for Fujiyama's great success internationally.

Though it's pretty obvious that parasols fold up much smaller than their full size, when the team of Fukai and Kimika begin plucking them out of the air onstage, it soon becomes evident that they will never run out of them. In a matter of minutes they can fill an entire stage with colorful parasols from the size of dinner plates to monstrous ones that are arranged in cascades and release masses of sparkling confetti everywhere. These are attractive people who have specialized, to their great advantage and to our delight.

Jewel Aich is a writer, teacher, and magician in Bangladesh who tours a full evening show, assisted by his wife Bipasha. He specializes in mental effects as well as major illusions, some of which are his own inventions. He has done four world tours and is well known to his colleagues in magic all over the globe.

CHAPTER 30

MODERN WIZARDS

ROBERT HARBIN

There are few artists in magic who earned as excellent a reputation among peers as Robert "Ned" Harbin. Born in South Africa, he took up permanent residence in England, where he became well known for his cabaret and television work.

He was a performer, inventor, innovator, and creative genius. Above all, he was generous and caring to all. One of the most popular and effective illusions now being used onstage, the Zig-Zag Girl, is his creation. The subject is placed in a standing position inside a narrow upright box, and metal blades are inserted from side to side just above her middle and just below. The middle section of the lady is slid over to one side, effectively dividing her into three zigzagged pieces! As usual with these operations, all is made right again—with any luck.

I first met Harbin and his wife, Dolly, when they arrived in Canada to astound Toronto audiences; I was a teenager then. In his hotel room, Ned patiently taught me a version of a classic card-trick that I still perform to this day. Every time I perform this minor miracle I think of his kindness.

Harbin wrote books on origami, the Japanese art of paper-folding. He was quite adept at it, and at one time had his own weekly television show in Britain demonstrating and teaching the process. He took genuine delight in creating birds and other animals from scraps of paper and giving them away to young folks who even today treasure these souvenirs.

Robert Harbin's contributions were remarkable indeed. He inspired many of us and left behind him many wonderful memories.

Top left: Milbourne Christopher was a performer, writer, historian, and collector in the magic field. He was a president of the Society of American Magicians and his colleagues honored him in every way possible for his contributions to the art. Top right: Frederick Eugene Powell, a teacher who changed into a magician, toured the U.S.A., South America, and the West Indies with large and small effects. He performed a spectacular cremation trick titled "She." Powell became known as the Dean of American Magicians. He died in 1938. Lower left: Mexico's Ali Kazam (Luis Roberto Rivas) casts his spell. Lower right: Jamy Ian Swiss describes himself as "An Honest Liar." A young man of prodigious skill, Jamy was born in Brooklyn and now lives in New York City. Constantly traveling, performing at industrial shows, nightclubs, and theaters around the world, he is a prolific writer and lecturer as well and a popular artist at magicians' conventions.

SHIMADA

A gift from Japan is the remarkable Haruo Shimada, who was first interested in magic when he got a job demonstrating tricks at the Tenyo Magic Shop in Tokyo. Not long after that, his act had developed to the point where he was invited to a command performance before Emperor Hirohito.

Shimada was one of the many young artists who was inspired by Channing Pollock and his innovative dove magic. He put his own distinctive touch on the manipulation of cards and billiard balls, and while touring with his show in Australia he met and married Deanna, who has been an important part of his act ever since. Together, they toured twenty countries over the next few years.

Up to this point, the act had been done in Western-style costume, a modified tail suit. Shimada decided that to satisfy his repeat customers, a second, Eastern-costumed and -styled act would have to be developed. That act, a very complex and colorful production, is spectacular indeed. Marvelous

Above left: Marco the Magnificent has been doing the Chinese Linking Rings for fourteen years in the show Le Grand David. Above right: Le Grand David and Company "family" show plays regularly in Beverley, Massachusetts. It has been running now for years, and shows no signs of slowing down.

masks and robes, fire and smoke, a full-size dragon, fans, and parasols fill the stage to dazzle the senses. At the end, no matter how closely you watch, you will be amazed at an instantaneous transformation in which Deanna becomes Haruo.

An anecdote here might take the reader behind the scenes a bit. Working on a special television show in Pittsburgh years ago with major artists like David Copperfield, Shimada, Richard Ross, and Ballantine,* I was performing the Milk Can escape. This involved my being locked into a large steel can full of water, after which a curtained enclosure was quickly dropped around it and the audience waited expectantly to see me make my exit from the enclosure. Now, I think I will not surprise you to admit that though my release from the device was accomplished rather quickly, I chose to remain atop the can for a bit longer to build the tension.

The stage configuration was such that neither the audience nor the cameras could see into the top of the curtain, so that was left open. However, there was a "catwalk" passing immediately above the whole affair, out of sight to everyone out front. As I emerged from the confinement and perched waiting for the exactly right moment to plunge through to the audience, gasping for breath (aren't we crafty devils?), I was shocked to hear, over the enthusiastically roaring orchestra, a voice saying, "Gee, David, that

*Carl Ballantine was also one of the stars of the TV series "McHale's Navy."

Top left: Multiple award-winner Michael Ammar's photo emphasizes the "golden hand" that has made him famous as a leading close-up performer. He's the son-in-law of the Falkenstein-Willard team. Just think of the kids who might soon be making an appearance on the magic scene with that DNA going for them! Top right: Scott Cervine is only one of many magicians using the Chinese Linking Rings to astonish his audiences. Scott, a multiple award-winner in the art, surprises everyone by ending his act floating above the stage! Lower left: The performer known simply as Angel combines rock music and magic in a colorful presentation that is rich in decibels, flames, smoke, and confetti. It certainly does manage to keep your attention. Angel breaks a few rules to achieve an exciting concept in the art. Lower right: If you can manage to disregard Paula Paul's remarkable beauty, you'll find that her magic performance is professional and captivating.

doesn't look too hard to do!" and looking up, I saw Copperfield and Shimada calmly leaning on the catwalk and witnessing the performance from an angle I'd never expected. "No, Shimada," answered Copperfield casually, "I think I'll put it in my next show." And the two magicians, dressed in their costumes in preparation for the grand finale that was to follow my number, turned and walked away, grinning as if their faces would break. Helplessly, I broke out laughing and had to quickly suppress it as I staggered through the curtain to face my appreciative audience.

But I had my revenge, at least on Shimada. Months later I was in a Los Angeles TV complex to do an interview show, and a stagehand commented to me that Shimada was in the next studio setting up the Great Dragon act, which was a very long, involved process. Sensing an opportunity, I sneaked

Above left: Souvenir program of Germain the Wizard (Karl Mattmüller, 1878–1959) who retired from the stage at age thirty-three, studied law, and was admitted to the Ohio bar, then went blind. Above right: In his performance of the classic Metamorphosis trick used by Houdini, rock musician–magician Angel uses a wall of flame and smoke rather than a curtain to conceal the action for the few seconds required to make the startling transformation.

into that studio and saw Haruo stripped to his shorts and straining mightily to get the pieces of his dragon prop together, mumbling to himself what I assumed were terrible Oriental oaths. He was unaware of my presence and obviously having a difficult time.

I tiptoed to within a few feet of him and just as I did, the half-assembled dragon rolled over and fell into some half-dozen pieces. Seeing my chance, I struck. "Gee!" I said, walking by Haruo in his distress. "That looks like an easy act to do! I'll have to get me one of those dragon things!" And I continued strolling right off the stage and out into the hall, smiling like the Cheshire Cat. I didn't look back. You don't, at great moments like that.

By now, I think Shimada has forgiven me. But I still owe Copperfield. . . .

FRAKSON

Frakson was a perfect example of the "cabaret artist." It's a little difficult to define cabaret work. Nightclubs, usually with tiny stages awkwardly placed, at one time provided employment for many magicians. Resorts,with bigger and better stages, came along and attracted more such artists. Generally speaking, there were performers who did not regularly work legitimate theaters, choosing to specialize in smaller venues. Such acts would usually do about ten to twelve minutes of fast-moving action.

Frakson was born in Spain in 1891, and first worked professionally under

Left: The Great Virgil is seen here levitating his chief assistant and wife, Julie, just before he passes a solid metal hoop over her body. Below left: Siegfried & Roy hold Las Vegas audiences spellbound with their beautiful animals and spectacular stage effects, vanishing a Brahma bull and changing a man into this tiger.

the name "D'Olivarès." He soon attained fame as a cigarette manipulator, and his success at this specialty had much to do with popularizing it among magicians. Almost all of Frakson's publicity photos show cigarettes in one form or another, and at one time no one who practiced manipulation could hope to omit lit cigarettes from the repertoire. He also dazzled audiences with his Salt trick, performed with special cross-lighting that emphasized the salt grains as they poured from his hand. To perform, he would empty a salt shaker into his closed fist, then open it to show the salt gone. A moment

At the Black Cat, the Moscow magic theater, Rafael & Elena offer a lavish stage show in the grand manner. The team has earned several prizes at international magicians' conventions.

later he'd reach into the air, make a grasping motion, and a stream of salt would begin trickling from his fist, getting more and more copious until what seemed like several pounds of salt had cascaded onto a huge square of blue velvet laid on the floor before him.

Another of his featured tricks was the Vanishing Bird Cage, accompanied by his charmingly accented patter.

He retired to politically troubled Spain in 1931 with $300,000—a very large sum for that time and country—and prepared to settle down and enjoy life with his family, but one night he was warned by some friends that the Federales were on their way to lock him up, and he fled. All his property was seized by the Franco regime, as part of the funding for the coming Spanish Civil War. Without a peseta, he left Spain, fleeing first to France, where he borrowed enough money from a magician colleague to begin again. He recommenced performing, moving to the United States in 1937, where his opening date was the famous New York Palace, then the prime showplace for such an act.

He became a U.S. citizen in 1945. Even the straightforward process of attaining citizenship had a magical air when Frakson undertook it. He studied long and diligently the required subjects of U.S. history and the Constitution, while at the same time he was working as a magician at a hotel on Pershing Square in Los Angeles. Every Thursday, he noted, a very respectable elderly gentleman would occupy the same table at the restaurant where he performed, and they got to recognize one another and exchange greetings on a familiar basis. As the date for his examination for citizenship approached, Frakson crammed more and more data into his head, and when he presented himself at the quiz table, he was shaking with nervousness, though he felt sufficiently well informed that he could pass the test. He looked up as the examiner, a federal judge, entered the room. It was the same regular customer who had been to see Frakson every Thursday! The judge settled into his seat, looked over the applicants, and beckoned Frakson forward before everyone else. "You're the magician, aren't you?" he asked. Frakson just nodded. "Who was the first President of the United States?" the judge asked, peering over his glasses at the fuddled conjuror. "George Washington!" answered Frakson brightly. "Correct," said the judge. "Welcome to the United States of America. That's all."

Frakson was semiretired in 1951; he returned to his homeland in 1977, after Franco died and democracy had been restored.

PETER PIT

First as a juggler in a Dutch circus, then as a star of the "Ed Sullivan Show" in the USA with his wonderful Dancing Cane trick, the multilingual Peter Pit came to the attention of the magic world very early in his life. He now works at Las Vegas casinos, runs about the world attending magic conventions, acts in cinema, produces and directs television shows, and, when free from those activities, busies himself at the Academy of Magical Arts in California and at the Hollywood Magic Castle.

Until you've seen Peter performing his bewildering routine with a wooden chair, you've not been subjected to really major mind-boggling. A square wooden tube, just large enough to conceal the chair, is located on the stage. Peter drops the chair inside, turns the whole thing upside-down, and when he pulls the tube away, the chair is upright. The chair multiplies into two, then back into one. A sequence of impossibilities takes place that seems to have no explanation in a real world. To do this trick, I think Pit has sold his soul. If so, he got a good price.

Russia's Rafael & Elena look over their cauldron of magic tricks. Their Black Cat Theater is a popular Moscow attraction.

PACO MILLER

Mexico is now home to this artist, who once had a very large show with a forty-piece orchestra, seven Arab acrobats, and a total of 135 persons working on- and offstage.

Born in Ecuador in 1918, Eduardo Arozamena became Paco Miller when he first got bitten by the magic bug, often a fatal disease. That happened when he saw the famous Li-Ho Chang perform, a man he says he considered to be "a god." Paco began with ventriloquism and then took up magic, performing under incredibly difficult conditions on some occasions. He

Above right: Chenkai is a Mexican performer specializing in large illusions. Here he is at the conclusion of the Indian Basket trick. Below right: All-round magician Vince Carmen works with a remarkable range of animals from doves to tigers in his large stage show.

remembers well the times he had to walk between towns with his ventriloquial dummy and a few magic props in a cardboard suitcase, sleeping on newspapers in the dressing room (when there was one), and struggling to save money to build a bigger act.

Success came along eventually, and Paco began to be in demand for special occasions, one of which he recalls with great glee. An oil company in Brazil hired him to entertain field workers in the Mato Grosso, and after an arduous journey through the heavy jungle, Paco arrived at the back of a huge tent set up for the occasion. Peeking through the curtain at the very silent audience he was about to entertain, he discovered that they were near-naked Indians. He decided that the "vent" act would be most suitable, and he prepared accordingly. Moments later, he stepped out before his audience, holding a prop skull in his hand. The skull said hello to the assembled Indians, and the whole tent suddenly emptied in a scramble of flailing brown limbs. It was the shortest show he'd ever done.

Another time, Miller could not find his regular pistol, which fired a blank shell at a large, ornate star to cause five preselected cards to instantly appear at the five points of the figure. He asked to borrow a pistol, but only a shotgun could be produced, and he was given a blank shell for it. When the moment came, he aimed and fired at the star, only to have the whole thing vaporize into tiny fragments that flew everywhere. The "blank" shell had been filled with birdshot.

When he was well established as a theater performer, he got to know David Bamberg (Fu Manchu) very well. Now, that was a day when every performer jealously guarded his secrets from other magicians. David was an

Above left: Italy boasts many a distinguished conjurors, among them Silvan, an illusionist who is a familiar figure to television audiences in that country. He is a performer with great panache and dignity, equally a master of major stage effects and intimate magic. Above right: Texan Paul Driscoll hosted a weekly TV magic show in Houston while still in his teens. Now that he's all growed up (he's 6 feet, 8 inches tall) Paul is seen at major corporate shows, on cruise lines, and at the Hollywood Magic Castle, doing every sort of magic.

Right: Iiro Seppänen displays a sparkling, puckish approach to well-developed sleight-of-hand close-up performances. His mobile face and the confident attack of his work are positive attributes. He is from Finland. Below right: Finnish performer Jyrki Niemi works in classical costume with doves, silk handkerchiefs, and billiard balls. He has a striking stage persona and, obviously, a great future in magic.

inveterate joker, and one night when Paco was in the middle of his full evening show in Mexico, with a huge, ornate prop box at center stage, he was startled to see David, dressed like a detective in a raincoat and fedora and accompanied by his associate Edmund Spreer, casually walk onto the stage. David took a tape measure to the box and began reading off measurements to Spreer, who copied them into a notebook. They finished, nodded to Paco, and walked offstage. He was speechless.

Paco Miller has had a rich and rewarding life in magic, and like Scheherazade, could fill a thousand and one nights with stories of wonder.

STEWART JAMES

Stewart James has spent most of his life in his home near Sarnia, Ontario, but his influence in magic has reached around the world. He is an exceed-

Left: Italy's Albert Sitta is anything but Chinese, yet careful attention to costume, makeup, and deportment, allows him to be very convincing in his portrayal of the "Oriental" wizard "Chun Chin Fu." Right: Ever frustrated, the Great Tomsoni bravely pursues the Muse of Magic, never to catch up with her. In addition, the gum-cracking "bimbo" assistant, Pam, torments the Great One at every opportunity. Behind the seeming bungles, artistry of a very high order is at work here.

ingly creative man, now in his eighties, who says he is "to magic as a playwright is to theater." He is sought out by magicians from far and wide, who visit him at home like a respected guru. The author Martin Gardner, of *Scientific American* fame, a recognized connoisseur of conjuring, says that James' originality is a puzzle in itself. "Where he gets his ideas is one of those mysteries of creative energy. It's like asking how Bach got his ideas for fugues."

Canada also gave the magic world Doug Henning, Celeste Evans, Dai Vernon, Ross Bertram, Sid Lorraine, and Dean Gunnarson. These magicians have made their personal impact upon the art, but it is amazing how many performances of artists all over the globe today incorporate, unseen and unnoticed, the principles developed by Stewart James. I've had occasion to demonstrate to colleagues a simple but highly effective method of linking two rings in the Chinese Linking Rings trick that I read about in some journal many, many years ago. It was described there by James, and I began using it as soon as I learned about it as a teenager. That obscure mention in print has escaped the attention of every magician to whom I've demonstrated the method, showing just how much Mr. James has written and contributed to the art of magic in his decades of dedicated service.

No, you'll not see the name Stewart James on a marquee. But you'll see his genius at work in the hands of magicians everywhere.

ROY BENSON

Roy Benson was one of the very first magicians I met after entering the United States. He and his wife, Connie, were active in the very busy "club date" field of the forties and fifties; there were few Friday afternoons when they were not off to the Catskills north of New York City, where the resorts demanded a huge spectrum of variety acts to entertain their customers, fortifying the program each weekend to accommodate additional patrons. Stars like Liberace, The Temptations, Johnnie Ray, Eartha Kitt, Victor Borge, Henny Youngman, Danny Thomas, Peggy Lee, and a skyful of others headed up the bills, and we magicians were often employed to "open" for them. Occasionally, a magician was top of the bill. Harry Blackstone, Sr., Dunninger, John Calvert, and a very few other conjurors enjoyed top billing.

Benson was incredibly funny, as well as technically brilliant. He had a handsome, boyish face with a quite manic set of expressions he could call upon at will. Typically, Roy would simply lie down on the stage in the middle of his act, leaning up on one elbow. His purposely corny magician's table—the sort of pedestal-type of velvet-draped affair with a fringe of white pom-poms that every aspiring magus was sure to feel a need for—would be immediately above his head as he ponderously addressed the audience on some inanity that had seemingly just popped into his mind. Suddenly, he would be distracted by the pom-poms, and reaching up, he'd pluck one like a piece of fruit, examine it curiously, and toss it into his mouth. He'd chew a bit, pluck another one, and hold it out to the front row. "Marshmallows!" he would announce with childlike glee. "Here, try one!" He'd throw it out to the audience.

Abruptly, Roy would flop over on his back and continue to pick miniature marshmallows, telling the audience, "As I said to my psychiatrist just the other day, I said, 'Tante . . .' "

Yes, I guess you had to be there. Roy's humor was very much like Dick Shawn's. I saw Shawn, in front of a packed house in the Catskills, lose a full third of his audience within the first fifteen minutes of his routine, simply because he wasn't relating to them in the way they might have expected. After the chaff had thus been winnowed away, he got down to business and spent a full two and a half hours delivering himself of a tour de force that was, in my experience, unequaled. I left the theater weak from laughter that had never stopped, along with others who were wiping their eyes and still in a daze from what they'd gone through. But not one of them could effectively repeat any substantial part of what had happened on that stage, in an attempt to tell someone else what was so funny. Again, you really had to be there.

Roy Benson's manipulatory skills were peerless. In his hands, a simple routine with a billiard ball and a small leather cone, came as close to supernatural as anything I ever saw performed. At the court of Pharaoh Khufu, he would have been a god.

Roy did it the hard way: He practiced. He made all of his own equipment in a breakaway workshop he contrived to set up in a tiny apartment in the New York City borough of Queens. The ever patient Connie, herself a talented dancer and contortionist who worked the circuits with Roy, managed to run the household among the soldering materials, spray paint, and glue pots. Perhaps her ability as a contortionist assisted in that process.

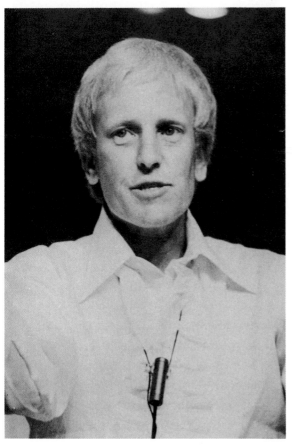

Above left: Peter De Paula has been a "pro" since his teens. He depends a great deal upon his mime talents (he studied with Marcel Marceau) to sell magic. Once the star of the road version of The Magic Show *originated by Doug Henning, Peter is now often seen in Las Vegas and in nightclubs all over the world. Above right: "Magic Christian" from Austria, is not only a competent professional magician, but an industrial designer as well. He designs and produces various secret devices and routines for magicians in between his travels around the world. Below left: Bob Little runs a busy, successful magic business from his headquarters in Hatboro, Pa., and is seen at any major convention of magicians anywhere in the world. He convulses his colleagues by poking gentle fun at their pretensions: In his hands, the illusion known in the trade as the Broom Suspension, in which a lady is suspended horizontally in the air with her arm resting upon a standing broom, reverses itself so that the broom slowly rises away from the lady and is "suspended"!*

It was my privilege to help Roy in designing the sideshow illusions for the Broadway musical *Carnival*, based upon the movie *Lili*. That show was highly successful, with the magic sequences coming in for special attention. Roy had a way of thinking directly and clearly to the end result that was required by the producers of such a show, bypassing all the philosophical baggage with which I was then loaded. I watched, and I learned from him.

In 1978 Roy Benson died of emphysema, brought on by heavy smoking and a careless disregard for his own health.

WILLARD THE WIZARD

The Willard family history started, somewhere around 1860, in Ireland with a series of performers all named "Willard the Wizard." From the look of the advertising material used by the last of the line, Harry Francis Willard, there was great economy practiced in posters and handbills. Paper printed well into this century by Harry looks as if it was in use in the mid-1800s.

Harry Willard chose to spend his entire career working "under canvas." Rather than renting theaters, he took a tent show through the American South and Southwest. At one time, seventeen trucks carried around his equipment and tent, including a calliope. Every single prop he used was handmade by himself, right down to the puppets he used in the act. He was the consummate "trouper," hardworking, fierce in discipline, dedicated in technique, and tireless to a fault.

His daughter, Frances, whom you met back in Chapter 26, recalls his instructions to the assistants, of whom she was one:

> Never, never turning our backs to the audience was not only considered good manners, but he always said, "It's bad luck to turn your back to the audience. Besides, they might wonder what you're up to. Always face the audience, and step backwards when you exit, bowing slightly. Try to remember when you are in front of an audience that you are just like a lion tamer in a cage. Never turn your back on the animal. Never let your guard down, for magic is a jealous art. It demands your full, undivided attention."

Willard's show set a very moral tone. He avoided the "leggy" look of the usual girl assistant, and assured prospective clients in his advertising material that "all entertainments will be kept up to the high standard of Morality and Respectability." He promised "Wonderful Talking and Dancing Dolls," and a "Troupe of Royal Martinettes," as well as "Comic Songs, Laughable Dialogues, Gymnastic Feats, Etc." as part of every show. His strongest number, the one that brought them back every time he passed through town, was the Willard Spirit Cabinet, based upon the Davenport Brothers' act.

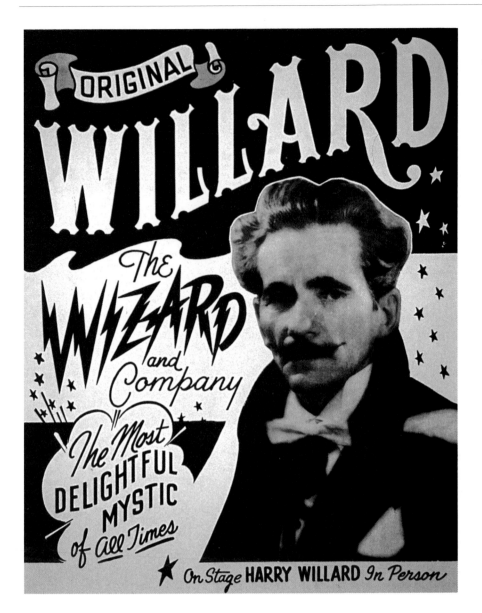

An effective, very satisfactory full stage show was the product that Willard the Wizard offered his enthusiastic audiences. Today, his daughter, Frances, is successfully performing his Spirit Cabinet illusion, aided by her husband, Glenn Falkenstein.

A good part of Willard's show depended upon his Ghost Walk. It's hard to say what a modern audience would think of the routine, but as Frances describes it, it was pretty scary. "It wasn't Casper," she says. The "medium" was securely tied within a velvet-curtained enclosure, and the cabinet was closed. It was hardly sealed when a ghostly figure strode forth, fully visible in vivid green light, walking down among the audience. This macabre form returned to the cabinet; the curtain was immediately pulled back and the ghost was nowhere to be seen, but the medium was still tightly tied in place, not a hair out of position.

I doubt that there is still an act of this kind in existence anywhere today, and perhaps we are now too sophisticated to accept such a show. When Willard went away, we lost that naïveté forever.

JOHN CALVERT

The ever-youthful John Calvert has been an active magician since about 1930, and seems to have no limit to his range of talents. Aside from being a major magic star, he was the star of a number of 1940s *Falcon* films (*Devil's Cargo*, with Rochelle Hudson, was one of them), in which he played a debonair detective.

His yachts have been an abiding passion of John's life. He has been through tropical storms at sea, even losing one yacht when it was wrecked off northern Australia. He has owned, and of course piloted, airplanes too. Flying his crew to a show date in Nashville, he put the craft down on a field instead of the airstrip, breaking his own leg and injuring some of the passengers. True to the show-business tradition, they opened on schedule the next night, with John on crutches.

John does an amazing manipulation act, plucking endless cigarettes from the air, then solemnly informing his audience that he doesn't smoke—"hates the things"—and warning against their use.

In their "big" show, his lovely wife, Tammy, is seen to be playing the electric organ while levitated by John. Like everything he does, it's done "big." John doesn't know any other way.

One of the dependable artists of our trade, John Calvert has done it all, and it seems he will continue to do so. His presence is a privilege for us to enjoy.

MARCO TEMPEST

A few years ago, in Madrid, I witnessed a remarkable performance by two young Swiss gentlemen who worked as The United Artists. This was a clever idea in which one stood directly behind the other, illuminated straight from the front. This made it appear as if there were only one artist onstage, working with four arms; objects disappeared from one hand and reappeared in any of the other three. The coordination required to perform in this way was of course attained only after long hours of practice. The team of Martin Cottet and Marco Tempest broke up, and now these artists are performing as "singles."

Tempest has innovated some features that have simply never been heard of or even imagined in the magic business. Happening upon some X-shaped boomerangs in a toy store, he set to work and put them into his act. At one point he folds up a square of white paper to form the traditional origami bird, which then turns into a real live dove flying over the heads of the audience. Highly successful with this act, particularly in Japan, Marco has now turned to computer technology and 3-D techniques to create a totally new idea in conjuring. Laser beams, projection video, and digital animation all

assist him in his task of creating illusions. He has the audience interacting, in real time, with his computer program and himself.

I seldom agree a hundred percent with the publicity releases that magicians send out, but I cannot argue with Marco's claim that he has "created an experience far beyond the limits of traditional magic."

MARTIN COTTET

Half of the clever but now defunct United Artists, Martin Cottet (pronounced "co-tay") has taken his natural dancing ability to the stage and combined it with such traditional and usually conservative tricks as the Chinese Linking Rings. With carefully designed lighting and stage effects, he is seen whirling the silver rings in ever-changing configurations and patterns as they seductively join and fall apart in his hands.

His talents reach beyond magic. Martin is a poet and musician, and the music he wrote specifically for his own show has been produced in a compact disk format. He has performed in places as far apart as the Hollywood Magic Castle and the Casino in Monte Carlo, and his unique style has won him awards at major competitions.

In 1991, for a special magicians' convention, the United Artists were briefly resurrected as Tempest & Cottet. As a team or as singles, these two young gentlemen, who first met as break-dancers in the streets of Zurich, are going to open your eyes.

Above left: John Calvert, in about 1940. This remarkable man, born in 1911, still tours the world in his yacht, Magic Castle II, *and performs a vigorous and demanding show. Above right: That airborne lady playing the electric organ is Tammy, who trusts husband John Calvert to keep her safely aloft.*

Martin Cottet of Switzerland combines modern choreography with the Chinese Linking Rings, one of the oldest tricks in recorded history, freshly and excitingly presented in the Space Age. Facing page, left: Brilliant, innovative choreography, and a decided Oriental flavor are trademarks of Marco Tempest, from whose fingertips boomerangs fly out over the audience in an exciting show, The Key of Imagination. *This photo illustrates his use of computer-generated 3-D images in his show. Facing page, right: The latest of a line of magical Davenports, Roy has adopted a striking and original costume that suits his rapid, exciting performance. Silver dollars rain from his fingers, and metal rings are linked in midair in bewildering ways.*

ROY DAVENPORT

Fergus Roy performs under the name Roy Davenport. No relation to the Davenport Brothers of spiritualist fame, he is the current generation of the famous Davenports of London, who have run their magic shop in that city for ninety-three years now. The magic Davenport family began with George Ryan, who at age seventeen began a retail magic business and changed his name to Lewis Davenport. As a performer, he became famous for his sleight of hand, specializing in billiard ball manipulation. He used solid ivory balls two and a half inches in diameter, multiplying them in both hands. Lewis claimed to have performed for Maskelyne & Devant's show at St. George's Hall, London, over two thousand times, and he was widely respected there. J. N. Maskelyne himself wrote of Lewis, "He is the most accomplished professor of pure sleight-of-hand ever seen in this, or any age."

Though it has moved about a bit during the years that it has served the conjurors of the United Kingdom, Davenport's magic shop remains a major source of supply for props, old and new books, posters, and other items that are needed in the trade.

The Davenport tradition of magic has been passed down from Lewis through Gus, George, Betty, and now Fergus Roy, who is just about to celebrate his tenth anniversary as a professional performer. He began at age ten to entertain with magic, hardly hampered by the family business. The family built a special studio for his rehearsals, and that investment has certainly paid off. The Davenport home is jammed with prizes and awards of all sorts that Roy has earned for his work as a conjuror.

"Frenetic" is the one word that pops to mind when describing Roy's performance. He enters like a speeding train and proceeds to litter the stage with coins, cards, and billiard balls produced at his fingertips in rapid suc-

cession. His handling of the classic Chinese Linking Rings trick is hugely innovative, the joining of two rings often occurring in midair in some strange way.

Departing radically from the traditional conjuror's costume, Roy Davenport appears in a blazing modern patchwork outfit that complements very well his unusual approach to magic. He is an exciting young new star from an old family in magic, an appealing personality and a welcome, refreshing addition to the galaxy.

ABB DICKSON

When affable Abb is not tending to the family business in Atlanta, Georgia, he's off somewhere with his full stage show, "Presto." With a cast of thirty highly trained people, the show has toured the mainland United States, Canada, Hawaii, and Puerto Rico. Abb himself has also appeared in films as a character actor.

In 1966 he was chosen as master of ceremonies and performing magician for an eleven-country tour sponsored by the U.S. Department of State. He was also a technical consultant for Broadway's *The Magic Show* starring Doug Henning. His knowledge of magic is extensive, and he has often advised other professionals.

KIO

In Russia, a country where belief in real magic has always been very strong, conjurors have always been popular. Many magicians from all parts of the world went there to make fortunes during the days before communism.

One Sunday morning in November of 1990, millions of Soviet television viewers stayed up until two A.M. to see the fate of a man bearing a famous magical name. Igor Kio, a son of Emil Kio, who performed very large and spectacular illusions for the Moscow State Circus, stepped from a cream-colored Mercedes limousine in front of 15,000 freezing spectators gathered around an iced-over pond. The forty-six-year-old wizard, dressed in his trademark light-colored suit, was tied into a large bag, locked into a steamer trunk, and hoisted above the pond by a helicopter. As the trunk reached the center of the pond, it was released to crash through the ice and into the black water. Minutes went by as the crowd chanted, "Ki-o, Ki-o," and then a suspiciously dry Kio stepped from the Mercedes, moving slowly, as if in a trance. The crowd was impressed.

The official Communist newspaper *Pravda,* then in the middle of a desperate campaign to regain the popularity it had lost with the advent of perestroika, trumpeted that Kio had outperformed the American Houdini. There were important facts that *Pravda* missed. First, Houdini never did the through-the-ice stunt that popular biographies have repeated, and when he emerged from a submerged trunk during the many times he performed *that* stunt, he was actually in the water. Quite wet.

Igor Kio, also a star of the Moscow State Circus, carries on the family show with the valuable assistance of his mother, Emil's wife, as chief assistant. They have performed all over the world, including in New York's Madison Square Garden. Another brother, Emil Junior, works with another unit of the State Circus.

The Kio show uses a great number of assistants (thirty have been counted!) along with striking costumes, smoke and flame effects, large cages, boxes and cannons, and a full-sized circus band. It is old-time circus razzmatazz at its best.

HARRY MAURER

This man works. All the time. Harry Maurer is booked ahead as far as he can see, and that's to be expected, judging by the recognition he's received from his peers and the public alike.

It all started for him when he was five years old and his grandfather pulled coins from his ears. To little Harry, that seemed like a good idea, and before long he was learning to do the same miracle. In his early teens, he worked with the "Show Biz Kids" of New Jersey, entertaining just about any place

Russia's Kio in a fiery circus number that "incinerates" a young lady for the sake of art.

that would allow the group in. By sixteen, he was in local restaurants, doing close-up magic at tables.

In high school, he was granted a special privilege. At lunchtime, he could leave school to perform the matinee show at the Thunderbird Hotel on the Jersey shore; then he'd return to school to finish the day. At eight he was back at the Thunderbird for the evening show.

Harry Maurer studied theater at Rutgers University while commuting to New York City to entertain at a prominent nightspot. He did 1,300 shows in two years at the Playboy Club—more than any other solo act.

In Atlantic City, he was nominated as "Atlantic City's Entertainer of the Year—Best Opening Act." In 1976 he had an audience of 60,000 persons as he conjured on the fifty-yard line of a football game!

The casinos in Atlantic City spell "home" to Harry Maurer, whom is known as a dependable, consistently excellent performer. His audience rapport is second to none, and he leaves 'em laughing.

JOAQUIN AYALA

Certainly, this young man is currently Mexico's most famous magician. Joaquin began as a regular dove worker dressed in traditional tails, then switched to a "period" presentation in which, costumed and bewigged as

Facing page, left: Joaquin Ayala and Lilia, Mexican show-stoppers in Las Vegas. This exciting new act uses flames, smoke, and explosions to punctuate a fast-moving act in which Lilia is vanishing, appearing, floating, and transforming in mind-boggling sequences. Facing page, right: The Bombino Brothers of Florida feature Alfredo, Carina, Francisco, and the mysterious Dijon. They offer a full spectrum of conjuring, juggling, tumbling, skating, unicycling, and general family enjoyment. Photo by Rick Diaz Photography.

Mozart, he did only tricks that used music or musical items. A flute (no doubt the Magic Flute?) floated in midair, music sheets were torn into scraps and then restored, and Joaquin's music stand soon filled up with rows of bewildered birds that seemed to have come from nowhere.

Then Joaquin developed an ultra-modern, fast-paced illusion act costumed in space-age form that has created a sensation with the public. With the lovely Lilia, his wife, he now presents a fast-moving and colorful stage act with a real live snow leopard and a number of tried-and-true "oldies" dressed up for the twenty-first century so that they could never be recognized. He is currently working in Las Vegas and Lake Tahoe and is preparing several specialty presentations for industrial trade-show applications.

At an age when she was barely able to speak, the Ayalas' little daughter, Nadia, was asked by an interviewer what she would like to do when she grows up. Having stood backstage so many times while her parents were doing their thing (she'd watched her mother Lilia leaping out of a huge basket after Joaquin had skewered it in all directions with flaming lances), she didn't need to think long about her answer. "I would like," she firmly announced, "to hide in a basket like my mommy!" We do not have a record of the lecture that was later delivered to this small person by her parents.

THE BOMBINO FAMILY

It seems that you can't keep certain dominant genes from emerging eventually. The Guerra family owned a circus in Cuba two generations ago; then the family dropped out of show business when the next generation merely produced an electrician. Things changed when the third generation, Francisco Bombino, came along in 1968. Driven by some basic urge, he began taking lessons in gymnastics from a Florida pro named Paul Anderson, and studied juggling as well. There was a circus class connected with the school, and his younger brother Alfonso began dabbling in juggling at age twelve. Already the insidious forces were at work. By age sixteen, Alfonso had become so advanced as a juggler that Fran left that specialty to him and took up magic.

Francisco declined a scholarship to study medicine in Nebraska, and opted for studying theater arts in Florida. He opened a "clown college" for aspiring jesters who either wanted only to expand their range of expression or were serious about the comic business.

By now, Alfonso was so proficient that he took second prize in Baltimore at the International Jugglers World Championship conference. Cousin Eddie was attracted to this life, too, and when the three began performing locally the audience began calling them the Bambinos. Taking the cue, Francisco altered the word a bit and decided that they would be known professionally as "The Bombino Brothers." And so they are today.

Then along came Dijon, a citizen of Switzerland who frankly admits that he took the name from a jar of mustard. A skating pro who has appeared at the Lido in Paris, La Scala in Barcelona, and Las Vegas, Dijon is also a film actor—he played the part of Frankie in *La Dolce Vita* and supporting roles in many other films—and is now one of the Bombino Brothers as a mentalist and close-up magician. The group is rounded out nicely by Carina Tinozzi, a young lady who is anything but a brother. Eddie Forero creates special music for the act, and Susan Torres, one of the graduates of Fran's own clown school, is out selling the Bombino Brothers show to clients when she's not festooned with her red nose.

The Bombino Brothers act is certainly an anachronism, a "family" group working together in a circus mode, able to perform as trampoline artists, mimes, jugglers, gymnasts, musicians, and magicians, sharing duties and responsibilities. That's the way it used to be done, with great success. Let's hope the Bombinos never discover that such an activity is old-fashioned and very passé. We need them.

CHAR

We expect to be seeing more of our Russian colleagues, who have developed with difficulty in the partial vacuum that existed behind the Iron Curtain, but who are now able to attend international magic conventions freely. One

Russian artist is Alexander Vorobiev, who works professionally as "Char," has a mother who was in show business, and a scientist father. His early childhood in India began his interest in magic, and he was able to study theater arts under Leonid Melnikov, a well-known Russian artist. Specializing in the manipulation of coins—"They're always available!" he says—Char has been awarded many honors for his work.

With his degrees in engineering and mathematics, Char nevertheless opted to pursue magic professionally. Now interested in mentalism, he performs assisted by his two sons, Youri (fourteen) and Andrei (nine) and does spoon-bending tricks and the duplication of drawings secretly made by the audience. Though he is careful not to claim supernatural powers of any kind, Char has a certain belief in ESP and in faith healing.

The first official Ring of the International Brotherhood of Magicians in Russia was formed in 1990, and its proud president is Char. He is also president of the Russian Magic Society formed in 1991 with 350 members. Char and his colleagues promise to become better known to audiences around the world.

DOUG HENNING

Henning is a Canadian from Winnipeg who at an early age was awarded a government grant to study magic. Hopping on his motorcycle and heading south, he studied with two master conjurors: Dai Vernon, another Canadian-become-American renowned especially for card magic, and Tony Slydini, a sleight-of-hand master. The report Doug made of his study was interesting but naïve, since he chose to believe some authorities rather uncritically.

Doug abandoned the top-hat-and-tails costume so long favored by magicians, and chose to perform in a T shirt and blue jeans, embellished with "flower child" emblems and adornments. He created a show called *Spellbound*, which played for a record-breaking run at the Royal Alexandra Theater in Toronto. Seen by American promoters, the show was adapted for Broadway as *The Magic Show* in 1974 and had a long four-and-a-half-year run there. Henning was the first magician to run a series of yearly magic specials on television, receiving an Emmy Award and seven nominations for these shows. An ambitious later Broadway show called *Merlin*, was spectacular indeed, and highly entertaining, but was so expensive to operate that it closed in a few months.

Henning has been featured in Las Vegas and Lake Tahoe, has designed magical effects for leading musical groups, and has been featured in major television commercials. His series of annual U.S. television specials was remarkable for being broadcast "live," an element that was calculated to eliminate the possibility of editing tricks being performed. It was a daring innovation. Doug is one of the best-known magicians in the business, in spite of not having been seen in recent years.

It is generally agreed that Doug's revival of magic on Broadway marked the beginning of a new era for the art, rekindling a public awareness of conjuring. His clean, young image did much to interest agents in the commercial applications of magic to their advertising and public-image needs.

Performing magic lost a bright star when Doug fell in with Maharishi Mahesh Yogi and the Transcendental Meditation movement. Dedicated to that cause, he gave up his profession, sold all his props, and moved to India to pursue Infinite Bliss. He is missed.

FANTASIO

Essentially retired now from active performing, Fantasio is pleased that his daughter, Jackie, has entered the business. He became interested in magic when he saw Fu Manchu at a very early age in his homeland, Argentina.

Fantasio became a legend in magic for his masterful handling of lit candles and walkingsticks. A seemingly endless number of these objects would materialize during his act, filling his tables and bringing continued gasps of delight and astonishment from his audience. When he retired a few years ago, he entered the retail end of the trade, and has enjoyed great success operating from his home in Coral Gables, Florida.

One of the true gentlemen of the business, Fantasio is an inspiration to us all.

Below left: Russian magician Alexander Char has done much to bring his country's magicians into contact with their Western colleagues. Below right: Canadian Doug Henning provided a fresh, modern, and youthful approach to the magic art. The Magic Show *ran on Broadway for almost five years, and Doug won an Emmy Award and seven nominations for his superb TV specials.*

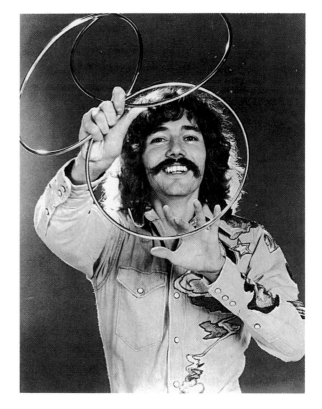

JEFF McBRIDE

Jeff, whose publicity material provides birthdates of 1959, 1960, 1961, and 1962, is a serious innovator in magic. His fascination with the Japanese art of Kabuki has led to his extensive use of masks and highly specialized make-up in his revue, *Mask, Myth & Magic.* Worldwide recognition has come his way, from Japan to Las Vegas. It is a tribute to his ability to hold an audience that stars such as Diana Ross, Billy Crystal, and Tina Turner have chosen him as an "opening act" for their own shows.

While one never knows just how much of a magician's brochure can be accepted as fact, and how much should be attributed to creative writing, Jeff's publicity material runs on and on about his mysterious investigations into "real" and "higher magick" [*sic*], including annual journeys to strange places during which he and a guru, "Marlin," go "to see what's on the other side of the veil." He tells his considerable following that the rest of us are "tricked into thinking magic [is] just illusion, sleight of hand, hokum . . . it's much more." He also admits that in his childhood he was "terrified of monsters—under my bed, in my closet, in the cellar, in the woods." I can't recall that I was ever thus terrified, so perhaps for that reason Jeff and I cannot share the same explanations of the world.

At the age of eight, this superstar of the craft began to dress up as a magician, and was soon performing a rudimentary act for local clubs. At sixteen, he was invited to tour Japan as part of a larger show, and thus began his exposure to Kabuki and to Japanese culture in general. He trained with the choreographers of the Kabuki theater and has since had the distinct honor of performing his individually adapted act before many Japanese audiences, to great acclaim and acceptance.

Jeff whirls through the "Dance of the Red Lion," "Unmasking," and any number of carefully themed routines that he says have deep lessons to teach. I'm sure they do, though I'm not privy to the messages, but I can tell you that they are highly entertaining, well designed, and startling. One leaves the theater completely exhausted and with mind racing.

I hardly need add that numerous attempts have been made to blatantly copy Jeff McBride's act. Lots of luck, guys.

PENN & TELLER

Though Penn & Teller have appeared as actors in separate films, and their personal lives and life-styles are decidedly different, this team is inseparable as a theatrical entity. Teller, a quiet intellectual sort, was formerly a Latin teacher. Penn, with his hair tied back in a small ponytail (for this current season, anyway) and just one fingernail enigmatically painted blood-red, spends his holiday time playing bass guitar with major musical groups, while

Above left: Fantasio is well named. Now essentially retired from active performing, he runs a very successful business supplying magicians from all over the world with the tools of their trade, especially certain items that have always been a specialty of Fantasio's own performance. Above right: Jeff McBride, in Mask, Myth & Magic *with one of his numerous colorful masks. Note the carefully designed custom makeup. Left: Denmark's Viggo Jahn is billed as "The Man with the Black Gloves." He has traveled the world, performing a routine in which an endless number of walkingsticks appear and he removes their knobs to multiply and otherwise manipulate them while wearing black gloves for greater visibility. Viggo is still actively involved in magic.*

Above: A very, very strange character has just handcuffed himself to a startled Penn. The confrontation makes for high drama and typical Penn & Teller weirdness. Right: While Penn reads "Casey at the Bat" in rapid-fire, his partner, Teller, struggles out of a straitjacket. If he's not out and standing when Penn finishes and stands up to take his bow, he ends up in the spikes. He usually makes it.

Teller is scuba diving on the other side of the globe or listening to classical music.

Together as a team since 1974, when for six years they called themselves the Asparagus Valley Cultural Society, Penn & Teller specialize in bizarre, original presentations. The bigger one of the two, and I mean *big*, is Penn. The other is simply Teller. Penn does all the talking. The introduction is always the same: "I'm Penn Jillette, and this is my partner, Teller." And when these two start doing their thing, stand back.

Most of the other magi don't quite know how to handle these problems called Penn & Teller. They either hate them or adore them. Count me in the latter camp. And make that, worship. Though P & T don't ever advertise themselves as magicians, they most certainly are. The team is hugely successful, booked up literally for years in advance, and these chaps are very much in control of their tumultuous careers.

Nothing takes place on their stage that is not carefully planned, designed, and rehearsed. It has to say, quite clearly, "Penn & Teller," or it doesn't work for them. On one of their television specials, they promised to produce more live animals than any other magician had ever even attempted to produce, and they did. Under a screened enclosure, with a well-protected cameraman in appropriate costume, they manifested tens of thousands of live, noisy, and angry honeybees. Stung many times during this daring number, they were protected from serious harm by the fact that they'd been immunized against the bee venom. Penn & Teller are daring, but they're not fools. I say this in spite of the fact that they ended that same television program with Penn driving a huge trailer truck over Teller as he lay out in front of Radio City Music Hall on New York's Sixth Avenue.

Whether the ever-victimized (but always victorious) Teller is being drowned—fully dressed—in a tank of water, or both performers have just had a full-sized refrigerator dropped on them, the audience accepts the zany, provocative pair as a refreshing new influence in the theater arts. Even when they are exposing the modus operandi of some item in the conjuring repertoire, it is done with a distinct reason, and in excellent taste. Furthermore, the audience is just as ready to be thoroughly confounded by the next magician who shows them the very same trick.

Penn & Teller have taken the stuffing out of stuffy magicians and have created an exciting challenge as the new guys on the block. They are original, exceedingly talented, daring, and hardworking. They have a devoted following and in my opinion, they're the best thing that has happened to the art of magic in a generation.

THE MEDVEDEVS

Oleg and Katya Medvedev are a young brother-and-sister team. Oleg's first professional engagement was at the Twelfth World Youth Festival in Moscow. Then, in 1987, Katya took the first prize and Oleg the second prize in "micro-magic" at the First All-Union Magic Competition. The following year, the team took first prize at the same competition, and Oleg carried away the top prize in the "up to sixteen" category for manipulation. The Third All-Union Festival awarded them two first prizes and one second prize. They are prizewinners of the Moscow Student Festival and the Second All-union Folk Art Festival as well, and have appeared many times on Soviet television and in the newspapers.

Kate is making a good name for herself as a close-up magicienne, while Oleg is adept at billiard ball manipulation and hopes to continue to perfect his art in that direction. He has a rather frenetic, fast-moving attack to his work, so much so that you have to avoid blinking so you don't miss anything!

ANDRÉ KOLE

André is a prolific inventor of magical effects, having created a number of important ones for such stars as David Copperfield. His show is sponsored by the Campus Crusade for Christ, an evangelical group. The first half of his show is excellent straightforward magic in the grand style and the second half a message—told through conjuring—of his religious beliefs.

André Kole has just compressed a young woman rather dramatically. Yes, that's a real woman you're looking at, and no trick photography. What you see is what you get.

André's son and daughter, Tim and Stacey, are both working magicians often seen starring in Las Vegas.

It must be told: The one trick you'll never see André Kole perform is the Bunny from the Hat. He's highly allergic to rabbits.

ROSS SKIFFINGTON

Australian Ross is a trained actor who specializes in stagecraft and theater magic. He has very firm ideas about what makes a magician. "I can't say many magic conjurors have inspired me," he says. "Too many people think you can go into a shop, buy a bag of tricks and call yourself a magician." Truer words were never spoken.

A poll of magicians by *Australian* magazine (June 1990) found him to be the conjuror "most respected by his peers."

LANCE BURTON

Ask me to show you what magic is all about, and I'll show you a videotape of Lance Burton in one of his television appearances. Many adjectives come to mind. The first is "flawless." Lance used that quality to win the top prize at the prestigious Grand Prix of magic in Switzerland (the first American to do so) and he was the first to win the International Brotherhood of Magicians' Gold Medal, in 1980.

Lance's idol is Channing Pollock, the artistic father of so many fine per-

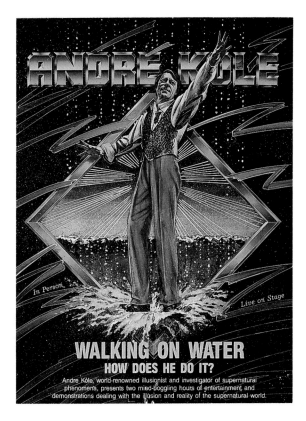

WALKING ON WATER
HOW DOES HE DO IT?
Andre Kole, world-renowned illusionist and investigator of supernatural phenomena, presents two mind-boggling hours of entertainment and demonstrations dealing with the illusion and reality of the supernatural world.

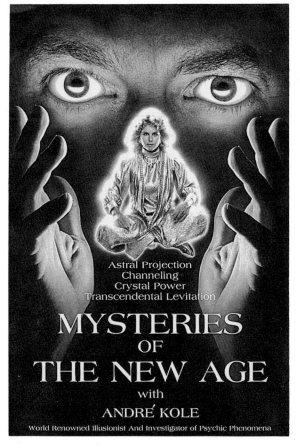

Astral Projection
Channeling
Crystal Power
Transcendental Levitation

MYSTERIES
OF
THE NEW AGE
with
ANDRÉ KOLE
World Renowned Illusionist And Investigator of Psychic Phenomena

Above left: Magician André Kole uses a novel approach to Levitation in which he himself floats through a doorway, seated in the lotus position. André is the inventor of many new presentations for illusionary effects. Above right: Kole, sponsored by Campus Crusades for Christ International, borrows from biblical miracles for many of his themes. Below left: His poster may give the impression that the customer will see the advertised wonders. In actuality, André shows his audience the fallacy of such beliefs.

Above left: The image of Lance Burton is strong, sharp, and effective. A winner of many awards from his colleagues, Lance has proven himself to be a technical perfectionist and a superb artist. To see him work is to understand what magic is all about. Above right: The young Mexican stage magician and close-up artist Alejandro Martinez works professionally as Alemaro. He's a multiple prize-winner in both categories.

formers in magic. Pollock has a very high opinion of Lance, and says that he is "the epitome of the perfect magician." That endorsement is not in any way an exaggeration, and you only need one exposure to the young man's talent to prove it true.

Lance Burton broke the unspoken Las Vegas rule that a magician had to have at least a leopard or a small tiger to compete with other acts. He walked onstage, began to make doves, candles, and playing cards appear at his fingertips, and won everyone in the house. A parakeet in a spherical cage floated from his hands, around the stage, and into a waiting box. It was the Floating Ball of Okito, not only resurrected but vastly improved on by the ingenious Burton.

Excellent appearance, a commanding approach, and a technique beyond improvement have been combined to make Lance Burton the magician every young neophyte wants to become. Then too, his effect on old-timers in the business has been demonstrated many times over. He established the record for the longest appearance ever on the "Tonight Show." Seeing him in rehearsal, Johnny Carson asked him to do his entire twelve-minute act, an unprecedented length of time on that show. He's been on the "Tonight Show," at last count, nine times.

Burton has advice for magic hopefuls. He tells them, "You have to be an actor, inventor, producer, director, lighting designer, costumer, philosopher, psychologist." Yes, and you have to work at each of these things twenty-four hours a day. Or more.

Lance has a great deal of personal charm, untainted by the fame that has rewarded his efforts. Success has not affected his personal attitude toward fans and friends. In a profession that demands hard work and sacrifice, he has paid his dues and enjoys the rewards.

DAVID COPPERFIELD

Today's preeminent international magic star is, without any doubt, David Copperfield. He started out in 1968, at age twelve, as "Davino," working with the usual silk handkerchiefs, birds, and playing cards. By 1975 he was the star of *The Magic Man*, a stage play based on a magician's adventures. The experience gained in that vehicle obviously served him well.

He has had twelve network TV specials to date, doing sensational stunts such as Vanishing the Statue of Liberty and Walking Through the Great Wall of China. Those programs have been syndicated worldwide and have

The leading figure in stage magic today, David Copperfield weaves his wonderful illusionary effects into enchanting tales in person and on internationally broadcast television specials. One wonders if the ideas and the miracles will ever run out.

Marvin Roy, assisted ably by his wife Carol, is billed as "Mr. Electric." Carol is caused to appear inside a gigantic light bulb, Marvin swallows handfuls of tiny bulbs and some wire, then pulls them from his mouth, strung and lighted, and a large bulb lights itself magically in the hands of Mr. Electric. Another act by these two artists features endless quantities of jewelry.

established his reputation throughout Europe and the Far East. In the United States, David has been a headliner at Caesar's Palace twice and is in constant demand in between his busy tours.

Often, an artist in person is somewhat less than the image generated on the video tube, but the Copperfield stage show matches the expectations generated by the television performances. Well designed and managed, it is a classic live presentation that has inspired more than one young person to pursue a career in magic. Copperfield himself comes across as a magnetic personality with great charisma and full stage skills.

A famous illusion that Bautier De Kolta originated about 1875, the Vanishing Lady, was an astonishing effect whereby a lady seated in a chair onstage was covered by a large cloth and simply evaporated instantly as the cloth was whisked away. As evidence that she had not somehow quickly dropped through the stage, magician De Kolta had spread several newspapers beneath and around the chair. Copperfield has presented this same illusion in a new and more convincing setting. His version has an attic scene with a chair standing atop a table, the same newspapers present but the audience now able to see right underneath the chair and the table. Still, the lady evaporates according to plan.

In 1992, Copperfield's fans were astonished to see the ultimate levitation effect performed in full light onstage. David achieved a "flying" process that is not apt to ever be surpassed.

In 1991, David Copperfield purchased—for $2,200,000—the famous Mulholland collection of magical literature and memorabilia, which had been housed at the New York Players Club and was later moved to Los Angeles. This valuable collection, consisting of tens of thousands of books,

Borrowing from mythology to suggest demonic assistance, "Direktor" Kassner was a German illusionist popular at the beginning of this century in Europe.

photographs, clippings, blueprints, scripts, posters, letters, contracts, and other rare historical material relating to the history and technology of magic, had been amassed by Mulholland throughout his lifetime. Entire collections belonging to other aficionados, which they bequeathed or sold to Mulholland, were organized into this remarkable enchanted time capsule.

The whole accumulation was put up for sale by the U.S. government by court order in settlement of certain legal debts incurred by an owner. The Library of Congress had bid for the treasure, but was outbid by Mr. Copperfield, who has announced that access to this treasure trove of conjuring secrets will be allowed only to qualified scholars and researchers.

So there it is. The chronicles of this most secret art, Magic, gathered through decades of dedicated research and loving labor by many, many caring curators, now rests in the hands of a major artist who has contributed so much to that record. Mr. Copperfield is, we know, well aware of his new responsibility. What cunning ideas, brilliant innovations, untested principles and presentations are concealed there? The tears, the applause, the honest sweat, the triumphs, and the laughter that went into creating that massive archive will not show as the pages are turned. Nor can I myself hope that in this book I have given you anything but the slightest glimpse behind the heavy curtain that must needs remain drawn over our dearest mysteries.

I have briefly shown you the performers. Now, somewhat more aware of their humanity, go and see the products of their skill. I will let another wizard, Prospero, close this volume for me:

Be cheerful, sir.
Our revels now are ended. These our actors,
As I foretold you, were all spirits and
Are melted into air, into thin air;
And, like the baseless fabric of this vision,
The cloud-capped tow'rs, the gorgeous palaces,
The solemn temples, the great globe itself,
Yea, all which it inherits shall dissolve,
And, like this insubstantial pageant faded,
Leave not a rack behind. We are such stuff
As dreams are made on; and our little life
Is rounded with a sleep. Sir, I am vexed.
Bear with my weakness: my old brain is troubled.
Be not disturbed with my infirmity.
—WILLIAM SHAKESPEARE
The Tempest
ACT IV

SPECIAL THANKS

Frances and Jay Marshall were most generous in giving me great help in preparing this book. "Magic, Inc.," their shop in Chicago, is one of the great purveyors of magicians' supplies, books, and advice. Lessons in magic are offered there to neophytes of all ages, and many have gone forth from those sessions to become satisfied subjects of the Muse of Magic.

Packed in stacks of boxes in the labyrinth of Magic Inc. I found literally thousands of photos, posters, show cards, and banners representing the careers of magicians great and small. Many were still as fresh as the day they were printed, and all brought the history to life in some way. The Marshall library was also an endless source of information, and Jay never tired of finding important dates, facts, and accounts for me in the hundreds of volumes dedicated to the subject.

George Johnstone, who served as assistant to Harry Blackstone, Sr., enlightened me on many points. I hope that I have done justice to his boss in these pages.

The late Dr. Morton Smith, emeritus professor of religion at Columbia University, generously advised me on the history of early wonder-workers, particularly in Greece and Rome. His comprehension of the social aspects and impact of conjuring was enlightening to me.

As many times before, the staff at the Fort Lauderdale Public Library was most helpful. So, too, were the folks at the Library of Congress (though I do wish they would get around to repairing those dreadful photocopying machines!). The New York Public Library and The British Library supplied valuable data.

I shamelessly took from many of the sources listed in the bibliography, and I recommend that the interested reader follow up the many individual histories that have been lovingly assembled and published by magic buffs. *The Encyclopedia of Magic and Magicians*, a fascinating reference work by T. A. Waters, was especially useful to me. *Milbourne Christopher's Illustrated History of Magic* and his *Panorama of Magic* are highly recommended reading that served me well. Maureen Christopher immediately responded to my requests for information about her late husband, and reminded me of several items of interest that would otherwise have escaped my attention.

Max Maven, with his very specialized knowledge of the modern Japanese scene, generously arranged for photos and information to be supplied and gave me the benefit of his advice.

Special data on the Houdini escape in Russia was generously provided by Alexander Char.

As always, my valued colleague Michael Hutchinson was more than generous with his time and labor, and Al Cohen of Al's Magic Shop in Washington, D.C., provided photos for my use.

Bobby Bernard, tireless researcher of magic and magicians, provided information from the U.K. that rounded out many points for me. I am grateful for his help.

The great Paco Miller loaned me photos of magicians he'd known and told me anecdotes about Fu Manchu and the other Bambergs. I spent pleasant hours with him in Mexico.

Craige Snader welcomed me to his home in Mexico City to share with me much information about David Bamberg and his colleague, Edmund Spreer. It was a valuable contact for me and a generous gift of Craige's time. His friend and mine, Mandrake, made his photo collection available for my use, to my delight.

The extensive library at the Hollywood Magic Castle was made available to me by curator T. A. Waters. We are all grateful to Bill and Milt Larsen for creating and maintaining this facility.

As always, my thanks to Fifi Oscard and Kevin McShane.

My editor at St. Martin's Press, Bob Weil, worked with me to produce this book, and I hope that he is pleased with the results. I would also like to thank the staff of St. Martin's Press, including Dan Burrows, Karen Gillis, Twisne Fan, Judy Stagnitto, Meg Drislane, and the designer Janet Tingey, all of whom labored at their respective tasks to bring out the fun and enchantment of our subject.

Finally, Mr. Jian Ding kindly provided me with reference material and translations of Chinese writings on the subject. It has been my delight to know this unusual young man since my visit to China years ago. He is a valued friend.

DEFINITIONS OF
SOME TERMS USED IN MAGIC
AND STAGE WORK

ACT: A performer (such as a magician), or the performance itself, as seen by the audience.

AGA: Specifically, a Levitation presentation in which the floating lady rises and then returns again to the original position; compare the Asrah version.

AMATEUR: A respected member of the conjuring field, often highly skilled and sometimes contributing to the art by originating techniques or devices that are used by professionals. Magic clubs all over the world take in eager members who aspire to no more than the occasional performance before their peers.

APRON: The area of the stage that protrudes into the audience area.

ASRAH: Specifically, the Levitation presentation in which the floating lady vanishes. The invention of Servais Le Roy. See *Aga*.

BACKSTAGE: The area behind the stage which is not seen by the audience.

BIRD WORKER: A magician who specializes in working with birds, such as doves, parrots, and parakeets.

BLACK ART: A method of presenting actors dressed in light-colored costumes against a dead black background. All sorts of transformations are possible in this format.

BLINDFOLD ACT: Any of a variety of performances involving the blindfolding of the artist, who then drives a car, reads fine print, navigates a maze, or otherwise acts as if able to use the power of vision. Used as early as 1885 by mentalist John Randall Brown and brought to a fine art by Kashmiri performer Kuda Bux.

BOARD-TOSSING: The act of operating a three-card monte game. Also rudely called broad-tossing, since the sought card in the game is the Queen.

BOX JUMPER: An assistant, almost always female, who is sawed, chopped, vanished, produced, or otherwise victimized, usually by means of a garish "box" prop of some sort. A long-suffering species.

CHINESE LINKING RINGS: See *Linking Rings*.

CLOSE-UP: A type of magic that is done in close proximity to the spectator(s), often with the conjuror seated at a table. It is a specialized and highly respected style of performance.

CLUB ACT: An act developed for, and suited to, small stages such as those in nightclubs and lounges.

COLD DECK: A deck of cards that is introduced fully shuffled and untouched by the performer.

COLD READING: In mentalism, the ability to confront an unknown spectator and reveal details to him or her apparently not known to the performer. Distinguished from situations in which the spectator has been asked to write out or discuss details that are later revealed.

DE KOLTA CHAIR: Also known as the Vanishing Lady. The trick in which a person is seated in a chair, covered by a large cloth, and vanishes. Named after the French magician Joseph Bautier de Kolta.

DIP: Slang term for *pickpocket*.

DOUBLE: A two-person act; see *single*.

DOWNSTAGE: The front part of the stage, nearest the audience. See *upstage*.

EFFECT: In magicians' use, the trick as seen by the audience. The term can refer to a small or large trick.

ESCAMOTEUR: French for "conjuror," "juggler," "pickpocket."

ESCAPE ACT: As invented by Harry Houdini, the process of extricating oneself from bonds, manacles, straitjackets, boxes, prisons, and the like. A specialized form of the magic act, requiring very specific abilities but using many of the standard conjuring techniques.

FAKIR: In India, a street performer usually featuring self-inflicted discomforts as a means of religious propitiation. Sometimes used generally to designate a street performer of conjuring in that country.

FIND THE LADY: Also known as three-card monte. A popular card trick played on the street for money, in which the operator manipulates three facedown playing cards, one a Queen, the others not. The object is to locate the Queen (lady) to take the wager.

FLYER: A single-sheet advertising handout, usually specifically concerned with one show or artist.

GAFF: Same as *gimmick*.

GIMMICK: (a) A device, usually small, whereby a trick is accomplished. (b) A secret method used to accomplish a trick.

ILLUSION: Though this term refers to any deception, it is most often applied to visual deception, and is used in the trade to designate any large trick for stage use. Often involves one or more assistants for performance. See, for example, *Sawing in Half*, *Levitation*.

ILLUSIONIST: In the trade, a conjuror who specializes in large tricks. See *illusion*.

IN ONE: The area of the stage in front of the front curtain.

JADU-WALLAH: Same meaning as "Fakir," except that the self-mutilation theme, if present at all, is not prominent. An Indian street performer of conjuring.

KARNAC: The name given by Harry Kellar to his Levitation presentation.

KEY-BENDING: See *spoon bending*.

LEGERDEMAIN: From the French *léger de main* or, loosely, lightness of hand. Sleight-of-hand.

LEVI: Short for "Levitation."

LEVITATION: Strictly speaking, an illusion whereby a person rises into the air. Differs from the Suspension illusion. Invention of the Levitation illusion is credited to John Nevil Maskelyne.

LINKING RINGS: A classic trick of Oriental origin in which a set of rings (usually three to eight) is linked and unlinked in a variety of shapes and figures. Rings vary in diameter from four inches to twelve inches. Also called Chinese Linking Rings.

MENTALISM: The art of the mentalist, consisting of a variety of conjuring acts that appear to be the result of mental powers. Prediction, ESP, psychokinesis (affecting objects by mind alone), clairvoyance, psychometry, and divination are examples.

MENTALIST: One who performs *mentalism*.

MISDIRECTION: The art of directing the spectator's attention away from the actual subterfuge. Accomplished by any of several means, such as fixing the attention on the wrong hand, turning away, creating a diversion, or establishing eye contact.

PALM: The act of concealing an object or substance in the hand so that it is not noticed.

PATTER: The stream of talk and banter delivered by the magician. Sometimes it is essentially impromptu, rather than strictly scripted.

PICKPOCKET: One who surreptitiously removes objects from the pockets and persons of victims. A criminal activity and, when presented onstage, also a form of entertainment.

PLANT: An unrecognized assistant planted in the audience to facilitate the performance. Use of a plant is usually frowned on by professionals.

PRODUCTION: Any trick in which a material, object, or substance is made to appear.

PROP: Short for "property." Any piece of equipment or stage dressing. It might be an illusion box or a small hand-held gimmick.

SAWING: Short for "Sawing in Half."

SAWING IN HALF: A classic illusion, attributed to P. T. Selbit, in which a person is severed with a saw and then restored. Modern varieties include a giant buzz saw (as developed by Goldin and popularized by the Blackstones) and sawing in eighths, dramatically performed by David Copperfield.

SHILL: See *stick.*

SILK: Often used by the magician as a noun designating a handkerchief, often of silk.

SINGLE: Refers to a one-person act; see *double.*

SLEIGHT OF HAND: See *legerdemain.*

SPOON-BENDING: The general trick whereby spoons and other cutlery—and other objects such as keys—are deformed and sometimes broken by casual manipulation. Developed by the famous Uri Geller, but now performed in close-up and stage performances by many artists.

STEAL: In magicians' terminology, to obtain, secretly, any object or prop during performance. Used as a noun, the act of stealing.

STICK: An unrecognized assistant who places bets or otherwise secretly assists a street worker. Same as "shill."

STREET MAGIC: Conjuring—often combined with juggling—performed in the open, in parks and public areas, usually for contributions.

STREET MAGICIAN: A performer of street magic.

SUSPENSION: An illusion in which a person is seen to be suspended in the air, yet attached to some sort of upright (broom, sword, microphone stand, stick) rather than floating free. It is commonly done in India. See *Levitation.*

SWORD BOX: Any of a great variety of cabinets through which swords, rods, tubes, or other objects are passed, while a person occupies the box.

THAUMATURGE: A performer of miracles.

THAUMATURGY: Early term for magic and/or conjuring. From the word *thauma,* Greek for "a wonder."

THREE-CARD MONTE: See *Find the Lady.*

TRANSPOSITION: An exchange of position between two persons or objects.

TREAD THE BOARDS: Take up acting.

UPSTAGE: The far end of the stage, so named because the classic stage slopes down slightly from the back to the front edge to provide a better view of the actors. For this reason, furniture and other properties were often made with somewhat longer legs in front.

VANISH: Any trick in which a material, object, or substance is made to disappear.

VANISHING LADY: See *De Kolta Chair.*

VENT ACT: Short for "ventriloquist act." A dummy is a "vent figure."

WINGS: The areas on each side of the stage adjacent to the open stage area, but unseen by the audience.

ZIG-ZAG: A popular "box" trick in which a standing assistant's middle section is severed and displaced to one side. The invention of the remarkable Robert Harbin.

BIBLIOGRAPHY

Andrews, Val. *A Gift From the Gods,* Warwickshire: Goodliffe, 1981.

Bamberg, David. *Illusion Show.* Glenwood, N.J.: Meyerbooks, 1991.

Bayer, C. P. *The Great Wizard of the North John Henry Anderson,* Ray Goulet's Magic Art Book Co., 1990.

Blackmore, Kent. *Oscar Eliason.* Sydney: self-published, 1987.

Braddon, R. *The Piddingtons.* London: Werner Laurie, 1950.

Christopher, Milbourne. *The Illustrated History of Magic.* New York: Crowell, 1973.

———. *Milbourne Christopher's Magic Book.* New York: Crowell, 1977.

———. *Panorama of Magic.* New York: Dover, 1962.

Dawes, Edwin A. *The Great Illusionists.* Secaucus, N.J.: Chartwell Books, 1979.

Dawes and Setterington. *The Encyclopedia of Magic.* New York: Gallery Books, 1989.

Dexter, Will. *Chung Ling Soo.* London: Arco, 1955.

Doerflinger, William. *The Magic Catalogue.* Toronto: Clarke, Irwin, 1977.

Faulkner, Simpson, and Wente. *The Literature of Ancient Egypt.* New Haven, Conn.: Yale University Press, 1972.

Fischer, Ottokar. *Illustrated Magic.* Toronto: Coles, 1980.

Fisher, John, ed. *The Magic of Lewis Carroll.* New York: Bramhall House, 1973.

———. *Paul Daniels and the Story of Magic.* London: Cape, 1987.

Frank, Gary R. *Chung Ling Soo: The Man Behind the Legend.* Hades Publications, 1987.

Frost, Thomas. *The Lives of the Conjurors.* London: Tinsley Brothers, 1876.

Gibson, Walter B. *The Original Houdini Scrapbook.* New York: Sterling Publishing, 1976.

Gilbert, and Rydell. *The Great Book of Magic.* New York: Abrams, 1976.

Grohmann, Karl F. *Frauen in der Zauberkunst.* Germany: self-published, 1981.

Hammond, P. *Marvelous Méliès.* London: Fraser, 1974.

Harris, Ben. *Gellerism Revealed.* Calgary: Micky Hades, 1985.

Hopkins, A. A. *Magic: Stage Illusions & Scientific Diversions.* New York, 1897; reprinted 1977 (New York: Arno).

Lead, and Woods. *Houdini the Myth Maker.* Self-published, 1987.

Maskelyne, J. *White Magic.* London: Stanley Paul, 1936.

Meissner, H. O. *30 Januar 1933.* Heyne, Germany: 1979.

Michalski, M. *Das Grosse Ravensburger Zauberbuch.* Ravensburg, West Germany: 1987.

Mulholland, John. *Beware Familiar Spirits.* New York: Scribners, 1979.

Nilsson, C. *Trollare och andra Underhållare.* Sweden: Spektra, 1990.

Reilly, James V. *Darling Jennie.* Hamilton, New Zealand: Magicana, 1991.

Reynolds, C. and R. *100 Years of Magic Posters.* New York: Darien House, 1976.

Sharpe, Sam H. *Salutations to Robert-Houdin.* Calgary: Hades, 1983.

Sorcar, P. C. *Indian Magic.* Orient Paperbacks, 1970.

Taves, E. H. *Trouble Enough.* Buffalo: Prometheus Books, 1984.

Waters, T. A. *The Encyclopedia of Magic and Magicians.* New York: Facts on File, 1988.

Whaley, Bart. *Who's Who in Magic.* Oakland, Cal.: Jeff Busby Magic, Inc.,1990.

Witt, W. *Taschenspieler-Tricks.* Hugendubel Munich: Verlag, 1986.

A LIST OF MAGICIANS, THEN AND NOW

The curtain opens once more to admit a long parade of magicians who have contributed to the art. As they cross the stage before you, think of the tens of thousands who were not able to make it to this final bow. Their names may be unknown, their fame fleeting. They may have played their parts but slipped by without coming to my attention. Or that remorseless editor who shaped these pages may have scissored them out. Applaud, if you will, those who were booked to appear here. And who knows, maybe *next* season . . .

Aich, Jewel 1950–

Alan, Alan (Alan Rabinowiz) 19–

Albano, Tony 1964–

Alemaro (Alejandro Martinez Rosas) 1970–

Alex (Sándor Horváth) 1971–

Alexander, C. A. (Claude Alexander Conlin) 1880–1954

Alexander, David 1943–

Ali Kazam (Luis Roberto Rivas) 1965–

Ali the Fakir ?

Alipio (Alipio Rabazo) 1958–

Ammar, Michael 1956–

Anderson, Harry 1952

Anderson, John Henry 1814–1874

Andrus, Jerry 1920–

Angel (Chris Sarantas) 1969–

Annemann, Theodore (Theodore John Squires) 1907–1942

Ayala, Joaquin 1963–

Ballantine, Carl (Meyer Kessler) 1917–

Bamberg, David (Fu Manchu) 1904–1974

Bamberg, Tobias (Theodore) Leendert (Okito) 1875–1963

Bellachini (Samuel Berlach) 1827–1885

Bengtsson, Tom 1968–

Benson, Roy (Edward McQuade) 1915–1978

Berglas, David 1926–

Bernardi (Bernhard Eskilsen) 1902–1946

Berry, Jay Scott 1960–

Bertram, Charles (James Bassett) 1853–1907

Bishop, Washington (Wellington) Irving 1856–1889

Blackstone, Harry, Jr. 1933–

Blackstone, Harry, Sr. 1885–1965

Blitz, Antonio 1810–1877

Bloom, Gaëtan (Jean-Louis Blum) 1953–

Bombino, Fran (Francisco Guerra) 1968–

Bongo, Ali (William Oliver Wallace) 1929–

Borra (Borislav Milojkovic) 1921–

Borra II (Dragisa Milojkovic) 1918–

Borra III (Vojislav Milojkovic) 1923–

Borra, Charly (Karl Milojkovic) 1945–

Bosco, Giovanni Bartolomeo 1793–1863

Bosco, Leon?

Brandon, James 19–

Brandon, Joan ca. 1920–

Brindamour, George (George Brown) 1870–1941

Brown, John Randall 1851–1926

Buchinger, Matthias 1674–1735 (?)

Burger, Eugene 1939—

Burton, Lance 1960–

Bux, Kuda (Khuda Bakhsh) 1905–1981

Cagliostro, Conte Alessandro di (Balsamo, Giuseppe?) 1743–1795

Calvert, John (Elbern Madren Calvert) 1911–

Cardini (Richard D. Pitchford) 1899–1973

Carlton (Arthur Philips) 1881–1942

Carlyle, Francis 1911–1975

Carney, John 1958–

Cartelini (Jörge Kitlinski), 1972–

Carter, Charles 1874–1936

Cervine, Scott 1962–

Char, Alexander (Alexander Vorobiev) 1953–

Chang, Li-Ho (Juan José Pablo Jesorum) 1889–1972

Ching Ling Foo (Chee Ling Qua) 1854–1922

Christopher, Milbourne 1914–1984

Chung Ling Soo (William Ellsworth Robinson) 1861–1918

Cleopatra (Valeria Kasfikis/Cherni) ?

Comte, Emmanuel Apollinaire 1788–1859

Comus (Nicolas Philippe Ledru) 1731–1807

Comus II ?–1820

Cooke, George Alfred 1852–1904

Copperfield, David (David Kotkin) 1956–

Cottet, Martin (Gottet) 1963–

Cyprian, Father Murray 1938–

Daniels, Paul (Newton Edward Daniels) 1938–

Dante (Oscar Eliason) 1869–1899

Dante (Harry August Jansen) 1883–1955

Davenport, Ira Erastus and William Henry 1839–1911; 1841–1877

Davenport, Lewis (George Ryan) 1883–1960

Davenport, Roy (Fergus Roy) 1971–

David, Le Grand (David Bull) 19–

De Kolta, Bautier (Joseph Bautier) 1848–1903

De Yip Loo 19–?

Dedi ca. 3500 B.C.

De Paula, Peter 1953–

Devant, David (David Weighton) 1868–1941

Dickson, Abb (Abner Pope Dickson) 1948–

Dingle, Derek 1937–

Döbler, Ludwig Leopold 1801–1864

Dominique (Dominique Risbourg) 1932–

Downs, Thomas Nelson 1867–1938

Driscoll, Paul 1958–

Dunn, Ricki (Fred Revello) 1929–

Dunninger, Joseph 1892–1975

El Neco, Hector (Nils Sture Hector) 1900–1965

Evans, Celeste 19–

Falkenstein, Glenn 1932–

Fantasio (Ricardo Roucau) 1936–

Fawkes, Isaac ca. 1675–1731

Fay, Anna Eva (Anna Eva Heathman) 1851–1927

Flosso, Al (Albert Levinson) 1895–1976

Fogel, Maurice J. 1911–1981

Fox, Karrel 1928—

Frakson (José Jimenez Seville) 1891–1981

Frikell, Wiljalba 1818–1903

Fu Manchu, (see *Bamberg, David*)

Fujiyama, Shintaro 1954–

Gali–Gali, Luxor (Mahguob Mohammed Hanafi) 1902–

Garcia, Frank 1927–

Geller, Uri 1946–

Gentleman Jack (Tommy Willy Jörgen Iversen) 1921–

George, The Great (Grove C. George) 1887–1958

Germain, Karl (Karl Mattmüller) 1878–1959

Gertner, Paul ?

Giordemaine, Johnny (Giovanni Giodmaina) 1898–1973

Giovanni, "Dr." (Adolph Herczog) 1896–1977

Glow, Brian 1957–

Gogia Pasha (Dhanapat Rai Gogia) 1910–1976

Goldfinger (Jack Vaughn) and Dove 1949– and 19–

Goldin, Horace (Hyman Elias Goldstein) 1873–1939

Goldston, Will (Wolf Goldstone) 1878–1948

Goshman, Al 1921—1991

Gotson, Steve (Bonfils, Jean–Paul) ?

Green, Lennart 19–

Gunnarson, Dean 1964–

Gwynne, Jack 1895–1979

Hamman, Bro. John 1927–

Hanussen, Erik Van (Herschel Steinschneider) 1889–1933

Harbin, Robert (Edward Richard Charles Williams) 1909–1978

Hardeen, Theodore 1876–1945

Heimbürger, Friedrich Alexander (The Great Herr Alexander) 1819—1909

Heller, Robert (William Henry Palmer) 1826 (1829?)–1878

Hellström (Axel Vogt) 1893–1933

Henning, Doug 1947–

Herrmann, Leon 1867–1909

Herrmann, Carl (Compars Herrmann) 1816–1887

Herrmann, Alexander 1843–1896

Herrmann, Mme. Adelaide (Adelaide Scarcez) 1854–1932

Hertz, Carl (Leib Morgenstern) 1859–1924

Hilden, "Miss" (Hildegard Neureiter/Ohlsson) 1906–?

Hoffmann, Professor Louis (Angelo John Lewis) 1839–1919

Hofzinser, Max (Josef Levin) 1885–1955

Hofzinser, (Dr. Johann Nepomuk H.) 1806–1875

Horowitz, Sam 1894–1971

Houdini, Harry (Ehrich Weiss) 1874–1926

Hull, Burling (Burlingame Gilbert Hull) (Volta) 1889–1982

Hume, (or Home) Daniel Dunglas 1833–1886

Ionia (Elsie De Vere/Williams) 1885–?

Jahn, Viggo 1917–

Jaks, "Dr." Stanley (Herbert Siegbert) 1903–1960

James, Loyal (James Pyczynski) 1953–

James, Stewart 1906–

Jarrow, Emil 1875–1959

Jay, Ricky (Ricky Potash) 1948–

Jhoni (Juan Sánchez Flores) 1939–

Jon, Finn (Finn Hauser) 1939–

Joseph (Joseph Gabriel Wierzbicki) 1958–

Kalanag (Helmut Ewald Schreiber) 1903–1963

Kaps, Fred (Abraham Pieter Adrianus Bongers) 1926–1980

Kassner, "Direktor" 1887–1970

Katterfelto, Gustavus 1730–1799

Keating, Fred 1898–1961

Kellar, Harry (Heinrich Keller) 1849–1922

Keops, Fernando (Fernando Otero T.) 19—

Kim Yen Soo, see *Kuma*

Kio (Emil Feodorowitsch Hirschfeld–Renard) 1894–1965

Kio, Emil Jr. (Emil Emilievich Kio) 1938–

Kio, Igor Emilievich Renard 1944–

Kole, André (Robert Gurtler) 1936–

Kolta, Bautier de 1848–1903

Koran, Al (Edward Doe) 1914–1972

Kreskin (George Joseph Kresge, Jr.) 1935–

Kuma (or Kim Yen Soo) (Kinjiro Tanko Kumajo) 1884–1963

Labero, Joe 1963–

Lafayette (Siegmund Ignatius Neuburger) 1872–1911

Lady Frances (Frances E. Hess) 19–

Larsen, William Walter 1904–1953

Le Roy, Servais (Jean Henri Servais Le Roy) 1865–1953

Leipzig, Nate (Nathan Leipzinger) 1873–1939

Lenert, Tina 1948–

Levante, Les (Leslie George Cole) 1892–1978

Lorayne, Harry 1926–

Lorraine, Sid 1905—1991

Lupo, Vito 1960–

Maeda, Tomohiro 1965–

Majax, Gérard (Gérard Fater) 1943–

Malini, Max (Max Katz/Breit) 1873–1942

Mandrake, Leon 1911–

Marco the Magi (Dr. Cesáreo Pelaez) 1932–

Marshall, Jay (James Ward Marshall) 1919–

Martinez, Daryl 1955—

Marvelli, Fredo 1903—1971

Maskelyne, John Nevil 1829–1917

Maskelyne, Nevil 1863–1924

Maskelyne, Jasper 1902–1973

Maurer, Harry 1960–

Maven, Max (Phil Goldstein) 1950–

McBride, Jeff 1959?–

McComb, Billy 1922–

Méliès, Georges 1861–1938

Melinda (Melinda Saxe) 1965–

Menna, Lisa 1963–

Mercedes (Joseph Cohen) 1888–1966

Miller, Paco (Eduardo Arozamena) 1918–

Moretti, Hans (Johannes Cewe) 1928–

Mulholland, John 1898–1970

Müller, Ralf, 1966–

Murray (Leo Norman Maurien Murray Stuart Carrington-Walters) 1901–

Napoleons (Parte Koishi and Bona Ueki) 1952– and 1952–

Neff, Bill 1905–1967

Nielsen, Norm 1934–

Niemi, Jyrki 1974–

O'Dell, Dell (Nell Newton) 1902–1962

Okita (Julia Ferret) 1852–1916

Okito, see Bamberg, Tobias (Theodore) Leneert

Palaez, Cesareo 1932–

Palladino, Eusapia (Minerverno Murge) 1854–1918

Pasha, Omar 1905–1975

Pasha, Gogia 1910–1976

Paul, Johnny (John Paul Zielinski, Jr.) 1912–

Paul, Paula (Paula Slape) 1954–

Pavel (Pavel Pomezny) 1945–

Payne, William Charles (Professor Du Payne) 1852–1919

Pendragons (Claude Douglas Yarbrough and Charlotte) 1953– and 1954–

Penn & Teller (Penn Jillette and Raymond Teller) 1956?– and 1949?–

Philadelphia, Jacob (Jacob Meyer) 1735–1795

Philippe (Jacques–André–Noé Talon) 1802–1878

Piddingtons, Sydney and Lesley (later with Robyn) 1918–, 1925–, and 1947–

Pinetti (Giuseppe Merci/Willedal de Merci/Wildalle) 1750–1800

Pit, Peter (Hermann Claassen) 1933–
Polgar, Franz 19–
Pollock, Channing 1926–
Potassy, Paul 1923–
Powell, Frederick Eugene 1856–1938
Punx (Ludwig Franz Wilhelm Hanemann) 1907–
Rameses (Albert Marchinski) 1876–1930
Randi, James (Randall James Hamilton Zwinge) 1928–
Ray, Jimmy 19–
Raymond, The Great (Morris Raymond Saunders) 1877–1948
Richiardi Aldo (Aldo Izquierdo Colosi) 1923–1985
Richiardi (Ricardo Izquierdo) 1885–1937
Robert-Houdin, Jean Eugène 1805–1871
Robin (Henri-Joseph Donckèle) 1811–1874
Robinson, William Ellsworth, see *Chung Ling Soo*
Rocco (Rocco Silano) 1959–
Rooklyn, Maurice 1905–
Rosini, Paul (Paul Vucci) 1902–1948
Ross, Richard (Richard Rozenboom) 1946–
Roth, David 1952–
Roy, Marvin (Marvin A. Levy) 1925–
Sam, Long Tack 1885–1961
Scarne, John (Orlando Carmelo Scarnecchia) 1903–1985
Scotto, Girolamo 1572–1602
Seabrooke, Terry 1932–
Selbit, P.T. (Percy Thomas Tibbles) 1881–1938
Seppänen, Iiro 1975–
Shaw, Steve 1960
Shaxon, Alan (Alan Arthur Howson) 1933–
Sheridan, Jeff 1948–
Shimada, Haruo 1940–
Siegfried & Roy (Siegfried Fischbacker and Roy Horn) 1943– and 1945–
Silvan (Aldo Savoldello) 1937–
Skiffington, Ross 1948–
Slade, Henry ca. 1840–1905

Slydini, Tony (Quintino Marucci) 1901–1991
Sorcar, Pradip Chandra (Sarcar) 1946–
Sorcar, P. C. (Protul Chandra Sarcar) 1913–1971.
Steiner, Robert 19–
Swiss, Jamy Ian 1952–
Takayama, Cyril 1974–
Talma, Mercedes (Mary Ann Ford) 1861–1944
Tamariz, Juan (Tamariz-Martel Negrón) 1942–
Tampa (Raymond S. Sugden) 1888–1939
Tempest, Marco 1964–
Ten Ichi (Shokyokusai Hattori) 1852–1912
Ten Ichi (Tenji) ?–1948
Ten-i-Chi (Jules De Nijs) 1893–1967
Tendo, Mahka (Takao Yabushita) 1960–
Tenkai (Sadajiro Ishida) 1889–1972
Tenko (Isao Hikita) 1934–1979
Tenko, "Princess" (Mariko Itakura) ca. 1959–
Tihanyi (Franz Czeiler) 1916–
Thurston, Howard 1869–1936
Tomsoni & Company (John Thompson and Pam Thompson) 1934– and 1936–
Tucker, Tom and Liz ca. 1915–1991 and ?
Uferini, Alfredo 1863–1934
Vera, Armando 1970–
Vernon, Dai (David Frederick Wingfield Verner) 1894–
Virgil (Virgil Harris Mulkey) 1900–1989
Warlock, Peter (Alec William Bell) 1904–
Willard, Frances 1940–
Willard the Wizard 1896–1970
Wilson, (James) Mark 1929–
Wonder, Tommy (Jacobus Maria Bemelman) 1953–
Wong, "The Great" (Ng Bo Oen) 1908–
Yedid, Meyer 1960–
Zancig, Julius and Agnes (J. Jörgensen & A. Claussen) 1857–1929 and ?–1916 (also Ada Zancig)
Zimmerman, Diana 1949–
Zeigler, Steve 1963–

A LIST OF MAGIC DEALERS

These businesses listed are often "mail order only" locations, while others are actual walk-in shops where the merchandise may be demonstrated to potential buyers. It is advisable to call first, to ascertain business hours. Most will offer comprehensive catalogs of their tricks, manuscripts, and books, for a few dollars each. If there is not a listing here of a dealer near you, consult your classified telephone directory under the heading, "Magician's Supplies." Those marked * do not do business by telephone.

IN THE U.S.A. AND CANADA:
Abbott's Magic Co.
Colon, MI 49040

Al's Magic Shop
1012 Vermont Avenue NW
Washington, DC 20005

Bert Easley's Fun Shop
509 West McDowell Road
Phoenix, AZ 85003

Biscayne Magic & Joke Shop
1680 NE 123rd Street
Fort Lauderdale, FL
(305) 891-7224

Collector's Workshop
Misty Morning Farm
Rte. 1, Box 113A
Middleburg, VA 22117
(703) 687-6476

Cosmar Magic
6765 El Banquero Place
San Diego, CA 92119
(619) 287-3706

D. Robbins & Co., Inc.
70 Washington Square, 9th floor
Brooklyn, NY 11201

Fantasio Magic Products
1002 Country Club Prado
Coral Gables, FL 33134
(305) 264-3321

Flosso/Hornmann Magic Shop
45 West 34th Street
New York City, NY 10001
(212) 279-6079

Guaranteed Magic
27 Bright Road
Hatboro, PA 19040
(215) 672-3344

Hank Lee's Magic Factory
24 Lincoln Street
Boston, MA 02111

Hank Lee's Magic Factory
P.O. Box 789
Medford, MA 02155
(617) 482-8749

Hollywood Magic, Inc.
6614 Hollywood Blvd.
Hollywood, CA 90028

House of Magic
2025 Chestnut Street
San Francisco, CA 94123

Lee Jacobs Products
P.O. Box 362
Pomeroy, OH 45769

Louis Tannen, Inc.
6 West 32nd Street
New York City, NY 10001-3808
(212) 239-8383

Magic Unlimited
619 Somerset Street West
Ottawa, Ontario K1R 5K3
Canada

Magic, Inc.
5082 Lincoln Avenue
Chicago, IL 60625
(312) 334-2855

Magical Moments
8317 West Atlantic Blvd.
Coral Springs, FL 33075
(305) 755-8586

Marvello Enterprises
982 Bennington Street
Boston, MA 02128-1137
(617) 569-7737

Mecca Magic, Inc.
9 South Harrison Street
East Orange, NJ 07018

Micky Hades
Box 476
Calgary, Alberta T2P 2J1
Canada

Moorehouse Magic
954 West Cross
Ypsilanti, MI 48197

Morrissey Magic Ltd.
927 St. Croix Blvd.
Ville St. Laurent, PQ H4L 3Y9
Canada

Owen Magic Supreme
734 North McKeever Avenue
Azusa, CA 91702
(818) 969-4519

Patry Magic Productions
62 Washington Manor
West Haven, CT 06516
(203) 932-9586

Stevens Magic Emporium
3238 East Douglas
Witchita, KS 67208
(316) 683-9582

Yogi Magic Mart
217 North Charles Street
Baltimore, MD 21201

IN THE U.K.:
*Martin Breese
1 Northumberland Park Industrial
    Estate
76-78 Willoughby Lane
London N17 0SN
081 885 2447

Camtrix Magic Ltd.
187 Gilbert Road
Cambridge, Cambs.
0223 356204

L. Davenport & Co.
7 Charing Cross Underground
        Shopping Arcade
The Strand, London, WC2N 4HZ
071 836 0408

Peter Diamond Co.
214 Brockholes View
Preston, Lancs. PX1 4XJ
0772 793173

Hamley's Ltd.
188 Regent Street
London, W1
071 734 3161

International Magic Studio
89 Clerkenwell Road
Holburn, London, EC1R 5BX
071 405 7324

The Kaymar Magic
106A High Street
Billericay, Essex CM2 1HT
0277 630470

Kovari Magic Products Ltd.
465 Watford Way
London NW4 4TR
081 203 4539

Mark Leveridge Magic
29 Wrefords Close
Exeter, Devon EX4 5AY
0392 52000

*Magic Books by Post
29 Hill Avenue
Bedminster, Bristol BS3 4SN
0272 774409

Vic Pinto (Videos)
252 Finchley Road
London NW3
071 794 7636

Repro Magic
46 Queenstown Road
London, SW8 3RY
071 720 6257

Supreme Magic Co.
Supreme House
Bideford, Devon EX39 2AN
0237 479266

*COUNTRIES OTHER THAN
U.S.A., CANADA, AND U.K.*
Ben Harris Magic
GPO Box 860
Brisbane, Queensland 4001
Australia

Braunmüller Zauberstudio
Steinbeisplatz 3
D-8000 München 21
Germany

Casa Magicus
Diputacio 274
08009 Barcelona
Spain

DeLarnos International Magic
    Centre
P.O. Box 190
Petersham, NSW 2049
Australia

Dick Marvel Magic Studio
Apartado 101
4501 Espinho Codex
Portugal
02/72-3345

El Rey de la Magic
Calle Princesa 11
3 Barcelona
Spain

Escamoteo Estudios
Casilla 5179 Central
Buenos Aires 1000
Argentina

Exclusive Magical Publications
Apartado Postal 12-655
Mexico D.F. 03020
Mexico

Franco Contigliozzi
Curiosita & Magia
70 Via In Aquiro
00186 Roma
Italy
06/678-4228

Harries
Box 102
S-601 03 Norrkoping
Sweden

Magic Fukai
2-15-16 Daizoji
Takatsuki-Shi
569 Osaka
Japan
0726/88-0618

John McLean & Associates
GPO Box 907
Melbourne, Victoria 3001
Australia

Magic Versand Galaxis
Bahnstrasse 10
A-2633 Pottschach
Austria

Tayade's Magic Shop
64-65 Bhatia Bhuvan
Ash La, Dadar Bombay 453893
India

Thaim Huat & Co.
231 Bain Street, #02-81
Bras Basah Complex
Singapore 0718

Tokyo Magic Co. Ltd.
2-10 Kiba 2 Chome Koto-Ku
135 Tokyo
Japan

W. Geissler-Werry
In den Benden 13
D-5160 Düren-Niederau
Germany

A LIST OF MAGICAL PERIODICALS AND ORGANIZATIONS

I suggest that you write to these organizations for information on how you might either become a member or subscribe to the magazines. In some cases you may have to be sponsored by one or two other magicians, who might be contacted through local magic dealers. Some publications are only available to members of magical organizations.

Abracadabra (weekly magic magazine)
150 New Road
Bromsgrove, Worcestershire B60 2LG
U.K.

Genii magazine
P.O. Box 36068
Los Angeles, CA 90036
U.S.A.

International Brotherhood of Magicians
103 North Main Street
Bluffton, OH 45817-0089
U.S.A.

The Linking Ring (magazine)
International Brotherhood of Magicians
Kenton, Ohio 43326
U.S.A.

Magic
4067 Hardwick Street
Suite 322
Lakewood, CA 90712

The Magic Circle
13 Calder Avenue
Brookmans Park, Herts AL9 7AH
U.K.

Magic Manuscript (magazine)
6 West 32nd Street
New York City, NY 10001
U.S.A.

Magicrama (magazine)
Caixa Postal 746-ZC-00
20,000 Rio de Janeiro-RJ
Brazil

Magicus Journal (magazine)
Lagarrigue, 81109 Castres
France

MUM (magazine)
Society of American Magicians
P.O. Box 510260
St. Louis, MO 63151
U.S.A.

Society of American Magicians
P.O. Box 368
Mango, FL 34262-0368
U.S.A.

Society of Young Magicians
P.O. Box 375
Nashua, NH 03061
U.S.A.

INDEX

ABOUT THE AUTHOR

James Randi is a professional magician (The Amazing Randi), author and lecturer, amateur archaeologist and amateur astronomer. Born in 1928 in Toronto, Canada, he received his education there. He was naturalized as a United States citizen in 1987, and now lives in Florida with a mellow old red cat named Charles, several untalented parrots, numerous other unnamed creatures, and the occasional visiting magus and/or apprentice. Understandably, he is single.

Mr. Randi was host of "The Randi Show" on radio in the mid-1960s, and he has had his own television specials in Italy, England, Belgium, Canada, Japan, Australia, and the United States. He has appeared in a great many TV documentaries, interview shows, and variety productions in France, Germany Hungary, Italy, Japan, and the U.K., and other countries. He has done three world tours as a performer and lecturer through the Far East, Europe, Australia, and North and South America; in 1974, he performed at the White House. He spends much of his time traveling between performances, and he lectures all over the globe.

Mr. Randi's writings (articles, essays, stories, book reviews) have appeared in many different periodicals. In 1983, he was awarded the Blackstone Cup of the International Platform Association as Outstanding Speaker in his category for his lecture "Science & the Chimera," and became the only second-time recipient of this award in 1987. He was 1984 Regents Lecturer at the University of Califormia at Los Angeles, and he has conducted several similar seminars at other colleges in recent years. Then, in 1986, he was awarded the prestigious MacArthur Fellowship in recognition of his pursuit of the truth about psychic claims.

In 1987, the Academy of Magical Arts and Sciences in Los Angeles created a Special Fellowship for James Randi in recognition of his contributions to preservation of the art of conjuring as a form of entertainment, as opposed to the use of deception for purposes of fraud. He was appointed to the Hall of Fame of the Society of American Magicians (SAM), and was also named an International Ambassador of Magic for the SAM, reporting to the Society from all over the world on developments in techniques and new talent discoveries.

The author's own participation in and contributions to the art of magic are told throughout this book as part of the narrative rather than being isolated in a particular section. He chose this method of telling his own story so that he might be more properly permitted to provide his personal insight into this history of the strange, fascinating characters who constitute Magic.

This book is Mr. Randi's ninth.

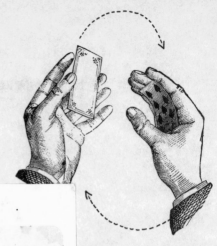

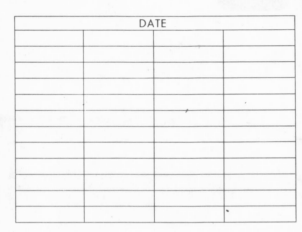